Tolkien and Modernity
1

edited by
Frank Weinreich & Thomas Honegger

2006

Cormarë Series

No 9

Series Editors

Peter Buchs • Thomas Honegger • Andrew Moglestue

Library of Congress Cataloging-in-Publication Data

Weinreich, Frank and Thomas Honegger (editors)

Tolkien and Modernity 1

ISBN 978-3-905703-02-3

Subject headings:

Tolkien, J. R. R. (John Ronald Reuel), 1892-1973 – Criticism and interpretation
Tolkien, J. R. R. (John Ronald Reuel), 1892-1973 – Language
Fantasy fiction, English – History and criticism
Middle-earth (Imaginary place)
Literature, Comparative.
Modernism

All rights reserved. No portion of this book may be reproduced, by any process or technique, without the express written consent of the publisher.

for my mother (1920-2006) (F.W.)

for Jana (T.H.)

Table of Contents

Frank Weinreich & Thomas Honegger
Introduction — i

Anna Vaninskaya
Tolkien: A Man of his Time? — 1

Maria Raffaella Benvenuto
Against Stereotype:
Éowyn and Lúthien as 20th-Century Women — 31

Laura Michel
Politically Incorrect:
Tolkien, Women, and Feminism — 55

Bertrand Alliot
J.R.R. Tolkien: A Simplicity Between
the 'Truly Earthy' and the 'Absolute Modern' — 77

Jessica Burke & Anthony Burdge
The Maker's Will ... Fulfilled? — 111

Frank Weinreich
Brief Considerations on
Determinism in Reality and Fiction — 135

Jason Fisher
"Man does as he is when he may do as he wishes"
The Perennial Modernity of Free Will — 145

Thomas Fornet-Ponse
Freedom and Providence
as Anti-Modern Elements — 177

Alexander van de Bergh
Democracy in Middle-earth:
J.R.R. Tolkien's *The Lord of the Rings*
from a Socio-Political Perspective — 207

Index — 237

Introduction

Tom Shippey's *J.R.R. Tolkien: Author of the Century* was not the first, but certainly the most prominent study to claim Tolkien and his literary work for the 20th century. It does not lack a certain irony that the impetus to such an approach had come, once again (*pace* Rosebury), from a philologist. Professor Shippey's, Dr. Rosebury's and the other scholars' arguments have since then been taken up, modified, elaborated, criticized, emulated, and developed by various literary critics. As a consequence, an increasing number of literary scholars who are not primarily (or even secondarily) 'Tolkienists' have begun to treat Tolkien's works as 'mentionables'. Hard-core Tolkienists have to get used to the fact that a critic may not know the difference between light-elves and dark-elves or between Westernesse and Eriador, but that s/he, nevertheless, is able to contribute relevant points to the understanding of the literary quality of Tolkien's work. Books like *Reading The Lord of the Rings*, edited by Robert Eaglestone, illustrate the strengths (and minor weaknesses) of such a development.

The present volume(s) grew out of the wish to further the exploration of Tolkien as a 'contemporary writer', i.e. an author whose literary creations can be seen as a response to the challenges of the modern world. This does not mean that we should disregard or even consider obsolete the other, hitherto dominant approaches, such as the exploration of Tolkien's 'roots' in the medieval and philological traditions, his Victorian/Edwardian background, his Catholicism, etc. The shift of focus from Tolkien as 'the Other' towards Tolkien as a contemporary character has been overdue for a long time and complements these earlier approaches. Furthermore, such a development is profitable for all involved and if we want to see and appreciate the 'tree' in its entirety, then it is necessary to look at it from as many points of view as possible.

The current volume, being the first of two dedicated to 'Tolkien and Modernity', comprises papers that focus on the following themes:

Tolkien and the 20th Century, feminist theory, time, creativity, and freedom. Although one could argue that most of these topics have been discussed since the beginning of literature, it is with the shaping events of the first half of the 20th century – the World Wars, Einstein's theory of relativity, totalitarianism and the atomic bomb – that they gained a new and immediate relevance. The rise of totalitarianism and the abominations carried out under the regimes of Stalin and Hitler, for example, seemed to expose the notion of Free Will as an illusionary concept. Man felt pushed helplessly into a way of life superimposed on him by forces remote and of anonymous structure, as was, for example, observed in the most important works of Kafka and Camus. For many this resulted in an inescapable feeling of helplessness, even meaninglessness of existence, that could surface in the smallest of events, as W. H. Auden has shown brilliantly in *The Age of Anxiety*. The pioneering discoveries of sciences in the 20th century on macroscopic as well as microscopic levels fortified the experience of the heteronomy of being. The question is whether experiences like these (and others), which are typical for modernity, can be traced and pinpointed in Tolkien's fictional work.

The time in which Tolkien lived and worked, as it shows itself in the mirror of literary reflections from late-Victorian and Edwardian nostalgia to the experiences expressed in the literary works of the inter-war period and shortly after, form the background of Anna Vaninskaya's essay. In her article she aims to point out contemporary writings as analogues for Tolkien's work. Their influences are identified and presented as factors which ground Tolkien the author in the 20th century by showing that his work has roots also in the primary world – without robbing his literary creation of its uniqueness or devaluing the Tolkienian cosmos.

A narrower topic of the 20th century is examined by Maria Raffaella Benvenuto, who concentrates on Éowyn and Luthien as potential embodiments of modern feminist attitudes. This may not only be seen in the obvious qualities of strength and independence discernible in both characters, but also in a more fundamental way by expressing (female) creativity as a life affirming trait. Thus models from older literary traditions and mythology are reconciled with contemporary feminist issues. This topic is furthermore investigated by Laura Michel's article on women in Tolkien's work. Her study endeavours to point out the elements of the author's sympathetic understanding of women through an analysis of the figures Éowyn and Erendis in comparison with other female characters and the women Tolkien knew closely in real life. Thus Michel shows that Tolkien's female characters are modern characters and that the work as a whole is not particularly androcentric.

Time, change, and timeless aspects of Tolkien's writing govern the arguments of Bertrand Alliot's study on simplicity and the opposing forces of comlexity in the modern world. Alliot starts by discussing simplicity as a value in itself, which can be deduced even at first sight from the values propagated, for example, in all topics related to Hobbits. On a deeper level, however, Alliot seeks to show that Tolkien, even though was well aware of the impossibility of recovering a pre-modern simplicity, he nevertheless sets out – and succeeds – in creating a new kind of simplicity which establishes a bridge between older (and possibly illusionary) nostalgic wallowings and absolute modernist world views which threaten to lose contact with deepset human values and needs. Deepset human values and, in a sense, timlessness and timeless values are also the topics of Jessica Burke and Anthony Burdge's essay on creation and subcreation, the process which governed Tolkien's work more than anything else. They first examine the process of subcreation and the importance Tolkien has seen in it. In a second step the author's beliefs are compared to current subcreative processes and the exposure to 'subcreative' works found in the modern world. They come to the conclusion that modern man suffers from a saddening loss of creative powers.

The next part of this volume comprises three papers discussing the closely related topics of determinism, fate, providence, and free will. First Frank Weinreich gives a short introduction to the relationship of determinism in reality and fiction, upon which the others aspects discussed in this section heavily depend. Then Jason Fisher identifies the question of freedom in Middle-earth as a perennial problem of humanity. After discussing free will as a religious and theological issue in general, and with regard to the Inklings in special, Fisher shows that Tolkien dealt with the topic in an exemplary way – clearly asserting the existence of free will as existent – which can be seen as a major reason for the unabated popularity of his work. Thomas Fornet-Ponse, then, scrutinizes in detail the roles of freedom, free will, determination, and providence in Tolkien's work. He discusses these themes in the context of Tolkien's deep-set Catholicism, which influenced his life and writing. Fornet-Ponse aims to show that the views on freedom and providence expressed in Tolkien's work neither contradict modern convictions of freedom, though challenging the proponents of naturalistic world views forcefully, nor do they contradict the possibility of a creator and a creator's plan. They thus reflect more or less traditional theological concepts of the interaction between providence and free will.

The volume closes with a study by Alexander van de Bergh on the socio-political perspectives in Tolkien's work. van de Bergh, in contrast to those studies that focus on individuals and their actions or omissions, examines the macroscopic structures of living in Middle-earth. He studies the governmental structures and forms of social life in Tolkien's creation and finds reflections of the radical changes in the real world, most of which happened in the period during which Tolkien sub-created Middle-earth. In conclusion, van de Bergh finds that although certain definite sympathies with certain societal structures can be identified, it is the individual and its choices that make up the core of the ethical convictions found in *The Lord of the Rings*.

A few remarks on the editorial principles. Although we did not take lightly the responsibility of editing the two volumes, we opted for a 'light editorial hand' approach. This means that we strove to unify, as far as possible, (bibliographical) references, that we proofread the papers and suggested alterations and emendations to the authors, and that we kept an eye on the papers on similar topics in order to prevent too much of an overlap. Yet we decided against too strong an intervention in matters of style and culture-specific scholarly traditions. Many of the papers therefore still show (as is intended by the editors) their 'cultural' roots in their selection of themes and in the way they approach a topic – and give a wider audience the opportunity to gain a glimpse of the multiple traditions of international Tolkien scholarship.

Frank Weinreich & Thomas Honegger
Bochum & Jena, Summer 2006

Tolkien: A Man of his Time?

ANNA VANINSKAYA

Abstract

This paper, first presented at *Tolkien 2005: The Ring Goes Ever On* at Aston University, UK, situates Tolkien in the cultural and literary context of his time, and argues that, Modernism aside, his work is representative of late nineteenth and twentieth century preoccupations. The aim of the essay is to sketch a picture of Tolkien's historical moment, concentrating on analogues rather than sources to demonstrate his place in the contemporary milieu. The paper looks at Tolkien in relation to the following: the romantic critique of industrial society, late-Victorian historical reconstructions, the fantasy tradition of Haggard, Chesterton and Morris, the rural nostalgia of the Edwardian period and the interwar years – both in its literary and sociological manifestations – the patriotic writing of the Great War, ideas of national character and Little Englandism, and political anti-statism of the Orwellian mould. Potential lines of further inquiry are suggested throughout.

INTRODUCTION

Let me begin with two quotations:

> Why has not England a great mythology? Our folklore has never advanced beyond daintiness, and the great melodies about our country-side have all issued through the pipes of Greece. Deep and true as the native imagination can be, it seems to have failed here. It has stopped with the witches and the fairies. It cannot vivify one fraction of a summer field, or give names to half a dozen stars. England still waits for the supreme moment of her literature – for the great poet who shall voice her, or, better still, for the thousand little poets whose voices shall pass into our common talk. (Forster 1910:789)

> This England, these shafted windows, the elm-trees, the blue distance – the past, the great past, crumbling down, breaking down, not under the force of the coming buds, but under the weight of many exhausted, lovely yellow leaves, that drift over the lawn and over the pond, like the soldiers, passing away, into winter and the darkness of winter .... For the winter stretches ahead, where all vision is lost and all memory dies out.[1]

The first of these quotations dates from 1910, the second from 1916, and neither is by Tolkien, though all who are familiar with his letters and early poetry will recognize the parallels with the famous 'mythology for England' letter to Milton Waldman,[2] and the 1915 version of the Warwick poem, *Kortirion Among the Trees* (Tolkien 1983:33-6).[3] I do not mean to imply that Tolkien had read E. M. Forster and D. H. Lawrence – the respective authors of the cited passages – a contention impossible to prove and frankly irrelevant to my purpose. What I would like to gauge is the extent to which Tolkien shared in the mood of his time, for if his works were indeed products of their cultural moment, it is to be expected that they should express widely held sentiments or independently arrive at conclusions already in circulation. Like David Doughan (1999) in his essay on Tolkien and Englishness, I am attempting to "indicate some of the intellectual atmosphere, some of the ideas [...] that were in the air" when Tolkien was writing, the context "of which he is

---

[1] D. H. Lawrence writing to Lady Cynthia Asquith in 1916 (qtd. in Lucas 1997:16).

[2] See letter 131: "I was from early days grieved by the poverty of my own beloved country: it had no stories of its own (bound up with its tongue and soil), not of the quality that I sought, and found (as an ingredient) in legends of other lands. There was Greek, and Celtic, and Romance, Germanic, Scandinavian, and Finnish (which greatly affected me); but nothing English, save impoverished chap-book stuff [...]." (Tolkien 1981:144)

[3] The melancholic atmosphere, the imagery of elm-trees, drifting leaves, the crumbling past, and the coming winter are almost uncannily identical.

unlikely to have been totally unaware [...] the material which may have helped him to build his coral reef." I cannot hope to undertake a cultural history of the dimensions this task would require in a single paper. Even the books and articles of Verlyn Flieger, Tom Shippey, and Brian Rosebury, who lead the way in the introduction of the modern intellectual context into Tolkien scholarship – whether with regard to the national reconstructions of nineteenth century writers or the language and time theories of Owen Barfield and J. W. Dunne[4] – leave much unsaid. This paper, therefore, will only suggest a few more directions in which such study could go. I have not read all the secondary literature listed in recent Tolkien bibliographies, but its seems to me that the critical approach I am proposing is one which Michael Drout and Hilary Wynne (2000) have left out of their classificatory survey of Tolkien scholarship: a study, in other words, concerned precisely with analogies (similarities that arise independently), in addition to homologies or sources. Nobody needs convincing of the presence of Anglo-Saxon and Old Norse elements in *The Lord of the Rings*, but an assertion of a similar kind with regard to the twentieth century still meets with suspicion.

---

[4] Flieger also looks at Coleridge, MacDonald, Du Maurier, Barrie, T. S. Eliot, Henry James, and H. G. Wells in *A Question of Time* (1997); see also *Splintered Light* (2002), and *Interrupted Music* (2005) for Joyce and Yeats. See Shippey's 'Goths and Huns: The Rediscovery of Northern Cultures in the Nineteenth Century' (1982), 'Grimm, Grundtvig, Tolkien: Nationalisms and the Invention of Mythologies' (2000b), 'Tolkien and Iceland: The Philology of Envy' (2002), and 'Light-elves, Dark-elves, and Others: Tolkien's Elvish Problem' (2004). I am not entirely convinced by Shippey's case for Tolkien as a post-war writer to be bracketed together with Orwell (made in Reynolds and GoodKnight (1995:84-93) and *Author of the Century*). One can also mention a number of other contributions: Patrick Curry's case for Weber, the essays in the *Proceedings*, and in the two Greenwood Press volumes (Clark and Timmons 2000; Flieger and Hostetter 2000), Jonathan Himes's 'What Tolkien Really Did With the Sampo' (2000), and the articles in *Tolkien Studies* 1, including Mark Hooker's 'Frodo's Batman' (2004), and Anne C. Petty's 'Identifying England's Lönnrot' (2004). I have not had the chance to read through issues of *Mallorn, Mythlore, Seven*, the *Inklings Jahrbuch* and other journals dedicated to Tolkien, and have probably missed much.

WHAT DOES IT MEAN TO BE REPRESENTATIVE

The reluctance may be due in part to the perceived Modernist associations of any such contention. I, however, do not intend to argue the 'modernity' of Tolkien's work or views, but to demonstrate, with as many examples as space allows, their representative status. To be representative, Tolkien need not have read a single Modernist manifesto. On the contrary, it is salutary to remember that Modernism was only one element in the literary scene of the time, and Tolkien's anti-modernism (both in the strictly literary and the philosophical sense) was in fact the more mainstream, not to say majority position. The woeful tale of Modernism's rise to absolute dominance in the academy – out of all proportion to its real historical significance – need not be told here, but it does appear as if the tide is finally turning.[5] Hopefully it will bring to an end the heroic but futile attempts to assimilate Tolkien to the Modernist mould in an effort to salvage his academic reputation:[6] that venerable last-ditch manoeuvre of all beleaguered champions of pariah authors and movements, from the much-maligned Georgian poets to the Edwardian realists dismissed by Virginia Woolf. To say that something was characteristic of its time, is not necessarily to imply that it was in any way self-consciously Modern with a capital M, avant-garde or cutting edge artistically, or politically progressive. Reactionary attitudes and artistic conservatism are often more characteristic, more democratic even, because they represent a bigger proportion of the population. But

---

[5] See the introduction to Baldick (2004), and the developments in the wake of the canon-breaking of the last generation, and the rise of book history and cultural studies.

[6] See the special Tolkien issue of *Modern Fiction Studies* (2004). Patchen Mortimer (2005) is correct to maintain that Tolkien must be placed in conversation with his contemporaries and be regarded as part of the literary current, but the identification of that current with Modernism seems to me to be misguided. Modernism was neither the only nor the main literary current of the time, and certainly not the one of most relevance to Tolkien. It would make more sense to focus on the differences like Verlyn Flieger in *Interrupted Music*.

even a minority view is representative if it could not have been held a century before or a century after, if it belongs to its time, grows out of and reflects its historical moment. Literary Modernism and the best-selling adventure romance – one very much a minority pursuit, the other a mass genre by definition – were both representative of the early twentieth century in this sense.

It is precisely to demonstrate this quality that a study of contemporary analogues is so indispensable, and so very different from the misguided search for spurious sources. In what follows, I am trying to assemble a picture of a period to see where Tolkien fits into it – arguing influences is not my primary purpose. If ten authors employ the same trope, it does not necessarily mean that they are borrowing from each other, it means that the trope is in common use and Tolkien's adaptation of it signals his participation in the prevalent literary discourse. Equally, to claim the relevance of specific historical developments – whether the rise of the Labour Party or the Nazi regime – to *The Lord of the Rings* is not the same as claiming that the book is an allegory of World War II or that Saruman's Shire is a straightforward critique of austerity-era England. Tolkien explicitly rejected both interpretations in his Foreword to the Second Edition, and Shippey has just as explicitly demonstrated how in a different sense they are both correct. Like Shippey and Rosebury, I am not referring to "coded reference[s] to specific contemporary events or phenomena but [to] the absorption into the invented world," consciously or not, "of experiences and attitudes which Tolkien would scarcely have acquired had he not been a man of the twentieth" (Rosebury 2003:163) and, I would add, the late nineteenth centuries. Before the siege of Minas Tirith Beregond tells Pippin that orders have come "that lights are to be dimmed within the City, and none are to shine out from the walls" (Tolkien 1995:754-755). No internal narrative logic can account for this detail as effectively as the fact of nightly blackouts during World War II, and Shippey (2000a:161-174) has adduced many more examples in this line. In the Foreword, Tolkien admits that "An author cannot of course remain wholly unaffected by his experience, [though] the ways in which a story-germ uses the soil of experience are extremely complex" (1995:xvii). In fact, the only way he can counter guesses about the allegorical significance of the Second World War and the post-1945 economic situation is by referring to other aspects of his historical context – World War I and suburbanization circa 1900.

By arguing that Tolkien was a man of his time I am assuming that it is possible to define this 'time' as at least to some extent a homogenous entity. Every period possesses a particular stock of accepted ideas or assumptions, certain models and moulds of thinking which permeate most discourses and disciplines, and around which all controversies revolve. No matter how bitter the disagreements between various ideological factions, the argument is usually over the interpretation of what is in essence a shared paradigm; and though responses may range across a broad spectrum, certain axioms are constant and form the common ground of the most widely divergent positions. Extremes of opinion are often two sides of the same coin, irreconcilable opposites that depend upon each other and are produced by the same society. The theological differences of the Middle Ages, for instance, presupposed a common belief in a deity; the Cold War was a conflict between two globalist ideologies; most theories or philosophies of modern times take for granted some form of relativism. In the late nineteenth and early twentieth centuries, historians, sociologists, politicians, and writers of different religious and political persuasions were as polarized on the fundamental issues as ever before or after, but they thought about them in the same period-specific terms: evolution vs. degeneration, individualism vs. collectivism, organic vs. mechanical, patriotism vs. cosmopolitanism, the common man vs. the elite, modern mass society vs. traditional localized community, and so on. Not all of these apply to Tolkien – no single person could have embraced all the existing cultural strands in their diversity – but it is possible to demonstrate just how much he shared in the received habits of thought.

EXAMPLE 1: ROMANTIC ANTI-INDUSTRIALISM

Instead of repeating *ad nauseam*, but without any kind of historical elaboration, the hackneyed fact of Tolkien's anti-industrialism, why not show exactly how Tolkien's letters, essays, and fictional works formed a part of the romantic critique of modern industrial society that was such an important strain in nineteenth and twentieth century English writing? Vociferations against the Machine, industrialism, suburbanization, and large impersonal structures both of state and capital, a corresponding turn towards the past, often in the form of medievalism, nature-worship, pastoralism, and the Simple Life, and the identification of these things with a true and unchanging 'Englishness', have a very long and varied pedigree: Carlyle, Ruskin, William Morris, Thomas Hardy, Edward Carpenter, C. R. Ashbee and other Arts and Crafts practitioners, the Georgians, G. K. Chesterton, Kenneth Grahame, E. Nesbit, E. M. Forster, D. H. Lawrence, Rudyard Kipling, G. M. Trevelyan, J. B. Priestley, George Orwell, politicians like Stanley Baldwin and Ramsay MacDonald ... the list goes on and on. Books have been written on the importance of this cultural stereotype for all media and in all spheres of society (literature, art, politics, advertisements) in the historical period which coincided with Tolkien's formative and adult years. It could be argued, in fact, that its heyday was the decade before the First World War when Tolkien grew up and imbibed many of his social assumptions. Yet no one, to my knowledge, has produced a full-length study of Tolkien in this context: neither in terms of his participation in nor of his transcendence and unique transformation of this literary-cultural complex. Vague references to an idyllic Sarehole childhood notwithstanding, the only thoroughly contextualized studies of Tolkien's thought and writing have been those dealing with the medieval and philological background of his work and with the impact of the Great War. A lot more remains to be done.

EXAMPLE 2: HISTORICAL RECONSTRUCTION

Even Shippey's and Michael Drout's excellent surveys of the philological scene could be filled out with considerations of that discipline in the context of contemporary anthropology, historiography, and comparative mythology, with which it was so inextricably entwined.[7] Tolkien did not study these subjects at Oxford, but he did know (and reject) the theories of Andrew Lang and Max Müller, and the models they and their peers in related disciplines developed permeated thinking about the 'asterisk' historical period which philology tried to reconstruct. Reading the historian Edward Freeman's description, in *Comparative Politics* (1873:33-35), of the original Aryan *Völkerwanderung* and dispersal – the march of the three kindreds into the west from their common birthplace, some pressing on ahead to the Ocean, others going off in different directions, "to meet [again] in far-off ages with their severed brethren" – one is reminded of nothing so much as the march of the Eldar from Cuiviénen. And what else but the Last Alliance of Elves and Men is evoked by Freeman's picture of the European "host which was to drive back the Turanian invader," when for the last time "the Roman and the Goth" marched "side by side, equal in might and dignity, emblems of the world that was passing away and of the world that was coming in its stead" (Freeman 1873:36). Tolkien need not have read Freeman's *Comparative Politics*, just as he need not have had any specific work of

---

[7] See Tom Shippey, *The Road to Middle-earth* (2004) and Michael Drout's edition of *Beowulf and the Critics* (Tolkien 2002). I have not had the chance to read Iwan Rhys Morus's "'Uprooting the Golden Bough': J. R. R. Tolkien's Response to Nineteenth Century Folklore and Comparative Mythology' (1990). Andrew Wawn's 'Philology and Fantasy Before Tolkien' (2002) is an excellent, though brief, treatment of the topic, focusing on E. R. Eddison and William Morris.

scholarship in mind when he was rewriting the European waves of westward migration in Middle-earth terms, culminating in the Rome-Barbarian parallels of Gondor in the Third Age.[8] But it must be recognized that several fundamental conceptions of Middle-earth history were rooted in late-Victorian reconstructions, and inherited certain aspects of their rhetoric.

THE LITERARY TRADITION: HAGGARD, CHESTERTON, AND MORRIS

Language and history, however, by no means exhaust the possibilities of comparative analysis. Certain authors in the late nineteenth and early twentieth century fantasy tradition provide ample material for comparison, though very little of the secondary literature on the genre is Tolkien-centered.[9] There are marginal cases of interest, like the People of the Hills in Kipling's *Puck of Pook's Hill*, who may be an unusual early analogue of Tolkien's Elves,[10] as well as George MacDonald's romances, children's books, and essays on the Imagination, which cast a revealing light on Tolkien's theory of sub-creation, despite Tolkien's

---

[8] See Judy Ann Ford, 'The White City: *The Lord of the Rings* as an Early Medieval Myth of the Restoration of the Roman Empire' (2005) for a detailed treatment of the analogies.

[9] Tolkien does usually get a chapter or at least a mention in most general fantasy criticism, but many of these works are deeply misguided, and none break any new ground in Tolkien studies proper. Richard Mathews's *Fantasy: The Liberation of the Imagination* (2002) is an exception, Shippey's introduction to *The Oxford Book of Fantasy Stories* (1994) is useful, and one wishes for a critical work on the lines of the anthology *Tales Before Tolkien: The Roots of Modern Fantasy* (Anderson 2003).

[10] Kipling's Old Things, Norse gods and Celtic faeries, also experience a fading of sorts, and hate to be confounded with "little buzzflies with butterfly wings and gauze petticoats [...] that painty-winged, wand-waving, sugar-and-shake-your-head set of impostors," (Kipling 1956:409-10). At the time this was written Tolkien had not yet entered his *Goblin Feet* phase, and was still several decades away from voicing Kipling's strictures. A more fruitful direction for inquiry may be the little-remarked but striking similarities of metre and rhythm in Kipling's and Tolkien's verse.

ambivalence about MacDonald as a writer. The names of H. Rider Haggard, G. K. Chesterton,[11] and William Morris are more significant.

The evidence for Haggard's direct influence is largely circumstantial. It is sometimes remarked that Tolkien borrowed the word "Kor" from Haggard's 1887 romance *She*, and that the starting conceit of a parchment in different languages appealed to him, as presumably did the book's mythological import, if C. S. Lewis's reactions are anything to go by. Tolkien and Lewis's shared interest in adventure tales with fantastical elements is well known. But though all of this remains at the level of speculation, anyone looking for analogies to Tolkien's work in contiguous genres cannot afford to pass Haggard by. One may mention, for instance, the parallels between Sam and the servant Job, who has an "honest round face" and waits on two bachelor gentlemen, Mr. Holly and his ward Leo (Haggard 1887:57). Job's speech patterns sound remarkably familiar: "I hope Mr. Leo won't meddle with no such things, for no good can't come of it" (Haggard 1887:54); "'Well sir,' answered Job, stolidly, 'I don't hold much with foreign parts, but if both you gentlemen are going you will want somebody to look after you'" (Haggard 1887:55). Mr. Holly, like Bilbo in *The Hobbit*, longs for his "comfortable rooms in Cambridge. Why had I been such a fool as to leave them? This is a reflection that has several times recurred to me since, and with ever-increasing force" (Haggard 1887:63). Perhaps these details are too commonplace to be revealing, though the facsimiles of the Sherd of

---

[11] See, most importantly, the special Tolkien issue of *The Chesterton Review* (2002); Joseph Pearce links Chesterton and Tolkien via Catholicism and distributism, and the two are frequently placed side by side in overviews of Christian fantasy. William N. Rogers II and Michael R. Underwood, 'Gagool and Gollum: Exemplars of Degeneration in *King Solomon's Mines* and *The Hobbit*' (Clark and Timmons 2000:121-131) make a good case for the importance of looking at Haggard, but their own analysis is not at all convincing. Jared Lobdell's chapter in *England and Always* (1981) on the *Lord of the Rings* as "an adventure story in the Edwardian mode" brings up both Haggard and Chesterton (as well as some authors I do not mention) and is the closest in method to my own analysis.

Amenartas are tempting prototypes for the Book of Mazarbul. But let's take a look at Haggard's Icelandic romance *Eric Brighteyes*, which would have appealed more readily to Tolkien's Northern imagination. Théoden's dispatching of Grima Wormtongue (Haggard 1891:145), Eowyn welcoming and filling Aragorn's cup (Haggard 1891:149) and later imploring him not to go (Haggard 1891:151), the company of the dead (Haggard 1891:309), Gimli's axe-work, Eomer tossing his sword in the air (Haggard 1891:310), outlaws like Barahir by Tarn Aeluin or Túrin on Amon Rudh (Haggard 1891:235-236), Túrin renaming himself son of Úmarth, or Ill-fate (Haggard 1891:197), the renaming of Cabed-en-Aras after Nienor's fall (Haggard 1891:*passim.*), Túrin speaking to his sword Gurthang and its answer (Haggard 1891:285-286): all these are scenes or images that have their exact counterparts in *Eric Brighteyes*. It could be argued that both Haggard and Tolkien drew on the same source material in the Icelandic sagas, and more likely than not the similarities are merely accidental, but none of this takes away the fact that Haggard's romances – considered together and in terms of plot – are distant precursors of Tolkien's legendarium.

Chesterton's relevance, though not as evident at the narrative level, is more substantial in other regards. It has always been known that there is an allusion to Chesterton in the essay 'On Fairy-Stories',[12] but no one seems to have bothered to read Chesterton's *Autobiography*, where the themes of humility, eucatastrophe, recovery, and consolation (Chesterton 1936:308), children and fairy tales (Chesterton 1936:42-44), democracy and monarchy (Chesterton 1936:269), and the metaphor of England as a railway station (Chesterton 1936:124), not to mention a condemnation of top-hats (Chesterton 1936:126), all make an appearance just a couple of years before Tolkien's landmark lecture. Chesterton was a very popular journalist and it is inconceivable that

---

[12] See Tolkien (2001:58, 64) for top-hats and railway stations.

over the thirty years of his omnipresence in the national press, which coincided with the first thirty years of the century, Tolkien would not have encountered his writing. He was certainly familiar with *The Ballad of the White Horse*, *Orthodoxy*, and at least some of Chesterton's essays (see letters 80, 186, 312: Tolkien 1981:92, 246, 402). Given Chesterton's well-publicized conversion to Catholicism, and his explicit interest in themes dear to Tolkien's heart, it is not surprising that he should have figured in the essay 'On Fairy-stories'. Tolkien mentions the "recovery of freshness of vision," the "queerness of things that have become trite, when they are seen suddenly from a new angle," as attributes of "Chestertonian fantasy" for the "humble," though why he does not address Chesterton's Christian theory of fairy tales more fully remains a mystery (Tolkien 2001:58-59). Perhaps that comparison still awaits its scholar. Chesterton and Tolkien came from roughly similar school backgrounds, and the resemblances between the T.C.B.S. and Chesterton's schoolboy clique of the previous generation would make for an interesting biographical investigation. Politically, as well, a case could be made for Tolkien's continuation of a certain strand of Chestertonian ideology, but before pursuing this connection, let us turn to a much clearer instance of literary paternity.

William Morris, who preceded Tolkien at Exeter College, Oxford by over fifty years, is one of the few clearly attested 'sources' among modern writers. But although his ancestry is universally acknowledged in studies of the fantasy genre, and Humphrey Carpenter, Tom Shippey, John Garth, Andrew Wawn, and Richard Mathews have all addressed aspects of his influence, no one has carried out a systematic comparison to assess the real extent of Tolkien's indebtedness. It is well known that Tolkien used his Skeat Prize money in 1914 to buy Morris's *The Life and Death of Jason*, *The Volsunga Saga*, and *The House of the Wolfings*; that same year, his first attempt to adapt the *Kalevala* took the shape of a Morris romance.[13] He carried *The Earthly Paradise* in the trenches (Garth 2003:185); he referred disparagingly to Morris's *Sigurd the Volsung* in his notes to the 1936 Beowulf lecture;[14] as a scholar he was familiar with Morris's and Magnússon's translations of the *Heimskringla*, and he even knew Morris's socialist utopia *News from Nowhere*. In fact, as Christopher Tolkien has confirmed, "his father owned nearly all of Morris's works," read *The House of the Wolfings* to Christopher as a child, and bequeathed him "11 titles of Morris's books of poems, translations, and fantasies [...] including *The House of the Wolfings*, *The Roots of the Mountains*, and *The Sundering Flood*, plus J. W. Mackail's two-volume *Life of William Morris* and A. Clutton-Brock's *William Morris: His Work and Influence*" (Mathews 2002:87). Most famously of course, Tolkien said that *The House of the Wolfings* and *The Roots of the Mountains*, Morris's two Germanic romances, were a bigger influence on *The Lord of the Rings* than World War I.[15] Yet where are the detailed studies of the Morrisian echoes in so many of Tolkien's Silmarillion writings, from the account of *Túor's Coming to Gondolin* to the *Wanderings of Húrin*? The Shire-muster and the muster of the Rohirrim, the moots of the hobbits and the Ents, but above all of the folk of Brethil, with their Moot-ring and Doom-rock and assembly of judgment, borrow not just the vocabulary, but the imagery of Morris's romances. Shippey

---

[13] See letter no. 1: "Amongst other work I am trying to turn one of the [*Kalevala*] stories – which is really a very great story and most tragic – into a short story somewhat on the lines of Morris' romances with chunks of poetry in between" (Tolkien 1981:7).

[14] See Tolkien (2002:255, 265) note 304: "he selected from all those available the one metre most foreign in mood and style to the original and not in itself a good metre"; also, Morris was not "a learned or a scholarly poet," he used a "living crib or interpreter" and had a "wild and willful way with them," though he was fortunate with Magnússon; his *Beowulf* translation was an "oddity."

[15] See letter 226: "The Dead Marshes and the approaches to the Morannon owe something to Northern France after the Battle of the Somme. They owe more to William Morris and his Huns and Romans, as in *The House of the Wolfings* or *The Roots of the Mountains*" (Tolkien 1981:303).

(1982) and Wawn (2002) have dealt with Tolkien's and Morris's philological reconstructions; Carpenter (2000:77-8, 98, 100), Mathews (2002:86), Rosebury (2003:95-96), and Garth (2003:34-35, 219, 224, 290, 296) have noted the influence of Morris's style and plotting on *The Fall of Gondolin* and *The Book of Lost Tales* as a whole, specifically the importance of Morris's elevated and archaic diction (though Garth's demeaning of Morris's literary gifts seems gratuitous); and Jessica Yates (2005) has considered Tolkien's probable borrowing of phrases like the "Sundering Flood," and "east of the sun, west of the moon." Yet there is enough material there – from plot parallels and recurrent motifs, to narrative devices, philosophical and biographical similarities – for a hefty monograph. Both men's opposition to industrial and mechanized modernity – the often-noted 'luddite' tendency – and the corresponding interest in the medieval North have already been mentioned. They were also both amateur calligraphers and manuscript illuminators, and though Tolkien was not a craftsman himself, the Morrisian emphasis on decorative arts and handicrafts is apparent in descriptions of Middle-earth. One need only remember the look of Théoden's hall, or the very character of the dwarves and the Noldor, who embody in their creative work Morris's artisan ideal. Most significant perhaps, is both writers' shared preoccupation with the theme of death and immortality: the central and defining theme, it could be argued, of their work.[16]

The original 1920 audience of *The Fall of Gondolin* was in no more doubt than Northrop Frye (1976) that Tolkien was "a staunch follower of tradition […] of such typical romantics as William Morris [and] George MacDonald," and it is indeed the case that Tolkien is best classified as a neo-romantic (audience report quoted in Mathews 2002:86). Despite the prevalent caricature of the tweedy don for whom

---

[16] See C. S. Lewis's essay on William Morris in *Rehabilitations* (1939), but also E. P. Thompson (1977).

literature stopped with Chaucer – despite even Tolkien's own modest protestations, which should be given as much credence as his deceptive repudiation of allegory – the nineteenth and twentieth centuries formed an indelible part of his mental landscape. Tolkien adapted Coleridge for his literary theory and echoes Keats in his poetry; debts to Dickens and images from Tennyson have been picked out by critics for analysis.[17] Closer to his own time there was the Catholic poet Francis Thompson – the young Tolkien's primary enthusiasm – and he was familiar with the writings of Walter de la Mare, Algernon Blackwood, Lord Dunsany, and E. R. Eddison, as well as with contemporary children's literature and science fiction, from H. G. Wells, Kenneth Grahame, and J. M. Barrie, to Isaac Asimov and Mary Renault (see Tolkien 1981:*passim.*). More surprising, given the entrenched stereotype, are Tolkien's references in his letters to *Arms and the Man* – George Bernard Shaw's play debunking military heroism – and to *Babbitt* – the 1922 novel satirizing bourgeois conformity by the American realist Sinclair Lewis.[18] But to speak only of literature is to take a strangely narrow view of what constituted Tolkien's historical moment. His contemporaries were engaged in many other cultural activities: country walking for example.

---

[17] See Rosebury (2003:93, 150-151) for references to A. E. Houseman, Swinburne, Yeats, Francis Thompson, Robert Bridges, Mark Twain, Fenimore Cooper, Dickens, Shelley, and Tennyson. Rosebury (2003:157) also mentions "neo-romantic earnestness." Lobdell (1981:11) takes it for granted that Tolkien was a romantic, as does Joe R. Christopher in 'Tolkien's Lyric Poetry', where he also argues for taking a larger view of what constitutes the twentieth century (Flieger and Hostetter 2000:144-145, 159-160).

[18] See letter 82: "We three have just come back [...] from a v. poor production at Playhouse of 'Arms and the Man', which does not wear well" (Tolkien 1981:94). "Babbitt has the same bourgeois smugness that hobbits do. His world is the same limited place" (qtd. in Carpenter 2000:168).

RURAL NOSTALGIA

Biographers tell us that Tolkien used to take country walks, with the two Lewis brothers or with other companions, and he would often stop to examine the things that grew by the wayside. Bilbo and Frodo, of course, also go on country walks around the Shire. But one can put this little-noted matter into context by recalling that country walking was a sociological phenomenon that reached unprecedented proportions in England in the interwar period. By the early 1930s there were half a million walkers or cyclists from London seeking out lanes with the help of guidebooks and Ordnance Survey maps. There were guided rambles, posters in railways advertising excursions, pamphlets, and a profusion of magazines like *Country Life* and 'beautiful England' travel books. The middle classes got into motor cars, and the working classes got onto bicycles, and both rode out to rediscover rural England 'as it really was', unspoilt and natural (Colls and Dodd 1986:83).[19] The landscape they were supposed to encounter according to these various publications was full of hills, fields, lanes, hedgerows and coppices – the cultivated farmland of the home counties, no less than of Oxfordshire and Warwickshire – or, described in exactly the same terms in chapter three of Book I, the landscape of the Shire.

Country walking was merely one of the tributaries feeding into the current of rural nostalgia that reached its highest tide in the pre- and post-World War I years. One finds that the most important tree of Tolkien's early writings – the elm – was at this time an "unofficial emblem of Englishness": from Morris's *Under an Elm Tree or Thoughts in the Countryside* to Forster's wych-elm 'comrade' (Lucas 1997:16). Rural writing of all kinds proliferated: from Richard Jefferies and W. H. Hud-

---

[19] See Alun Howkins's 'The Discovery of Rural England' (1986). There is a vast secondary literature on English ruralism and the countryside, from Raymond Williams onwards.

son, to George Sturt, Edward Thomas, and the Georgian poets, to Kenneth Grahame in *Pagan Papers* and *The Wind in the Willows*. Grahame was appalled by the "leprosy of suburbia, collieries, and railways invading the English countryside," and horror at the threat to countryside and village life posed by the spreading of the town – so familiar to readers of Tolkien with regard to Birmingham's absorption of Sarehole – was voiced by everyone from Forster to Edith Nesbit.[20] In the interwar period, the Conservative and Labour prime ministers Baldwin and MacDonald agreed that the real England was in the countryside: "England is the country and the country is England," as Baldwin phrased it (qtd. Colls and Dodd 1986:82). Tolkien's contemporary at Oxford, the socialist and labour historian G.D.H. Cole also took a lot of country walks and expressed his passion for the southern English landscape (Wiener 1981:118).[21] This was not surprising: the English socialists had a long-standing tradition of country rambling and cycling, going back to the Clarion Clubs of the 1890s and the Edwardian period.

The rural theme, it must be remembered, also related directly to the experience of the Great War. Wartime propaganda, not least in the pastoral poetry anthologies produced specifically for the use of soldiers, pictured 'home' as rural and southern – but the tendency was not entirely government-sponsored (Colls and Dodd 1986:80-1). During and after the war, poet combatants like Sassoon, Blunden, and Thomas also idealized the rural home: the rose-covered cottage and the village spire. One poem, T. P. Cameron Wilson's *Sportsmen in Paradise*, even identified rural England with Heaven.[22] Though Tolkien's iconography was

---

[20] See 'London's creeping' in *Howard's End*, Nesbit's articles in the Fabian *New Statesman,* and John Carey's *The Intellectuals and the Masses* (1992).

[21] See also Wiener (1981:chapter 4) 'The 'English Way of Life'?' for a thorough description of the rural and anti-industrial construction of Englishness in the period.

[22] "They left the fury of the fight, / And they were very tired. / The gates of Heaven were open, quite / Unguarded, and unwired. / There was no sound of any gun; / The land was still and green: / Wide hills lay silent in the sun, / Blue valleys slept be-

different – recall the Oxford, Warwick, and Lonely Isle (England) of his wartime verses – the nostalgic impulse of this type of poetry remained with him long after 1918. One need only think of Sam's "In Western lands beneath the Sun," and the symbolic weight that accrues to the Shire as the hobbits leave it further and further behind. Though it was the 'South Country' rather than Tolkien's West Midlands that predominated in the patriotic imaginary of the time, both could give young officers in World War I 'a vision of Englishness' and

> a model of society – an organic and natural society of ranks, and of inequality in an economic and social sense, but one based on trust, obligation and even love – the relationship between the "good Squire" and the "honest peasant." It was a model which admirably suited the relationship between the young infantry Subaltern and the sixty or so men under his command.
> (Colls and Dodd 1986:80)

I have come across no better description of the relationship between Frodo and Sam, who were, as Tolkien half-admitted in his letters, a picture of an officer and his batman (see Carpenter 2000:89 and also Hooker 2004). Sam in particular was a reflection of the privates whom Tolkien knew in the war and whom he recognized as superior to himself; and Sam's "love for his master" bears comparison with at least some soldiers' 'love' for their officers, as revealed in oral testimony. The trenches, like the trek to Mordor, fostered a "classlessness based upon a shared experience of suffering," and hearkening back to the pre-war ideal of a "united agricultural community" (Colls and Dodd 1986:81). This, and not the other literary stereotype of "old gardeners and servants,

---

tween. / They saw far off a little wood / Stand up against the sky. / Knee-deep in grass a great tree stood [...] / Some lazy cows went by [...] / There were some rooks sailed overhead – / And once a church-bell pealed. / 'God! but it's England,' someone said, / 'And there's a cricket field!'" (Bentley 1992:18)

family retainers [...] cap-fumbling workmen who cringe to their 'betters'," is the appropriate context for Tolkien's depiction of Sam (Abu-Manneh 2002).

THE NATIONAL CHARACTER AND LITTLE ENGLANDISM

At the very beginning of *The Lord of the Rings* Bilbo says: "I want to see the wild country again before I die, and the Mountains; but [Frodo] is still in love with the Shire, with woods and fields and little rivers. He ought to be comfortable here" (Tolkien 1995:32).[23] In the first decades of the twentieth century all of England was in love with the Shire, and all Englishmen were hobbits. The stereotypes of the English national character current in the twenties, thirties, and during the Second World War were often predicated on a myth of rural England, though some famous commentators like George Orwell and J. B. Priestley did not confine their definitions to the countryside.[24] It was frequently noted that English people were gardeners, and no wonder, since England itself was well on its way to becoming a garden with the foundation of garden cities and suburbs, and the growth of plot-lands after World War I.[25] The English people, furthermore, were slow, stupid, parochial, insular and xenophobic, unwilling to fight but brave and sturdy when forced to, private, decent, law-abiding, gentle, common-sensical, and averse to continental regimentation.[26] They had enduring traditions whose stability and con-

---

[23] The passage is also interesting for its juxtaposition of the sublime and the beautiful.

[24] See Raphael Samuel (1989), especially Volume I *History and Politics*, for the national character, Little Englandism, and romantic anti-capitalism.

[25] See Colls and Dodd (1986:82-3). Morris may not have had this in mind when he said that "England will become a garden."

[26] Cartoons in the *Daily Mail* and the *Daily Express* from the 1920s to the 50s featured stock figures like 'The Little Man': a self-caricature of the domesticated, middle-aged English everyman, put-upon but able to stand up for himself, sensible, pacifist, not concerned with foreigners or political nostrums, and above all small.

tinuity were rooted in the immemorial life of the countryside, and a strong attachment to home and locality, hobbies, and amateurishness, which ensured their rejection of imported abstract theory and government control. The greatest evil was central state planning, whether manifested in ribbon development or, for the non-socialists, in nationalization.[27] One only has to recall the hobbits' response to Sharkey's regime, their distrust of Buckland and the attitudes in Bree – a parochialism which Tolkien explicitly criticized in *Letters* (see Tolkien 1981:329) – their "plain hobbit sense," the hidden courage of Bilbo and Sam, and the pointed absence of crime and voluntary obedience to The Rules, to realize how perfectly in sync with the prevailing stereotypes Tolkien's portrait of his fellow Englishmen was.

In his Little Englandism, as well, Tolkien was entirely in tune with the times. "The bigger things get the smaller and duller or flatter the globe gets," he wrote.

> It is getting to be all one blasted little provincial suburb [...] Col. Knox says 1/8 of the world's population speaks 'English', and that is the biggest language group. If true, damn shame – say I [...] I think I shall have to refuse to speak anything but Old Mercian. But seriously, I do find this Americo-cosmopolitanism very terrifying [...]. I need to you hardly add that them's the sentiments of a good many folk – and no indication of lack of patriotism. For I love England (not Great Britain and certainly not the British Commonwealth (grr!)). (Tolkien 1981:65)

---

[27] This was the suburban and updated version of Tolkien's rustic late-Victorian hobbits.
See Julia Stapleton, 'Resisting the Centre at the Extremes: 'English' Liberalism in the Political Thought of Interwar Britain' (1999) and 'Nationalism and Patriotism in British Political Thought since 1850' (1998).

A little later he wrote: "I know nothing about British or American imperialism in the Far East that does not fill me with regret and disgust, I am afraid I am not even supported by a glimmer of patriotism in this remaining war [...]. It can only benefit America or Russia" (Tolkien 1981:115). A Little Englander, at least since the Boer War, was an English patriot who condemned jingoism and imperial extension, and not infrequently all aspects of mass society. He reserved his love and loyalty for the traditional English community rather than the British Empire, which was associated with international finance and the centralized state. Chesterton, with his anti-cosmopolitanism, local patriotism, and distributist belief in small peasant freeholdings was the prototypical Little Englander. Orwell's radical patriotic effusions drew on many of the same notions; J. B. Priestley wrote in 1934, "It is little England I love" (qtd. in Samuel 1989:xxiii); and all signs point to Tolkien's participation, consciously or not, in the same tradition. The fate of Númenor should be enough to indicate his attitude to imperial overreach, and certainly Tolkien shared the Little Englanders' pronounced rejection of both the Soviet and the American models. It is rarely recalled that in 'The Scouring of the Shire' he satirized not only socialist-style planning, but capitalist greed via the character of Lotho Pimple. Arthur Quiller-Couch expressed the essence of the concept when he said that for the source of true patriotism the Englishman looks to a

> green nook of his youth in [some] shire [...] where the folk are slow, but there is seed-time and harvest; [...] other nations extend, or would extend, their patriotism over large spaces superficially: ours [...] ever cuts down through the strata for its well-springs, intensifies itself upon that which, untranslatable to the

> foreigner, is comprised for us in a single easy word –
> Home. (qtd. in Colls and Dodd 1986:117)[28]

In light of this, not to mention the highly-charged associations of 'home' during the Great War, Christopher Garbowski's reading of the Shire as *Heimat* takes on a new relevance. And now consider the following words spoken by Sam in response to the Ring's temptation: "deep down in him lived still unconquered his plain hobbit-sense [...]. The one small garden of a free gardener was all his need and due, not a garden swollen to a realm; his own hands to use, not the hands of others to command" (Tolkien 1995:881). A statement of Christian humility? Yes, but if one influential version of the English mentality of the interwar period ever needed a creed – that would have fitted it to a tee.

ANTI-STATISM

One can turn finally to the subject of Tolkien and politics: the cause of much muddled thinking usually due to insufficient historical grounding. In a well-known 1943 letter to Christopher, Tolkien wrote:

> My political opinions lean more and more to Anarchy (philosophically understood, meaning abolition of control not whiskered men with bombs) – or to 'unconstitutional' Monarchy. I would arrest anybody who uses the word State (in any sense other than the inanimate realm of England and its inhabitants, a thing that has neither power, rights nor mind) [...] If we could get back to personal names, it would do a lot of good. Government is an abstract noun meaning the art and process of governing and it should be an offence to write it with a capital G or so as to refer to

---

[28] See Peter Brooker and Peter Widdowson, 'A Literature for England' (1986).

> people [...] it would go a long way to clearing thought, and reducing the frightful landslide into Theyocracy. (Tolkien 1981:63)

And here is Orwell, also writing in 1943 in his famous essay on *The English People*:

> English political thinking is much governed by the word 'They'. 'They' are the higher-ups, the mysterious powers who do things to you against your will. [...] The word 'They', the universal feeling that 'They' hold all the power and make all the decisions, and that 'They' can only be influenced in indirect and uncertain ways, is a great handicap in England.
> (Orwell 1943:17; 33)

The observation goes back at least to Orwell's *The Road to Wigan Pier* (1937:49):

> [The working man] feels himself the slave of mysterious authority and has a firm conviction that "they" will never allow him to do this, that and the other. Once when I was hop-picking I asked the sweated pickers [...] why they did not form a union. I was told immediately that "they" would never allow it. Who were "they"? I asked. Nobody seemed to know; but evidently "they" were omnipotent.

In 1957 Richard Hoggart, documenting working-class perceptions in *The Uses of Literacy*, wrote about "the world of 'Them'," "the world of the bosses [...]. a shadowy but [...] powerful group affecting [the workers'] lives at almost every point." "They" are the officials, the authorities, "'the people at the top', 'the higher-ups', the people who give you your dole, call you up, tell you to go to war, fine you [...] 'get yer in the end' [...] 'clap yer in clink' [...] 'treat y' like muck'" (Hoggart 1957:53-54).

"They" are the opposite of the local, the homely, the personal (Hoggart 1957:20, 57).

Enough has probably been said of the distrust of centralization and the dislike of the impersonal modern state to recognize the tradition to which all three authors belong. But it must be emphasized that the unfortunate and pernicious slide into "Theyocracy" was bemoaned by representatives of both ends of the political spectrum. Left or right, the libertarian and guild socialists from Morris to Orwell, the distributists like Chesterton and Belloc, the anarchists in the mutualist line from Kropotkin, were all proponents of small, devolved, local communities. And as romantic anti-statists they were all ranged together on one side against the encroaching Servile State represented by the bureaucrats, administrators, experts and efficiency-mongers, centralists and globalists, whether of the capitalist, the Fabian, or the communist variety. It has been observed before, though never in this context, that politically the Shire is a model anarchist commune.[29] Notwithstanding its pronounced social hierarchies and the historically-specific accoutrements of the English class system – which serve no identifiable political purpose – it is a self-governing, fully-functional community. No central government is necessary to maintain harmony, for the hobbits never fight amongst themselves. In fact, as the Prologue says regarding the "Ordering of the Shire," hobbits "had hardly any 'government'. Families for the most part managed their own affairs [...]. Estates, farms, workshops, and small trades tended to remain unchanged for generations." "There had been no king for nearly a thousand years," and in the Fourth Age the Shire is guaranteed continued local autonomy from the Gondorian monarchy (Tolkien 1995:9). Laws are kept of free will, the Thainship is "a nominal dignity," the elected Mayor – "the only real official in the Shire" – is chiefly ornamental, and the only centralized services are the

---

[29] See also Weinreich (2005).

Messengers and the Watch, though the un-uniformed police are mainly employed in dealing with stray animals (Tolkien 1995:10).

It is of course true that the Shire is not representative of the majority of Middle-earth societies; it is an anomaly even in terms of the textual evolution of the Silmarillion matter. There are many realms which extend over large territories, but most still conform to one of the two alternatives in the letter quoted above: they are either personal "unconstitutional" (and sometimes elected) monarchies or natural associations characterized by an "abolition of control". It is only the evil societies – Saruman's or Sauron's totalitarian industrial empires with world-state ambitions – that are recognizably contemporary 'Theyocracies', despite, or perhaps because of their basis in slavery. The orcs that Frodo and Sam encounter in Mordor use the most modern idiom in the book: theirs is distinctly the speech of twentieth-century soldiers, but also of government or party functionaries, minor officials in a murderous bureaucracy.[30] Shagrat and Gorbag talk of the "Big Bosses": "'It's going well, they say.' 'They would,' grunted Gorbag," who is aware of the official propaganda (Tolkien 1995:720-721). There is a sense of frustration with headquarters: "they couldn't get Lugbúrz to pay attention for a good while" (Tolkien 1995:721), but the two "have [their] orders," in the clipped language of army dispatches: "Prisoner is to be stripped. Full description of every article [...] to be sent to Lugbúrz at once [...]. And the prisoner is to be kept safe and intact, under pain of death for every member of the guard" (Tolkien 1995:723). The two tracker orcs Frodo and Sam observe from afar speak just like the Nazis on trial at Nuremberg: "'Whose blame's that?' said the soldier. 'Not mine. That comes from Higher Up'" (Tolkien 1995:904). "Higher Up," like "Big Bosses," like all the impersonal structures or forces of a Theyocracy, is

---

[30] This is not just the "closed militaristic culture" that Rosebury (2003:82) talks about.

capitalized. The orcs' conversation conveys a definite sense of a hierarchical party structure: "They've lost their heads, that's what it is. And some of the bosses are going to lose their skins too, I guess, if what I hear is true" (Tolkien 1995:904). In fact, if one did not know the context of the lines, one could be forgiven for thinking that this was a naturalistic novel of army life in one of the world wars, or better yet, a totalitarian dystopia. "'You come back,' shouted the soldier, 'or I'll report you!' 'Who to? Not to your precious Shagrat. He won't be captain any more.' 'I'll give your name and number to the Nazgûl'," threatens the tracker orc (Tolkien 1995:904), and the slave-driver of the column Frodo and Sam fall in with warns: "Deserting, eh? [...] Up you get and fall in, or I'll have your numbers and report you" (Tolkien 1995:909). The idea of soldiers, like prisoners, having numbers, no less than the concept of reporting insubordination to superiors whose own situation is precariously dependent on the favour of the big bosses, is entirely alien to the world of Middle-earth as originally conceived (in the Silmarillion writings of the 1920s and 30s and as late as *The Hobbit*). Yet few commentators ever remark that the glimpses of orc life in Mordor are completely at odds with the rest of the narrative, that the tone and atmosphere of these scenes have more in common with *Nineteen Eighty-Four* than with anything else in *The Lord of the Rings*.

CONCLUSION

It is possible to extend this study in many other directions, to consider, for instance, Tolkien's artistic output – both patterns and illustrations – in the context of Art Nouveau design. But hopefully, enough examples have already been provided to ground Tolkien thoroughly in his own time. The project is not intended to devalue the uniqueness of Tolkien's creation, on the contrary, it is only by recognizing how much he shared with his contemporaries that one can appreciate the extent of his originality. None of the other authors here considered thought of the

Straight Road or the Music of the Ainur; none invented Sindarin lenition based on Welsh or sent Chaucer's Vingilot journeying to far seas with Cynewulf's Earendil on board; not one saw the light of the Two Trees or conceived of death as a gift that would carry men beyond the circles of the world. But Niggle's tree did not spring rootless out of nothing, it grew in the rich and fertile soil of its time.

ANNA VANINSKAYA is a Marshall Scholar and D.Phil. candidate in English Literature at Oxford University. Her research focuses on late nineteenth and early twentieth century romance writing, historiography, and socialist propaganda. She is interested in the intersection between politics and genre, as well as in concepts of Englishness, and fantasy literature. Ms. Vaninskaya has published essays and articles on William Morris, George Orwell, and Robert Blatchford in conference proceedings and journals like *Utopian Studies* and *Contemporary Justice Review*.

Bibliography

Abu-Manneh, Bashir, 2002, *Fiction of the New Statesman, 1913-1939*, University of Oxford D.Phil. Thesis.

Anderson, Douglas A. (ed.), 2003, *Tales before Tolkien: The Roots of Modern Fantasy*, New York: Del Rey.

Baldick, Chris, 2004, *The Modern Movement: The Oxford English Literary History 1910-1940*, Oxford: Oxford University Press.

Bentley, James (ed.), 1992, *Some Corner of a Foreign Field: Poetry of the Great War*, London: Little, Brown and Company.

Boyd, Ian (ed.), 2002, *The Chesterton Review: J.R.R. Tolkien: Mythos and Modernity in Middle-earth* 28.1 and 28.2, Feb./May 2002, pp. 1-299.

Brooker, Peter and Peter Widdowson, 1986, 'A Literature for England', in Robert Colls and Philip Dodd (eds.), 1986, *Englishness: Politics and Culture 1880-1920*, London: Croon Helm, pp. 116-163.

Carey, John, 1992, *The Intellectuals and the Masses*, London: Faber and Faber.

Carpenter, Humphrey, 2000, *J.R.R. Tolkien: A Biography,* (revised edition, first edition 1977), New York: Houghton Mifflin Company.

Chesterton, G. K., 1936, *Autobiography*, (1959 edition), London: Arrow Books.

Clark, George and Daniel Timmons (eds.), 2000, *J.R.R. Tolkien and His Literary Resonances: Views of Middle-earth*, Westport, CT: Greenwood Press.

Colls, Robert and Philip Dodd (eds.), 1986, *Englishness: Politics and Culture 1880-1920*, London: Croon Helm.

Curry, Patrick, 1997, *Defending Middle-Earth, Tolkien: Myth and Modernity*, London: HarperCollins.

Doughan, David, 1999, 'England? Which England? Concepts of Englishness 1892-1954', in Richard Crawshaw (ed.), 1999, *Tolkien, A Mythology for England?*, Cambridge: 13th Tolkien Society Seminar, [email to author].

Drout, Michael, and Hilary Wynne, 2000, 'Tom Shippey's *J.R.R. Tolkien: Author of the Century* and a Look Back at Tolkien Criticism Since 1982', in *Envoi* 9.2, Fall 2000, pp. 101-167

Flieger, Verlyn, 1997, *A Question of Time: J.R.R. Tolkien's Road to Faërie*, Kent, Ohio: The Kent State University Press.

--- and Carl F. Hostetter (eds.), 2000, *Tolkien's Legendarium. Essays on The History of Middle-earth*, Westport, Connecticut and London: Greenwood Press.

---, 2002, *Splintered Light: Logos and Language in Tolkien's World*, (second edition, first edition 1983), Kent, Ohio: Kent State University Press.

---, 2005, *Interrupted Music: The Making of Tolkien's Mythology*, Kent, Ohio: Kent State University Press.

Ford, Judy Ann, 2005, 'The White City: *The Lord of the Rings* as an Early Medieval Myth of the Restoration of the Roman Empire', in *Tolkien Studies* 2, 2005, pp. 53-73.

Forster, E. M., 1910, *Howard's End*, in *Great Novels and Short Stories of E. M. Forster*, 1999, New York: Carroll & Graf, pp. 561-857.

Freeman, Edward, 1873, *Comparative Politics*, (second edition 1896), London: Macmillan.

Frye, Northrop, 1976, *The Secular Scripture: A Study of the Structure of Romance*, Cambridge, Mass.: Harvard University Press.

Garbowski, Christopher, 2000, *Recovery and Transcendence for the Contemporary Mythmaker: The Spiritual Dimension in the Works of J. R. R. Tolkien*, Lublin: Marie Curie-Sklodowska University Press.

Garth, John, 2003, *Tolkien and the Great War. The Threshold of Middle-earth*, London: HarperCollins.

Haggard, H. Rider, 1887, *She*, (2001 edition), London: Penguin Books.

---, 1891, *Eric Brighteyes*, (1895 edition), London: Longmans, Green, and Co.

Himes, Jonathan, 2000, 'What Tolkien Really Did With the Sampo', in *Mythlore* 22.4, Spring 2000, pp. 69-85.

Hoggart, Richard, 1957, *The Uses of Literacy*, London: Penguin Books.

Hooker, Mark, 2004, 'Frodo's Batman', in *Tolkien Studies* 1, 2004, pp. 125-136.

Howkins, Alun, 1986, 'The Discovery of Rural England', in Robert Colls and Philip Dodd (eds.), 1986, *Englishness: Politics and Culture 1880-1920*, London: Croon Helm, pp. 62-88.

Hughes, Shaun F. D. (ed.), 2004, *Modern Fiction Studies: J.R.R. Tolkien* 50.4, Winter 2004, pp. 807-1028.

Kipling, Rudyard, 1956, *Kipling: A Selection of His Stories and Poems*, Garden City: Doubleday.

Lewis, Clive S., 1939, *Rehabilitations: and Other Essays*, London: Oxford University Press.

Lobdell, Jared, 1981, *England and Always: Tolkien's World of the Rings*, Grand Rapids, Michigan: William B. Eerdmans.

Lucas, John, 1997, *The Radical Twenties: Aspects of Writing, Politics and Culture*, Nottingham: Five Leaves Publications.

Mathews, Richard, 2002, *Fantasy: The Liberation of the Imagination*, New York: Routledge.

Mortimer, Patchen, 2005, 'Tolkien and Modernism', in *Tolkien Studies* 2, 2005, pp. 113-129.

Morus, Iwan Rhys, 1990, '"Uprooting the Golden Bough": J. R. R. Tolkien's Response to Nineteenth Century Folklore and Comparative Mythology', in *Mallorn* 27, 1990, pp. 5–9.

Orwell, George, 1937, *The Road to Wigan Pier*, (1958 edition), New York: Harcourt Brace Jovanovich.

---, 1943, *The English People*, in Sonia Orwell and Ian Angus (eds.), 2000, *The Collected Essays, Journalism, and Letters*, Vol. 3, Boston: Nonpareil Books, pp. 1-37.

Pearce, Joseph, 1998, *Tolkien: Man and Myth*, London: HarperCollins.

Petty, Anne C., 2004, 'Identifying England's Lönnrot', in *Tolkien Studies* 1, 2004, pp. 69-84.

Reynolds, Patricia and Glen H. GoodKnight (eds.), 1995, *Proceedings of the J. R. R. Tolkien Centenary Conference*, Altadena, CA: Mythopoeic Press.

Rosebury, Brian, 2003, *Tolkien: A Cultural Phenomenon*, (revised and enlarged edition; first published 1992), Houndmills: Palgrave Macmillan.

Samuel, Raphael (ed.), 1989, *Patriotism: The Making and Unmaking of British National Identity*, London: Routledge.

Shippey, Tom A., 1982, 'Goths and Huns: The Rediscovery of Northern Cultures in the Nineteenth Century', in Andreas Haarder (ed.), 1982, *The Medieval Legacy*, Odense, Denmark: Odense University Press, pp. 51-69.

--- (ed.), 1994, *The Oxford Book of Fantasy Stories*, Oxford: Oxford University Press.

---, 2000a, *J.R.R. Tolkien: Author of the Century*, London: HarperCollins.

---, 2000b, 'Grimm, Grundtvig, Tolkien: Nationalisms and the Invention of Mythologies', in Maria Kuteeva (ed.), 2000, *The Ways of Creative Mythologies:*

Imagined Worlds and Their Makers, Telford: Tolkien Society Press, pp. 7-17.

---, 2002, 'Tolkien and Iceland: The Philology of Envy', in *Tolkien, Laxness, Undset Symposium,* 13-14 September, 2002, Reykjavik, Iceland: Sigurdur Nordal Institute, <http://www.nordals.hi.is/page/nordals-english>.

---, 2003, *The Road to Middle-earth,* (third edition; first edition 1982; second edition 1992), New York: Houghton Mifflin.

---, 2004, 'Light-elves, Dark-elves, and Others: Tolkien's Elvish Problem', in *Tolkien Studies* 1, 2004, pp. 1-15.

Stapleton, Julia, 1998, 'Nationalism and Patriotism in British Political Thought since 1850', in *Political Studies Association Conference Proceedings,* 1998, University of Keele, <http://www.psa.ac.uk/cps/1998/stapleton.pdf>.

---, 1999, Resisting the Centre at the Extremes: 'English' Liberalism in the Political Thought of Interwar Britain', in *British Journal of Politics and International Relations* 1.3, October 1999, pp. 270-292.

Tolkien, J. R. R., 1981, *Letters of J. R. R. Tolkien,* (edited by Humphrey Carpenter), London: George Allen & Unwin

---, 1983, *The Book of Lost Tales, Part I,* (edited by Christopher Tolkien), London: George Allen & Unwin.

---, 1995, *The Lord of the Rings,* (revised edition, first edition 1954-5), London: HarperCollins.

---, 2001, *Tree and Leaf,* (revised edition, first edition 1964), London: HarperCollins.

---, 2002, *Beowulf and the Critics,* (edited by Michael Drout), Tempe: Arizona Center for Medieval and Renaissance Studies.

Thompson, E. P., 1977, *William Morris: Romantic to Revolutionary,* (revised edition, first edition 1955), New York: Pantheon Books.

Wawn, Andrew, 2002, 'Philology and Fantasy Before Tolkien', *Tolkien, Laxness, Undset Symposium,* 13-14 September, 2002, Reykjavik, Iceland: Sigurdur Nordal Institute, <http://www.nordals.hi.is/page/nordals-english>.

Weinreich, Frank, 2005, 'Verfassungen mit und ohne Schwert. Impressionen idealer Herrschaftsformen in Mittelerde als Ausdruck des politischen Verständnisses von J.R.R. Tolkien', in *Hither Shore* 2, 2005, pp. 89-104.

Wiener, Martin, 1981, *English Culture and the Decline of the Industrial Spirit 1850-1980,* Cambridge: Cambridge University Press.

Yates, Jessica, 2005, 'William Morris's Influence on J.R.R. Tolkien as a Poet', in *William Morris Society Fiftieth Anniversary Conference,* 7-10 July, 2005, Royal Holloway, University of London, [email to author].

Against Stereotype:
Éowyn and Lúthien as 20th-Century Women

Maria Raffaella Benvenuto

Abstract

While female characters in Tolkien's fiction are indeed fewer and apparently less prominent than male ones, those which stand out are undisputedly among his most powerful creations. They also show quite clearly that the radical changes in the condition of women that happened during Tolkien's lifetime affected the author much more that one might be led to believe from a superficial reading of his work. This essay is mainly concerned with two characters that I consider to be closest to modern ideas of women's roles: the elf-maiden Lúthien and the warrior princess Éowyn. The image of modern femininity they both convey goes beyond the obvious aspects of strength and independence in order to embrace the fundamental value of creativity as a life-affirming force.

Introduction

One of the most frequent criticisms levelled against Tolkien's fictional work regards the scarcity of female characters and their minor role – when he is not targeted by outright accusations of misogyny, chauvinism, or even simple paternalism.[1] However, while stating that women in Tolkien's fiction are as plentiful or even as prominent as men would mean stretching the truth somewhat too far for comfort, it is also quite true that too many a critic has read Tolkien's work without bothering to take off the blinkers imposed by the current fashion for 'political

---

[1] The latter definition comes from Patrick Curry, a more than appreciative critic of Tolkien's work, who is nevertheless aware of the aspects which are more likely to go against the grain of the contemporary frame of mind: "Even with the characters of Éowyn, Galadriel and Shelob [...] Tolkien's paternalism if not patriarchy is unmissable." (Curry 1995:127)

correctness'. Therefore, any story with a prevalence of male characters would be quite likely to find itself at the receiving end of accusations of much the same kind, as would any story where women are not presented according to the image of how a 'modern' woman should behave.

On the other hand, the majority of contemporary fantasy writers have made a point of creating female characters which are not only independent and strong-willed, but very often hold positions of power and responsibility.[2] Such is the case of Robert Jordan's lengthy *The Wheel of Time* series,[3] where women amount to a good half of the main characters, and many are rulers of states in their own right, even enjoying absolute power.[4] Furthermore, many of the best fantasy writers of our times are women, whose work often displays more original, distinctive features than many of their male counterparts' output, all too often rooted in the 'heroic fantasy' tradition in the Robert E. Howard mould. These writers have brought a different outlook to a genre still plagued by stereotypes, such as the recourse to more or less graphic sex and violence, larger-than-life characters and clichéd plot lines. Their relationship with Tolkien, however, is often a rather uneasy one, aware as they are of "what they see as certain of Tolkien's premises: his acceptance of limitations on women's roles, as well as traditional acceptance of class" (Ringel 2000:157).

---

[2] Lisa Hopkins (1995:365), however, points out that "Power in the works of Tolkien is often to be found in the hands of a woman", then cites the examples of Galadriel, Melian, the Númenórean queens and the less well-known character of Meril-i-Turinqi in *The Book of Lost Tales*.

[3] The first volume of the series was published in 1990; at the time of writing, eleven volumes have been published so far (the latest in October 2005). The twelfth and very probably last episode of the series is scheduled for publication by the end of 2007.

[4] Possibly, the foremost example is the Empress of the warlike continent of Seanchan, a sort of semidivine figure who is not even supposed to be looked at by common mortals.

TOLKIEN'S WOMEN

Tolkien's rather conservative (though far from chauvinistic) stance towards women should not come as a surprise to modern-day readers. In fact, although Tolkien lived throughout most of the 20th century, he was the product of an upbringing still strongly influenced by Victorian and Edwardian values, which were quite different from those upheld by contemporary Western society. Therefore, trying to prove that Tolkien was in any way a 'hidden feminist'[5] would be a rather pointless exercise. His rare remarks about women prove quite clearly that he believed in traditional gender roles; besides, in one of his letters he mentioned feminism as one of the 'evils' inherent to the American influence on the whole world.[6] He also had reservations about women holding positions of responsibility, as in the case of the woman registrar mentioned in one of his letters to C.S. Lewis.[7] Then, in his notorious letter to his son Michael, he wrote that women's "gift is to be receptive, stimulated, fertilized (in many other matters than the physical) by the male" (letter No. 43, Carpenter 1995b:49), though they are very rarely creative in their own right – a remark that could be defined as politically incorrect, to say the least, and not likely to win him any admirers among true-blue feminists.

However, the biographical evidence available presents us quite a different picture of Tolkien's relationship with the female sex. At times we get the impression that, more than being genuinely convinced of women's inferiority (intellectual or otherwise), he may have felt somewhat uncomfortable around them, as it was typical of many men of his generation. Single-sex educational contexts were the rule at the time, so that men and women did not learn to deal with each other until later in

---

[5] See Donovan (2003:106) for a very similar remark.
[6] *Letters*, No. 53 (Carpenter 1995b:65).
[7] *Letters*, No. 49 (Carpenter 1995b:62).

life, when many preconceptions had already become rooted. This did not prevent men and women from falling in love and forming relationships based on genuine feelings of shared affection, as it was the case of Tolkien and his wife; however, once the barriers were set, it was difficult, if not impossible, to tear them down. Moreover, Tolkien's strong need for male companionship went hand-in-hand with his doubts about the possibility of real friendship between a man and a woman.[8] As a matter of fact, in the Oxford years his wife Edith often felt excluded from her husband's professional life and environment, and this led to frequent moments of tension between them.[9]

Interestingly, however, it seems that Tolkien's relationship with Edith herself, when they first met, was based just on the sort of companionship that, later in his life, he would mainly enjoy with other men. Even though their intellectual development had been very different, they evidently shared many interests (such as bicycle rides), got up to pranks together and, more importantly, genuinely enjoyed each other's company.[10] Though this friendship later bloomed into romance, it is all too easy to disregard the fact that Edith and Ronald began as friends who were completely at ease with each other. A very similar development can be observed in the relationship between Éowyn and Faramir, which starts as a friendship before turning into romance, as we will see in the following sections.

It is a well-documented fact that Tolkien corresponded with many women, never sounding patronising or disrespectful towards any of them. Some of his most interesting, detailed letters were in fact written to women, in some cases fellow writers such as Naomi Mitchison, or

---

[8] *Letters*, No. 43 (Carpenter 1995b:48): "In this fallen world, the 'friendship' that should be possible between all human beings, is virtually impossible between man and woman."
[9] See Carpenter (1995a:158-160).
[10] Carpenter (1995a:46-48).

keen readers of his work such as Rhona Beare.[11] We also know from reliable sources that he counted many women among his close friends,[12] and there is no evidence whatsoever of his being less than fair to his women students, one of whom, the Belgian graduate Simonne d'Ardenne, became for a time one of his closest collaborators.[13] She might have proved the exception to the rule, as Tolkien himself stated in the above-mentioned letter to his son; nevertheless, I think that someone really prejudiced against women would have carefully avoided any such form of partnership.

In my opinion, the best definition of Tolkien's view of women is possibly the one expounded by Lewis and Currie in their 2002 book, *The Uncharted Realms of Middle-earth*. According to the authors, Tolkien's opinions concerning women can be traced back to the so-called 'majority view', which prevailed in British society throughout the Victorian era up to the mid-1960s.[14] In a way, this view tended to idealise women and see them as creatures to be protected, receptive rather than creative, more suited to homemaking than intellectual activity. Even though we may recoil in horror before such opinions, we should not forget that, in spite of the enormous changes that have come about since then (not to mention the speed with which those changes have been effected), things were quite different in many European countries, including Britain itself, until no more than fifty years ago.

---

[11] See, for instance, No. 144 (to Naomi Mitchison), in which Tolkien speaks at length about some points in *The Lord of the Rings*; or No. 211 (to Rhona Beare), in which he answers many detailed questions about his fictional world.
[12] Carpenter (1995a:61).
[13] Carpenter (1995a:145).
[14] See Lewis and Currie (2002:183-188).

'MODERN' WOMEN

It should be clear from the start that anyone looking for 21st-century models of gender roles in Tolkien's fiction is bound to be severely disappointed. However, as usual, an ability to go beyond appearances (in this case, the idealised, medieval-style trappings so popular with right-wing groups)[15] is essential in order to understand that Tolkien was not as indifferent or hostile to social changes as it is commonly believed, and that what he wrote in his letters did not always reflect his actual behaviour.

As I stated above, in any discussion of Tolkien's female characters it should never be forgotten that he wrote in a historical period, which, though not so distant from ours in terms of time, was very contradictory as far as women's rights were concerned. Although British and American women had been able to vote for some time, and many of them worked outside the home, the situation in other European countries was not quite so rosy. Italian women were allowed to vote for the first time in 1946, and the '50s and '60s saw an all-time low in female employment. Those who did go to work usually chose typically 'feminine' careers such as teaching, nursing or office work. Women professionals, such as lawyers, architects or even medical doctors, were rare, and usually limited to urban areas. Until the early '70s, Italian men enjoyed many more rights than women in a married couple. Women's liberation movements fought long and hard for their achievements in the field of civil rights,

---

[15] The right-wing interpretation of Tolkien's writings would deserve a more thorough treatment of its own. In the 1970s it was a remarkably widespread phenomenon in Italy, as illustrated in Del Corso and Pecere's 2003 book *L'anello che non tiene* ("The Ring that Does Not Hold"). As a matter of fact, the authors mention that, in 1976, a magazine for women called *Éowyn* was founded by the foremost Italian right-wing party, Movimento Sociale. This publication wanted to convey an 'alternative' (i.e. not feminist) image of femininity, relying heavily on pseudo-medieval imagery, as well as strongly conservative ideals of women's role in society (see Corso and Pecere 2003:18-22).

which were constantly under attack from the Catholic Church and the more conservative components of society.[16]

As much as these attitudes may have changed in our times, stereotypes are hard to kill. With alarming regularity, we are treated to the latest 'scientific discovery' about supposed chemical differences between men and women, men's inborn tendency to sexual promiscuity, women's inferior ability in mathematics, and other such dubious matters. Women are still heavily discriminated in workplaces, not to mention the various forms of segregation and abuse to which they are subjected in many parts of the world. Nowadays, even in our enlightened societies, we cannot help noticing a worrying sort of backlash against everything that we have been taking for granted.

Tolkien may not have believed in women's liberation, and he may have paid lip service to the 'majority view' of his times; but he did not always practice what he preached, and his behaviour to women appears to have consistently been respectful and considerate. Moreover, his feelings for his wife Edith were genuinely deep and long-lasting, as witnessed by the beautiful, moving words he wrote to his son Christopher a few months after her death:

> I never called Edith *Lúthien* – but she was the source of the story [...]. In those days her hair was raven, her skin clear, her eyes brighter than you have seen them, and she could sing – and *dance*. But the story has gone crooked, & I am left, and *I* cannot plead before the inexorable Mandos.
> (Letter No. 340, Carpenter 1995b:420)

---

[16] For instance, in the 1970s the laws on divorce and termination of pregnancy were both the object of referendums promoted by conservative, Church-backed organisations.

SEX, LIES AND STEREOTYPES

In spite of enduring prejudice, Tolkien's treatment of his female characters is much more varied than one may believe – not really exclusively "restricted to the roles played by women in our primary world's medieval romances – object of the quest, mother, temptress, witch – or else absent [...]" (Ringel 2000:165-166). In the course of my research for this essay, I have come across some interesting observations in reference material aimed at the general public rather than at scholars and academics. Interestingly, such texts often reflect a strict 'politically correct' point of view, and as such tend to offer somewhat unsympathetic readings of Tolkien's female characters. The fact that Tolkien supposedly left sex out of his writings is something with which the contemporary mentality struggles and, in most instances, fails to accept. I found the following remarks quite revealing of this attitude:

> Sex sells. Everybody knows that [...] If it is the case, however, why on earth are Tolkien's books so popular with men and teenage boys? His fantasy is about as unsexual as you'll find in the genre. There's no character the least little bit like Barbarella here.
> (Harvey 2003:293)

The author then goes on to mention 'Middle-earth machismo' and the lack of 'spicy romance' in *The Lord of the Rings*, which is rather ridiculous if one thinks about it. Very few, if any, of Tolkien's characters can be actually described as 'macho' (Boromir being perhaps the obvious example); then, there are no rules stating that romance has to be obligatorily 'spicy', or even that men and teenage boys will not read anything not featuring sex scenes.

In an interesting, though somewhat biased article published on the Internet, Michael Skeparnides (1999:1) remarks that *"The Lord of the Rings* has a somewhat definitive and chauvinistic appraisal of women as 'maidens' who must adhere to 'male' protectionism", and berates

Tolkien for presenting his female characters (in this case, Éowyn) according to the "classic conventions of the male gaze" Skeparnides (1999:2) then pursues his point by stating that

> [...] women in Tolkien's world are portrayed as 'pure' and 'virginal' maidens very much in the tradition of Shakespeare, yet Éowyn portrays a subversion of this cultural norm, in perhaps an emphasis by Tolkien (and Shakespeare) on the potential of women in such a rigid patriarchal world to trick men and be able to achieve the same, if not greater glory, than their male counterparts.

It can be rather amusing to observe how, for some critics, Tolkien seems to be at fault for the mere fact of being a man of his times with an according point of view – which does not make him necessarily a chauvinist. As to Tolkien's women being all 'pure' and 'virginal' maidens, it is mainly a question of seeing what one wants to see. It is true that practically none of Tolkien's female characters are actually evil – unless we count the two monstrous spiders, Ungoliant and Shelob, which are indeed fascinating creations, although some of the things that have been written about them border on the ridiculous,[17] however, neither can they all be labelled as 'pure and virginal maidens'. It is the case of characters like Aredhel or Erendis, who show more negative features than positive ones,[18] though neither could possibly be defined as 'evil'; while Queen Berúthiel, an intriguing example of potential villainess, has unfortunately remained nothing more than a footnote in Tolkien's creation.

---

[17] For instance, in Armitt (2005:99), Sam's wounding of Shelob assumes sexual connotations, as he "penetrates the orifice in her lower belly right up to the hilt" with his sword. Besides, the whole episode of Shelob's lair has been sometimes interpreted according to Freudian models – which, in my opinion, makes for rather amusing reading.

[18] See Lewis and Currie (2002:200-202) for Aredhel and (2002:222-227) for Erendis.

On the other hand, even in secondary literature of a more popular slant it is possible to find people arguing in favour of Tolkien and trying to demolish the stereotype of his alleged misogynism:

> Even ignoring for a moment the radical idea that no one human being is required, in his public or artistic endeavours, to be accountable for anybody *else's* ideas of what may be right and proper [...], the text of *The Lord of the Rings* doesn't bear out for a moment the idea that Tolkien had any kind of derogatory opinion about women. Three things are clear: he was far from being a misogynist, the female characters in his masterpiece *collectively* represent all that's great about being a woman, and less representation does not equal less importance. (McNew 2003:115)

THE AMAZON AND THE GODDESS

After careful consideration, I have chosen to concentrate on the characters of Éowyn and Lúthien as the most representative of a modern vision of women in Tolkien's Middle-earth. The third most popular female character, Galadriel, is charged with implications which would lead us away from discussions of modernity in Tolkien's fiction.[19] Besides, these two characters embody two different but complementary conceptions of 'modern' femininity, which is one of the main reasons for their enduring fascination. They can also contribute to dismantling a series of common stereotypes about Tolkien's output, including the alleged lack of psychological depth of its characters.

---

[19] In fact, Galadriel is probably the best example of the figure of the 'fatal woman' in Tolkien's fiction, as shown by her words in the episode of her 'temptation': "All shall love me and despair!" I hope to have the opportunity to further explore this topic in the future.

Quite obviously, Lúthien and Éowyn are different characters, belonging to vastly different narrative contexts. According to Northrop Frye's definition,[20] *The Silmarillion* would occupy a middle ground between the mode of myth and that of romance; its heroes are either "superior in kind both to other men and to the environment of other men" (as in myth) or "superior in degree [not in kind] to other men and to their environments" (as in romance). Lúthien is evidently superior to Beren; she could even be said to possess many of the characteristics of a divine or semidivine being: superhuman beauty, immortality, magical powers. On the other hand, *The Lord of the Rings*, as Shippey points out (2005:238-239), borders on 'high mimesis', as its heroes are "superior in degree to other men but not to [their] natural environment". Therefore, Éowyn is beautiful, but not preternaturally so; she has no particular powers besides her above-average courage and strength of will, and she is definitely very vulnerable. In *The Lord of the Rings* we see much more of Éowyn's psychological makeup, even though it is often necessary to be able to read between the lines.

On the other hand, the very tone of *The Silmarillion* apparently leaves out any possibility of introspection or any other form of psychological treatment. Accordingly, Lúthien is presented in the style of myth or fairy tale, with a strong emphasis on her looks and mesmerising presence:

> Blue was her raiment as the unclouded heaven, but her eyes were grey as the starlit evening; her mantle was sewn with golden flowers, but her hair was dark as the shadows of twilight. As the light upon the leaves of trees, as the voice of clear waters, as the stars above the mists of the world, such was her glory and her

---

[20] All citations from Northrop Frye are originally contained in *Anatomy of Criticism: Four Essays* (Princeton: Princeton University Press, 1957); however, I have taken the above quotations from Shippey (2005:238-239).

loveliness; and in her face was a shining light.
(*Silm.* 193)

A creature of light and shadows, with a strong affinity to natural phenomena (as shown by the terms of comparison used by the author), Lúthien's beauty goes beyond the merely physical. She is part of a world far removed from modernity, the world of the First Age as narrated in *The Silmarillion*. As a character of legend and fairy tale, half-Elvish and half-angelic in nature, equipped with clearly superhuman characteristics, she seems to be light years away from any modern conception of femininity. She is also the protagonist of that old mainstay of poetry and legend, a doomed love affair between two apparently incompatible people, which ends with a *Liebestod* in the best romantic tradition (although with an unexpected twist). However, she is probably the single most important character in the fabric of Tolkien's mythology: her presence hovers in *The Lord of the Rings*, where her fate is paralleled by Arwen's choice.[21]

Éowyn has mythological implications as well, having been often compared to an amazon[22] or, especially, a valkyrie. She dreams of glory and great deeds, calling herself a "shieldmaiden", an archaic word suggestive of such legendary figures, or even of literary characters such as Ariosto's Bradamante or Tasso's Clorinda;[23] however, if we replace such

---

[21] See Aragorn's song in Chapter XI of *The Fellowship of the Ring;* moreover, his healing powers are clearly a legacy from Lúthien herself (Hammond and Scull 2005:584). Arwen mentions Lúthien's choice to Frodo in Chapter VI of *The Return of the King*.

[22] In his only detailed reference to Éowyn's character in the *Letters* (No. 244), Tolkien states that she is not "a soldier or 'amazon', but like many women was capable of great military gallantry at a crisis" (Carpenter 1995b:323).

[23] In Ludovico Ariosto's *Orlando furioso* (1532), Bradamante is a Christian warrior in love with Ruggiero, a young Saracen; from their union the noble house of Este will originate. Clorinda, one of the characters in Torquato Tasso's *La Gerusalemme liberata* (1575), is a pagan (Saracen) warrior who is loved by the Christian Tancredi, and is accidentally killed by him in a duel.

an unfashionable term with any contemporary professional title, the modernity of her character begins to emerge beneath the surface of the medieval imagery.

In fact, Éowyn's physical description and behaviour until her near-fatal duel with the Witch-king may suggest a kinship with these figures. In one of her first appearances, she is depicted as a cup-bearer, a typical occupation of both valkyries and nobly-born women in ancient Germanic societies.[24] Then, a few pages later, we see her invested as temporary ruler of her people, in full military regalia: "the sword was set upright before her, and her hands were laid upon the hilt. She was clad now in mail and shone like silver in the sun" (*LotR* 512). Like Lúthien, as Donovan (2003:123-124) observes, "Éowyn is portrayed in terms of the intensification of light common to the benevolent Germanic valkyrie figures." However, as Burns (2005:143-144) points out, "more than fact or literary convention lies behind Éowyn's character [...]. For Tolkien, in spite of his strong sense of established order and predetermined place, also had considerable sympathy for those whose lives are restricted and for those who are confined." Indeed, in his treatment of her Tolkien shows a psychological subtlety for which he is very rarely credited, and which has hardly ever been discussed in full – even though, without any doubt, Éowyn (together with Galadriel) is the female character who has been most often the object of critical attention.

BETWEEN LOVE AND PAIN: TOLKIEN AS PSYCHOLOGIST

As a matter of fact, there are almost as many interpretations of Éowyn's figure as there are essays and books written on Tolkien's work. However, a good deal of them seem to agree with Lewis and Currie's (2002:207) pithy statement that "its author got the jitters and dropped

---

[24] See Neville (2005:102), with particular reference to the character of Wealhtheow in *Beowulf*.

her back in the baby trap, quick." Once again, this shows how easy it is to be led astray by sterotyped views. Anyone thinking that Éowyn is just a token female figure inserted in a strongly male-oriented plot would be making a serious mistake in judgment. Through Éowyn's character, Tolkien found a way to harmonise his professional knowledge of medieval literature with his awareness of social and cultural issues.

Éowyn is introduced in *The Lord of the Rings* so simply and briefly, that at first the reader hardly notices her presence: she is just "a woman clad in white" (*LotR* 501) standing behind Théoden's chair; the king is by far the most important figure in this episode. Subsequently, when she is first addressed directly by her uncle, we see her in a different, more detailed perspective: "Grave and thoughtful was her glance [...]. Very fair was her face, and her long hair was like a river of gold. Slender and tall she was in her white robe girt with silver; but strong she seemed and stern as steel, a daughter of kings." (*LotR* 504) Though she looks completely in control of her emotions, Aragorn's presence affects her in some way, as it becomes evident as the narrative progresses: "As she stood before Aragorn she paused suddenly and looked upon him, and her eyes were shining. And he looked down her fair face and smiled; but as he took the cup, his hand met hers, and he knew that she trembled at the touch," (*LotR* 511)

At a superficial glance, Éowyn may come across like a rather stereotypical 'feminist': namely, a woman who wants to be a man (and that most macho of men, a warrior) and even likes to dress as one.[25] However, while in Gondor, before its decline, learning and the arts were highly prized, the society of Rohan has no other role models to offer to either men or women. In fact, the Gondorians have come to admire the

---

[25] Éowyn openly appears in masculine garb at least twice before disguising herself as Dernhelm: when she accepts Rohan's temporary rule from Théoden (*LotR* 512) and when the Grey Company departs for the Paths of the Dead: "She was clad as a Rider and girt with a sword" (*LotR* 767-768).

Rohirrim for their youthful vigor and heroism, as Faramir relates to Frodo and Sam: "And we love them: tall men and fair women, valiant both alike, golden-haired, bright-eyed and strong; they remind us of the youth of Men, as they were in the Elder Days", though they recognise that they "love war and valour as things in themselves, both a sport and an end" (*LotR* 663). It should not come as a surprise, then, that Éowyn's main aspiration is to prove her courage and martial skills in battle. Nevertheless, her vulnerability is also evident, as she struggles against the bonds imposed by her womanhood: "born in the body of a maid, she had spirit and courage at least the match of yours", says Aragorn to Éomer as she lies dying in the Houses of Healing (*LotR* 848-849). In spite of her undeniable beauty and good manners, at first she does not come across as a particularly appealing character, being on several instances portrayed as cold and detached.[26] Only when her hand trembles at Aragorn's touch do we get a glimpse of her innermost feelings. Before that, we see her look at Théoden with "cool pity in her eyes" (*LotR* 504), showing a somehow patronising attitude towards his weakness and dotage. Though later we come to realise how deeply she cares about him, we get nevertheless the impression of a young woman chafing at the bit, hating every minute of what she is obliged to do, and showing very little patience towards an older person's failures. However, we cannot help sympathising with her plight, since most people, at least once in their lifetime, have experienced feelings of frustration, unrequited love, even despair. Indeed, the heartwarmingly happy ending of her story (her personal 'eucatastrophe') follows a very close brush with death, very much resembling a failed suicide attempt.

On several occasions, Éowyn's supposed immaturity has been pointed out: indeed, Aragorn first perceives her as "fair and cold, like a morning of pale spring that is not yet come to womanhood" (*LotR* 504),

---

[26] For instance, Legolas refers to her as "the cold maiden of the Rohirrim" (*LotR* 856).

although we know her to be twenty-four. On the one hand, she has been forced to grow up in a hurry; on the other, she is emotionally immature, as is shown by her infatuation with an older, more sophisticated and experienced man – a far from unusual occurrence even in our times, based more on hero worship than on genuine feelings of love. Her process of maturation is slow and painful, achieved at great risk for her life and spirit. She has grown up as an orphan, in closer contact with men than with other women, and possibly in the shadow of a strong, warlike older brother. As the product of a culture which worships courage and physical strength, she evidently has some trouble in relating to her feminine side. We can also suppose that being the unwilling object of Gríma Wormtongue's desire disgusts her and makes her feel ashamed of her weakness and vulnerability.[27] Though not really shy, she does not seem to be aware of her own attractiveness, as she does not rely on her looks in order to attract Aragorn.

Éowyn's personality is much more complex than it seems, in spite of the common belief that Tolkien's characters are somewhat unidimensional. However, Tolkien's work requires from its readers an ability to read between the lines in an unbiased way. In Éowyn's portrayal, most readers will recognise a very familiar element, the frustration of one's aspirations. Though she realises that she has the potential to achieve much more than what the circumstances have forced upon her, such potential is stifled; moreover, something prevents her from expressing her feelings, as Aragorn tells Éomer:

> Yet she was doomed to wait upon an old man [...] and her part seemed to her more ignoble than the staff he leaned on. [...]. My lord, if your sister's love for you,

---

[27] According to Lewis and Currie (2002:212), this is the real reason for Éowyn's despair: she thinks "she is likely to become a female captive in the hands of the man who has treacherously destroyed her family and her people, facing the proverbial 'fate worse than death'."

and her will bent to her duty, had not restrained her lips, you might have heard even such things escape them. (*LotR* 848-849)

Speaking through Aragorn's words, Tolkien here reveals the unsuspected depth of his psychological insight. Aragorn, as Faramir later in the book, realises Éowyn's situation considerably better than those who have known her for much longer. Not only is she too proud to give way to her feelings, but she also probably thinks that no one would understand her plight. Even the person closest to her, her brother Éomer, appears to have been totally unaware of her suffering:

> [...] yet I knew not that Éowyn, my sister, was touched by any frost, until she first looked on you. Care and dread she had, and shared with me, in the days of Wormtongue and the king's bewitchment; and she tended the king in growing fear. But that did not bring her to this pass! (*LotR* 848)

Gradually, her infatuation with Aragorn leads her to act in a very uncharacteristic way for someone so proud and dignified, as when she kneels in front of him, begging him to take her with him on the Paths of the Dead. When the Grey Company departs, "it seemed to Gimli and Legolas [...] that she wept, and in one so stern and proud it seemed all the more grievous" (*LotR* 768). Éowyn's thin veneer is cracking, but she still cannot bring herself to ask for help: instead, she chooses disguise and rides in search of death. Only the meeting with a person who can really understand her can give her back her will to live, as Aragorn warns: "But to what she will awake, whether to hope, forgetfulness or despair, I do not know. And if to despair, then she will die, unless other healing comes which I cannot bring." (*LotR* 849)

POWERS OF CREATIVITY

Apparently at least, Lúthien is the polar opposite of Éowyn. Her character has little or no psychological depth, seen as she is mainly portrayed in terms of her appearance and actions. As a fairy-tale character, a heroine of epic and legend, we perceive her as being somewhat larger than life. One could not think of anything further from a real 20th-century woman: indeed, she is described in terms of such perfection as to seem wholly alien to the contemporary frame of mind. Like Galadriel in *The Lord of the Rings*,[28] she possesses all the features of the preternaturally beautiful, mesmerising woman idealised by Romantic writers, who can make even a strong, brave man like Beren utterly lose his head. Their encounter in the glade in Doriath might have been developed in rather a different way, as just another variation of the mortal-trapped-by-a-fairy theme, ending with the man's enslavement and subsequent loss of his immortal soul, or even with death (like the knight in Keats' *La Belle Dame sans Merci*).[29] As a matter of fact, Beren does fall under Lúthien's spell, and for a while is even unable to speak; this, however, does not result in his perdition. When he first arrives in Doriath, Beren is an exhausted, lonely and desperate man, wandering aimlessly in unknown lands: it is Lúthien's intervention that rescues him and gives back to him "the pride of the Eldest House of Men" (*Silm.* 195).

Once again, Tolkien surprises us by turning stereotypes neatly around. For one thing, Lúthien is no traditional 'damsel in distress' – just the opposite, in fact, seen as throughout the tale she is the one who protects the man and not the other way round. As Jane Chance (2005:35) aptly points out, she "functions as hero equally with her male lover, in fact transcending him in her artistic and heroic roles [...] Lúthien

---

[28] See, for instance, Armitt (2005:95-96).

[29] Interestingly, the title of Tom Shippey's *The Road to Middle-earth*'s Chapter 8 is "On the Cold Hill's Side"; on pages 317-319 it deals indeed with the topic of the mortal trapped in Faerie.

matches in knowledge or artistry whatever Beren accomplishes in brave feats [...]." Lewis and Currie (2002:196) add that "often it is her skills and knowledge that save them both." It is not surprising if, of all of Tolkien's female characters, Lúthien (even more than Éowyn) is the one who evokes the most enthusiastic responses from earnest supporters of modern conceptions of femininity, as this apparently naive remark by Challis (2003:140) clearly shows: "[...] Tolkien didn't have anything against women taking an active role and being risk-takers. Wow, that Lúthien! She defies her father, tracks down Beren, and seeks out both Sauron and Morgoth." Though this may sound a little simplistic, this observation contains a good deal of truth. Even the more scholarly-minded Lewis and Currie (2002:196) seem to agree on this point:

> Lúthien cannot be by any stretch of the imagination seen as a good little girl of the pre-1960s type. She is more like her father's nightmare of these days. She is active, not passive; she has her own creative powers; she knows her own will and is prepared to act upon it, even in defiance of her father.

Though she hardly ever appears in the tale before her meeting with Beren, Lúthien comes across as self-sufficient, quite happy to be on her own and pursue her artistic interests. Although "the most beautiful of all the children of Ilúvatar" (*Silm*. 193), she does not use her beauty in order to gain her own ends, but rather relies on her creative powers: singing, dancing, healing, weaving a cloak out of her hair, are all examples of creativity, contrasting with the often destructive environment of Middle-earth in the First Age. Like her physical aspect, her magical powers are strongly connected to nature and growth: at her birth "the white flowers of *niphredil* came forth to greet her as stars from the earth" (*Silm*. 99); while her song "released the bonds of winter, and the frozen waters spoke, and flowers sprang from the cold earth where her feet had passed" (*Silm*. 193).

Singing represents Lúthien's artistic creativity at its strongest.[30] Her songs have the power of the shamanic songs in the Finnish *Kalevala*: she can bring on the spring, put evil creatures to sleep, heal people's hurts. Éowyn, on the other hand, may seem the most unlikely character to engage in such activity: interestingly, though, singing is mentioned once in relation to her. When she finally melts and recognises her change of heart, she tells Faramir that she will "no longer take joy only in the songs of slaying" (*LotR* 943). As a matter of fact, in the culture of Rohan singing has quite a different function than for the Elves. We see the Rohirrim singing to celebrate someone's heroic death or to prepare themselves for battle, in the best tradition of the ancient nations of Northern Europe. It is indeed an artistic achievement, but one with a negative edge because of its connection with violence and death. Conversely, the Elves seem to delight in singing for its own sake: for instance, when Frodo, Sam and Pippin meet Gildor and his companions in the forest, the Elves sing and laugh at the same time, for the sheer pleasure of it (*LotR* 77).

In spite of any attempts at oversimplification, it can be said that Éowyn's new reason to live does not only involve the love of a sensitive, honourable man, but the discovery of her own creative powers as well. The supporters of the thesis of Éowyn's so-called 'taming' by Faramir[31] conveniently disregard the fact that, when she tells him that she "will be a healer, and love all things that grow and are not barren" (*LotR*: 943), she is referring to creative activities which are the polar opposites of her former aspirations towards power and glory. As some have argued, this may involve an acceptance of traditional feminine roles (like motherhood) on her part; however, it also means embracing

---

[30] Not surprisingly, the name given to her by Beren, Tinúviel, means 'nightingale', the bird with the sweetest voice, often celebrated as a symbol of poetic creativity.

[31] Éowyn's remark about Faramir taming "a wild shieldmaiden from the North" (*LotR* 944) is clearly ironical.

some definitely positive values generally considered as feminine, namely the refusal of violence, aggression and power for its own sake in favour of creativity and peace-making. As Harvey (2003:299) points out, "their union is based on the assumption that true peace can only be based on what people tend to think of, rightly or wrongly, as feminine virtues." Faramir does not suggest she stay at home while he pursues more traditionally masculine interests, but rather "let us cross the river, and in happier days let us dwell in fair Ithilien and there make a garden. All things will grow with joy there, if the White Lady comes" (*LotR*: 943-944). Once the pall of death and darkness is removed from Middle-earth, Éowyn literally 'sees the light' about herself and understands her priorities: "No longer do I desire to be a queen", she tells Faramir (*LotR* 943). She has gone beyond childish infatuation and hero worship to reach a more balanced outlook on life. Moreover, far from being just a suitor who pays her extravagant compliments, Faramir proves a true friend, forcing her to confront unpleasant truths about herself, yet at the same time offering his support and understanding.[32] Even if their conversations on the battlements of Minas Tirith are not related, we can imagine Faramir showing interest and appreciation towards Éowyn as a human being, not only as "a lady beautiful [...] beyond even the words of the Elven-tongue to tell" (*LotR* 943).

Though not exclusively a feminine prerogative, gardening, as healing, is a creative activity (and a very English one at that) which Tolkien loved, as witnessed by several of his letters[33] and by Sam's character. Although Faramir is an outstanding soldier (as Éowyn immediately realises on first meeting him), war is not his real vocation, as it is instead for his brother Boromir. As such, he is "more in touch with his feminine side" (Harvey 2003:299), thus a far cry from men like Éomer. In a

---

[32] *Letters*, (No. 244, Carpenter 1995b:232): "I think he understood Éowyn very well."
[33] See in particular *Letters*, No. 312.

certain way, Tolkien identified with Faramir, as they had much the same attitude towards war: although not a 'pacifist' in modern terms, Tolkien grew to detest it, as he knew firsthand the pain and misery it wreaked on people.[34] Consequently, Éowyn's true 'liberation' is not effected through the imitation of typically masculine ideals of power and military glory, gained at the expense of other human lives (symbolised here by the 'songs of slaying'): conversely, she refuses the values of destruction to embrace those of creation.

This is a point of view with which I am personally in very strong agreement, as I do not think it is in any way positive or 'liberating' for a woman to adopt models of behaviour which are negative for *all* human beings, be they male or female. Lúthien does not need to resort to any kind of violence to neutralise Morgoth or any other adversary, since she can rely on the 'magic' of her creative powers. On the other hand, while Éowyn gains renown from killing the Witch-king, it is almost at the cost of her life. As Aragorn rightly predicts, in order to find complete healing from the 'frost' which threatened to destroy her, she must reject death and open herself to life – as she eventually does.

CONCLUSIONS

With this essay, I hope to have proved that Tolkien was much more sympathetic to his female characters than he is usually credited for, and that in the characters of Lúthien and Éowyn he managed to reconcile literary models (taken mainly from medieval literature, mythology and fairy tales) with contemporary issues. Though this may not be immediately apparent, unbiased readers will be able to appreciate the way in which Tolkien, conservative and traditional as he was as far as 'the

---

[34] *Letters*, No. 64.

Woman question' was concerned, created two unforgettable female characters who are remarkably more modern than one may be led to believe.

MARIA RAFFAELLA BENVENUTO, born and based in Rome, Italy, has got a degree in English Language and Literature and is currently studying for a Ph.D. in Comparative Literature. Her interest in Tolkien dates back from the early '80s. She is one of the editors of the Italian translation of Tom Shippey's *The Road to Middle-earth*, which was published in December 2005. She has also contributed four articles to the forthcoming *The J.R.R. Tolkien Encyclopedia* (due in the autumn of 2006) and participated to Birmingham's *Tolkien 2005* conference with a paper on the Italian translation of *The Lord of the Rings*. At the time of writing, she is working on the Italian translation of Vincent Ferré's *Sur les rivages de la Terre du Milieu* and Verlyn Flieger's *Splintered Light*, as well as on several other projects based on Tolkien and related subjects, such as fairy tales.

Bibliography

Armitt, Lucie, 2005, *Fantasy Fiction. An Introduction*, New York/London: Continuum.

Burns, Marjorie, 2005, *Perilous Realms. Celtic and Norse in Tolkien's Middle-earth.* Toronto: University of Toronto Press.

Carpenter, Humphrey, 1995a, *J.R.R. Tolkien. A Biography*, (first edition 1977), London: HarperCollins.

Carpenter, Humphrey (ed.), 1995b, *The Letters of J.R.R. Tolkien.* London: HarperCollins. [*Letters*]

Challis, Erica ("Tehanu"), 2003, 'Quests, Myths and Heroines', in The OneRing.net (eds.), 2003, *The People's Guide to J.R.R. Tolkien*, Cold Spring Harbor: Cold Spring Press, pp. 136-142.

Chance, Jane, 2005, 'Tolkien's Women (and Men): The Film and the Book', in *Mallorn* 43, July 2005, pp. 30-37.

Curry, Patrick, 1995, 'Less Noise and More Green: Tolkien's Ideology for England', in Patricia Reynolds and Glen H. Goodknight (eds.), 1995, *Proceedings of the J.R.R. Tolkien Centenary Conference*, Milton Keynes and Altadena: The Tolkien Society and The Mythopoeic Society, pp. 126-138.

Del Corso, Lucio and Paolo Pecere, 2003, *L'anello che non tiene. Tolkien tra letteratura e mistificazione*, Roma: Minimum Fax.

Donovan, Leslie A., 2003, 'The Valkyrie Reflex in J.R.R. Tolkien's *The Lord of the Rings*. Galadriel, Shelob, Éowyn and Arwen', in Jane Chance (ed.), 2003, *Tolkien the Medievalist*, London/New York: Routledge, pp. 106-132.

Hammond, Wayne and Christina Scull, 2005, *The Lord of the Rings. A Reader's Companion*, London: HarperCollins.

Harvey, Greg, 2003, *The Origins of Middle-earth for Dummies*, Hoboken, N.J.: HungryMinds Inc.

Hopkins, Lisa, 1995, 'Female Authority Figures in the Works of Tolkien, C.S. Lewis and Charles Williams', in Patricia Reynolds and Glen H. Goodknight (eds.), 1995, *Proceedings of the J.R.R. Tolkien Centenary Conference*, Milton Keynes and Altadena: The Tolkien Society and The Mythopoeic Society, pp. 364-366.

Lewis, Alex and Elizabeth Currie, 2002, *The Uncharted Realms of Middle-earth*, Oswestry: Medea Publishing.

McNew, Cynthia L. ("Anwyn"), 2003, 'Men are from Gondor, Women are from Lothlorien', in The OneRing.net (eds.), 2003, *The People's Guide to J.R.R. Tolkien*, Cold Spring Harbor: Cold Spring Press, pp. 115-120.

Neville, Jennifer, 2005, 'Women', in Robert Eaglestone (ed.), 2005, *Reading The Lord of the Rings. New Writings on Tolkien's Classic*, London/New York: Continuum, pp. 101-110.

Ringel, Faye, 2000, 'Women Fantasists: In the Shadow of the Ring', in George Clark and Daniel Timmons (eds.), 2000, *Tolkien and His Literary Resonances*, Westport: Greenwood Press, pp. 159-171.

Shippey, Tom, 2005, *The Road to Middle-earth*, (first edition 1982), London: HarperCollins.

Skeparnides, Michael, 1999, 'A Reflection on Tolkien's World: Gender, Race and Interpreted Political, Economic, Social and Cultural Allegories', accessed via http://tolkien.cro.net/mskeparn.html.

Tolkien, John Ronald Reuel, 1999, *The Silmarillion*, (edited by Christopher Tolkien, first edition 1977), London: HarperCollins. [*Silm*]

---, 2002, *The Lord of the Rings*, (first edition 1954/55, second edition 1966), London: HarperCollins. [*LotR*]

Politically Incorrect: Tolkien, Women, and Feminism

LAURA MICHEL

Abstract

J.R.R. Tolkien has been accused of sexism more than once. Such an accusation can be easily proven wrong by analyzing strong, active female characters from his work, such as Éowyn, or protagonists that do not fit the (male) ideal of the submissive and self-sacrificing wife, such as Erendis. Furthermore, Tolkien's deep understanding of women and modern women's issues is also revealed in his other female characters, even those whose roles are more traditional and less active.

INTRODUCTION

Almost fifty years after *The Lord of the Rings* was published, a Mexican movie critic wrote in her review of Peter Jackson's *The Fellowship of the Ring* that the two most remarkable things about the film were, first, that it was a special-effects movie; and, second, that the original story was made to appeal to young boys. The rest of the review made it quite obvious that the critic had not read the book; still, her reaction was but an echo of other ill-founded words that had been said about J.R.R. Tolkien before: Edwin Muir's statement that Tolkien's characters were like children since they did not know anything about women, and the remarks of J.W. Lambert, who found no religion in the novel, and no women.[1]

What would make *The Lord of the Rings* a 'boy's book'? Apparently there are plenty of facts that might seem to support such a view: a 'lack' of female characters in prominent roles; the dealing with topics

---

[1] Carpenter (1990:244).

that, according to common beliefs, are of no interest to women, and the total absence of explicit sex. It has also been argued that Tolkien did not write about women (an absolutely false assertion) because he did not know them, or was not interested in them. All of that, of course, would hardly explain why Tolkien's books have attracted a steady and devoted female readership ever since they were first published.

For years, Tolkien has been criticized, attacked, explained, forgiven, and mainly misunderstood when it comes to the matter of women. Criticism on this topic has ranged from mild attempts to excuse Tolkien's points of view to truly violent accusations of misogyny and chauvinism, sometimes drawing completely unfounded conclusions about his private life. Those who try to exculpate Tolkien often justify his 'exclusion' of women as due to stylistic and generic constraints (the epic has never allotted important roles to women), or argue that it has to do with his education and his living in a male-dominated scholarly society.

It is amazing, though, to see that most of this criticism has very little to do with Tolkien's work itself and too much with a biased idea of what a 'boys' book' should be like (and a 'girls' book' as well). Claiming that a story of war, quests, and adventure cannot appeal to girls, one might as well contend that no boy could enjoy reading Ursula K. LeGuin's science-fiction novels, most of which are 'female' in their concerns. Still, Ms. LeGuin's fiction remains a favourite among male readers worldwide.

Could it be, then, that the critique of Tolkien and his women protagonists is not based on a careful reading and analysis of his work, but on certain misconceptions? Or that the fiction by Tolkien, a man of the 20th century, has not been examined from a fully modern perspective, but merely measured against the narrower standards of the latest views of political correctness and, not surprisingly, found wanting?

POLITICALLY CORRECT FEMINISM

As Edith L. Crowe (1995:272) quotes, from a letter Tolkien wrote to his son Christopher in 1943, he was uneasy about the global spread of, among other things, feminism. In another letter to C.S. Lewis (Carpenter 2000:62) he describes his attendance of a civil marriage ceremony and disapproves of the woman registrar. He had written to his son Michael before that women, in education, "can go no further, when they leave his [the teacher's] hand, or when they cease to take a *personal* interest in *him*," with "rare exceptions" (Carpenter 2000:49).

So, Tolkien was no feminist. But does this turn him automatically into a chauvinist? As Crowe suggests, it is not known how Tolkien himself would define feminism; she provides an interesting reflection on this matter when she states that "to say that Tolkien's work is completely incompatible with feminism is to accept not only too limited a view of Tolkien's writing, but too narrow a definition of feminism" (Crowe 1995:272). Feminism, as a movement, involves such a wide variety of ideas (on social, political, economical and moral questions) that it is impossible to give a simple, universally valid definition; but if we considered feminism not in the abstract, but rather the general idea of what feminism should be like in practice, especially when it comes to social roles and status, Tolkien's view of it seems, if not fully set forth, at least easier to understand.

Author Ursula K. LeGuin considers feminist ideology valuable, since it has forced women of recent generations to get to know themselves better, that is, "to separate [...] what we really think and believe from all the easy 'truths' and 'facts' we were (subliminally) taught about being female, being male, sex roles [...] etc. etc." (LeGuin 1978:142); in other words, to question the values of society that are often imposed, sometimes in (almost) dogmatic form.

However, LeGuin also points out the dangers of radical feminism: "If it is forced it leads to spitefulness and self-destructiveness; if it is faked it leads to Feminist Chic, the successor to Radical Chic" (LeGuin 1978:142).

One can only guess that, when rejecting feminism, Tolkien was aware of its long-term consequences, and its potential failure; for women's role in society to change, it is necessary for the role of men to change, too. Tolkien writes, in his above-mentioned letter to son Michael, that for a woman to be, on the one hand, economically independent, means, on the other hand, to be dependent on a male employer. If feminism started as something quite positive, it has been, over all these years, turned into another kind of dogma, something that must be followed without questioning. While a woman's social role was, in the past, to be beautiful, to give birth to and raise children, to be a housewife, and to take care of the domestic economy, a modern, liberated woman nowadays has to have a job, has to be economically independent – next to being beautiful, to have and raise children, to be a housewife, and (especially in poorer countries) to manage and contribute to the domestic economy (the present author fails to see any liberation in all of that). Feminism, in the beginning, helped female minds to wake up and fight for what they really wanted and believed in; now, it seems that those minds have been put back to sleep on an even harder mattress.

Since Tolkien's ideas on women (as they are presented in his letters) sound unabashedly derogatory – his remark that women's gift is to be "receptive, stimulated, fertilized (in many other matters than the physical) by the male" is a good example –, one can be sure that he spoke his mind and did not worry about being politically correct (*avant la lettre*, so to speak). There are many people who would use less offending, and less honest language to hide their 'politically incorrect' views. Yet even though Tolkien objected to feminism, he was in favour of seeing men and women as equals. He wrote that a woman is "*another* fallen human-being with a soul in peril" (Carpenter 2000:49; italics added); this also shows that he did not idealise women – an accusation that will be discussed later.

Tolkien's 'active' female characters, Éowyn and Lúthien, are bound to be praised by many feminists (though both of them seem, by the standards of radical feminism, to fail in the end); other women, such as Rosie Cotton and Arwen, are criticized for staying home and waiting, seemingly doing nothing.

Yet, according to LeGuin: "[...] it's one thing to sacrifice fulfillment in the service of an ideal; it is another to suppress clear thinking and honest feeling in the service of an ideology." Tolkien's female characters, whether they have chosen to stay home or to fight, may not be presented as apogees of unfailingly clear thinking, but they do not lack powerful honesty. They do not represent ideologies, but remain faithful to themselves, which is true for the shieldmaiden Éowyn as well as the stay-at-home mom-to-be Rosie Cotton.

THE 'MODERN' MOVIE LADIES

Director Peter Jackson's and co-writers Fran Walsh and Philippa Boyens' decision to add or beef up female roles, especially that of Arwen, can be seen as a sign that they share the view that Tolkien's fiction lacks sufficient women characters.

Jackson, in doing so, seems to follow a widespread tradition of 'book to screen' adaptations. The examples go back as far as fifty years ago, such as Henry Levin's *Journey to the Center of the Earth* (1959), where an active female character (Mrs. Goetaborg, played by Arlene Dahl) is added to Jules Verne's 'boys' tale', to more recent ones, with Disney's *Treasure Planet*, a sci-fi spin-off of Robert Louis Stevenson's *Treasure Island*, with Captain Smollet being transformed into a female leader (called Captain Amelia). In most of these movies, women seem to be there only to spark the romantic interest of a major male character (Mrs. Goetaborg wins the affection of the cold intellectual Professor

Lindenbrook and Captain Amelia marries Disney's version of Dr. Livesey) – a fact that should be quite offensive by itself; or they occur to provide the female audience with someone they could identify with ... again, in the middle of a love story of some kind.

Not that Jackson was trying to correct any fault of Tolkien's. He was clearly aware that his films had to live up to the standards of an audience different from Tolkien's original one. While Jackson's portrayal of Arwen as an elven warrior is not quite incompatible with her character as she appears in Tolkien's writing,[2] it is clear that he wanted to include the politically correct idea of a woman being at least as strong as any man (Arwen's completely odd gesture of putting a sword on Aragorn's neck is obviously designed to show that she is very much his match, at least physically), that women may also perform so-called 'male deeds'. But Liv Tyler's Arwen as a warrior in the movie was, if not 'catastrophic', mainly unnecessary, and, as Professor Tom Shippey (2004:237) says, "the heroic role that she is given rings a little hollow" – the hollowness of political correctness that one takes for granted, and is an 'anticipation' of Éowyn's role (as found in Morton Grady Zimmerman's faulty treatment in the first *Lord of the Rings* movie script that was presented to Tolkien).[3]

Arwen's planned appearance in the battle of Helm's Deep would only have made things worse. Even Liv Tyler was thankful when the whole scene was cancelled.

Jackson added another 'modern' element when he gave Rosie Cotton a job, just as if he were trying to justify her. Would it have been too much of a shock for female audiences to be presented with a young girl

---

[2] Michael Martinez (2003a:165) points out that, while Arwen never wielded a sword just like in the movies, she was used to cross the Misty Mountains when visiting Galadriel, the dangerous path where Arwen's own mother had been attacked and captured by Orcs. So it is quite suitable that she would possess, along with other knowledge, fighting skills.

[3] Carpenter (2000:273, Letter No. 210).

that does not work? Nothing would have, essentially, changed the story had Rosie stayed home to help mother or had Arwen not saved Frodo.

But would Tolkien have objected to these interpolations, which are motivated by the desire to live up to 'modern' standards? There is, of course, no way of knowing, but a good clue can be found in the Patricia Gray's theatrical adaptation of *The Hobbit* (1968), which was approved by the author himself: in it, instead of the king of the elves, we have a queen (Legolas' mother, perhaps?)

FEMININE CONCERNS

Female readers, no matter how devoted, would find that women in *The Lord of the Rings* are, as Cynthia L. McNew (2003:116) puts it, "terribly under-represented". This refers to two obvious facts: there are fewer female characters than male characters, and the roles they get to play are minor ones. But, McNew continues, "less representation does not equal less importance" (2003:115), and even when female characters – not only in *The Lord of the Rings*, but in all of Tolkien's fiction – may be outnumbered by men, most of the women are memorable.

There are outstanding characters such as Lúthien, Éowyn and, though less easily to accommodate, Erendis. Tolkien writes of Éowyn that "[…] she was also not really a soldier or an 'amazon', but like many brave women was capable of great military gallantry at a crisis" (Carpenter 2000:323). But there are also characters that, having not an active role, truly make evident the depth of Tolkien's understanding of women issues.

Erica Challis (2003:139) observes that "our society has changed since Tolkien wrote his tale hoping to create a 'Mythology for England', and I'm not sure the myth still fits us as we are today." One can agree with that only in part. It is possible that Tolkien's female characters are not as representative of modern women as, just to mention one example, those found in the more recent works of Louise Cooper or

Diana Wynne Jones. But it is possible, too, after a careful reading of *The Lord of the Rings*, *The Silmarillion* and the *Unfinished Tales*, to find examples of many women-related topics that have been discussed both in fictional and non-fictional contemporary literature. There are cases of family violence (Aredhel and Eöl), of possessiveness and jealousy (Morwen and Túrin), of sexual harassment (Éowyn), of great love in the face of greater sorrow (Ëarendil and Elwing), and, of course, of the colliding interests of men and women; a topic that, says Brian Rosebury (Pearce 2000:63), is a recurrent one in Tolkien's fiction – and there are no villains in that kind of struggle.

The conflict between Ents and Entwives, even though it is only mentioned a couple of times in *The Lord of the Rings*, remains fixed in the mind of many readers; although the mystery of the Entwives' fate has never been solved (Tolkien himself said he did not know what had happened to the Entwives; see Carpenter [2000:419]), the most interesting part lies in the conflicting points of view. The differences in character of Ents and Entwives cause all females of the species to depart from their original homelands, possibly to their deaths – an example of serious lack of communication between the partners. A similar problem is presented in the story of Aldarion and Erendis, discussed below.

Even characters in cameo or background appearances have something important to say on this topic. While Lúthien stands in the spotlight in her love-relationship with Beren, and is the focus of Thingol, her father's unyielding decision, it is her mother, Melian the Maia, who perceives clearly what is happening and its consequences: "[...] you" she tells her husband, "have devised cunning counsel. [...] For you have doomed your daughter, or yourself" (Silmarillion, Tolkien 1979:203). In the Houses of Healing, when things are getting desperate for Faramir, Éowyn, and Merry, it is in the 'old lore' of the aged nurse Ioreth that the first hope of the true king's coming can be foreseen, even though that lore is not valued by her male superior, the learned but unwise herb-master of Gondor.

WOMEN IN HIS LIFE

Using an author's biography as a tool to analyze his books, or to draw conclusions based on the interpretation of his personality rather than on his work itself, is generally fraught with dangers. An author's work should stand on its own and his personal life remain private. But, since Tolkien's way of living has been discussed before as a part of this essay and since it is necessary to refute the claim that he did not know women, I would like to comment on some details in his biography that are seldom noticed but still worthy of attention.

Professor Michael Stanton (2001:131) argues that "one has to call to mind Tolkien's birth in the late nineteen century and the prevalent standards of the day", and his living in the time of a "Victorian notion of 'separate spheres' of activity for men and women in the world" to understand that he was not "vitally interested in women." Other critics blame Tolkien's apparent lack of knowledge about women to the fact that he had only one love relationship, i.e. with his wife, and that at a very young age. Not every affirmation of this sort is necessarily negative; there is no malice in Dr. Jorge Ferro's (1996:28) claim that for Tolkien, as for any "chaste man, women are a great mystery." Nevertheless, it is possible to find in Tolkien's life facts that strongly contradict this.

The very first person to have a powerful and lasting influence on Tolkien was a woman of extraordinary strength, intelligence, and courage: Mabel Suffield, his mother. She was Tolkien's first teacher, and his love for languages, drawing, fairy tales, and nature came from her, as did, even more importantly, his religion and faith. Even though she died young, "worn out with prosecution, poverty, and, largely consequent, disease, in the effort to hand on to us small boys the Faith" (Carpenter

2000:353), Tolkien never forgot her. As Humphrey Carpenter once hinted, a glimpse of Mabel Suffield may be seen in Gandalf's admiration for another mother, the 'fabulous' Belladonna Took. We are not told what exactly made Bilbo's mother 'remarkable', but, if the Took family did to live up to their fame, then it had to do with courage and an adventurous spirit.

No man who has a wife, a daughter, and a granddaughter should be accused of not knowing women or not caring, and Tolkien was the father of one girl, and, just like G. K. Chesterton, a loving married man (Ferro 1996:28). Edith and John Tolkien's own love story was reflected in the tale of Beren and Lúthien, which was to become the centre of his mythology. Without going any deeper into Tolkien's married life, it is important to emphasize that Tolkien's vision of marriage was realistic enough to keep any kind of idealizing (which he is often accused of) from ruining a happy life; for him, the essential thing was not a life full of boundless joy and eternal indulgence, but the sharing of both sorrow and happiness, and the living dialogue between the partners.

Furthermore, while Tolkien is better known for his male friendships, he was also close to a number of female friends – among them former students and colleagues, such as Simonne d'Ardenne, Professor Helen McMillan Buckhurst, Elaine Griffiths, Stella Mills, Mary Salu, and later on, secretary Joy Hill.

George Sayer remembers (1995:21) that Tolkien would take on girls as pupils; they were sent to him by women's colleges because he was a married man and so they could visit him without a female chaperone. Those girls, he says, "spoke of him with affection" and some of them liked going to his house and taking care of his children; eventually, they became friends of his family. Sayer thinks that he continued tutoring girls even after chaperoning was not used anymore.

And it was two women, Ms. Griffiths and her friend Susan Dagnall, who played a crucial role in the publication of Tolkien's first novel, *The*

Hobbit. Ms. Dagnall was an Oxford graduate working for Allen & Unwin and she had heard from Ms. Griffiths about the story; after reading the unfinished manuscript, she encouraged Tolkien to complete it and presented the book to the editors.

Finally, Ms. Joy Hill was assigned by Allen & Unwin to be Tolkien's personal assistant during the difficult years following his rise to celebrity status. She was in charge of managing his fan mail, protecting the privacy of his family life and home, and, later on, even helping the Professor and his wife with the housework. From a very tense beginning, their relationship became one of true affection; she considered him a father figure, and, near the end of his life, he gave her as a gift a poem called 'Bilbo's Last Song'.[4]

So, Tolkien had more than one chance to talk to women and to gain first hand knowledge of their ideals, hopes and fears; but, again, this biographical evidence is hardly necessary since his books are a greater testimony of Tolkien's knowledge of woman's thoughts, character, and feelings.

IDEAL WOMEN AND COURTLY LOVE

In his essay 'The Rippingest Yarn of All', Kenneth McLeish first defines the essential nature of *The Lord of the Rings* as "the almost total absence of femininity" (in male characters, he points out later, as it can be found in another 'boys' story', Homer's *Iliad*). He then continues to argue that the few female characters of the story are "cardboard figures from Welsh legend." Stanton (2001:131) writes that "it seems clear that Tolkien [...] treats his women with an old-fashioned courtliness, or what in Victorian terms might have been called 'reverence for womanhood'." For Nick Otty (1984:176), Tolkien's women are healers (if human),

---

[4] Ms. Hill's recollections and some anecdotes can be found in Grotta's biography.

over-perfect (if Elvish) and humble helpmeets (if Hobbit), incapable of evil, with the exception of Shelob, whom, according to Otty, Tolkien uses as the receptacle of all negative characteristics – as if they were excised from all other female characters and transferred to this figure of "loathing and disgust" (Otty 1984:176).

But, as flattering as it may seem that Tolkien would consider women wonderful and special, the truth is that idealizing love was, for him, one of the most difficult situations a couple had to deal with. Even though, as he explains to his son Michael, the tradition of romantic, chivalric love can be ennobling, its danger is that, having started as an artificial game of courting, it would finally turn into the enjoyment of love for its own sake. A young man that plays that game would worship two "imaginary Deities, Love and the Lady" (Carpenter 2000:49), and will be incapable of considering "[…] women as they are, as companions in shipwreck, not guiding stars." Or, in the words of Canadian novelist Geoff Ryman, the courtly game would be "let me do everything for you. That way we can never be equals."

Tolkien says that women, who are much more practical, do not need guiding stars. Sometimes, however, they idealize their loved ones as heroes, or believe that they can change them. But when a love story that has been based on these (mis-)conceptions comes to an end, the consequences (hopelessness and, according to Tolkien, cynicism) can be devastating.

Tolkien also regrets that, due to idealization, the greatest tales of 'splendid love' do not deal with the marriage of two lovers, but with their 'tragic separation'; the audience gets the impression that love is interrupted only by death or worse, and the natural hardships of married life seem to be omitted in most stories. Tolkien tries to give the 'whole story' and, particularly in *The Silmarillion* and later works, he writes of numerous marriages and, albeit briefly, describes them in a rather realistic way; for him, marriage is not the end of hardships, but may well be the beginning of tribulations, as can be seen, among others, in the personal stories of Galadriel and Celeborn, Húrin and Morwen, and Melian and Thingol.

Tolkien also did not believe that women were good all the time. They, he points out, are human beings, and "therefore capable of perfidy", though not necessarily 'fair and false', as traditional male literature has often described them. There are female characters in Tolkien that, for one reason or another, may be considered villains (Erendis the Mariner's wife, for instance), but Shelob is not one of them. She is not, as Brenda Partridge claims, the proof of Tolkien's "inner fear or abhorrence of female sexuality."[5] Shelob is female for biological reasons: the females of some spider species devour the shorter-lived males after mating. Shelob, as a descendant of Ungoliant, may well have inherited this characteristic from the latter, and even though *The Lord of the Rings* is a fantasy story, laws of nature have to be respected, since "days are days, and weather is weather" (Carpenter 2000:272).

A quick and superficial reading may give the impression that Tolkien 'idealizes' women because they are often described as beings of outstanding beauty, virtue and power. However, this does not concern female characters only. For sure, it is very difficult for an ordinary woman to compete against Lúthien, Goldberry or Galadriel; but so it is for an ordinary man to try and emulate Aragorn or Beren.

Two characters that are almost opposites when it comes to their desires, aims, and personality, are of special interest in order to illustrate Tolkien's knowledge of women: Éowyn from *The Lord of the Rings*; and Erendis, from *Unfinished Tales*.

---

[5] Partridge's interpretation (1982:191) of Sam's fight with Shelob as a symbol of violent intercourse is certainly illogical, but also comical; and it only reveals an obsession with sex from which other accusations to Tolkien's fiction have derived. As Joseph Pearce (2000:155) says, Tolkien did not include sex in *The Lord of the Rings* because, for the thematic concerns of the work, it was not needed.

ÉOWYN

Éowyn represents Tolkien's view of a woman who is confronted with the very contemporary problem of frustration.

A long time before taking a sword and becoming a shieldmaiden in disguise, Éowyn has been facing, all by herself, many hardships that are familiar to contemporary women. Because of her great sense of responsibility, she accepted a task that does not satisfy her, i.e. tending her uncle, whom she loves dearly, but whose love has not made her sacrifice any easier. She feels helplessly trapped while knowing that she is capable of more. She sees how her brother and her cousin are doing what is generally regarded as most important (for some reason, household business has never been much appreciated, "yet the deeds will not be less valiant because they are unpraised" (LotR, p. 767), to quote Aragorn), and even has to suffer sexual harassment by Wormtongue. She has gone through all of this without breaking, but her silent and unspectacular heroism has been ignored. That Háma, Théoden's doorward, calls her "fearless and high-hearted" and says that she should be "as *lord* of the Eorlingas" (LotR, p. 512; emphasis added), is little comfort to her, because she is going to be left behind once more. Tolkien's view of Éowyn is both compassionate and understanding.

She is not, as Partridge says, driven to war by her unrequited love for Aragorn, but by her own desire to change what she thinks is an empty, dull life. Her passion goes beyond love, but she falls in love with Aragorn (to use more colloquial language, she has a 'crush' on him) both because she admires him strongly and maybe because she believes that marrying him could provide a way out of her present misery. She is mistaken in this, but then neither Tolkien's female nor his male characters are perfect.

The cause of Éowyn despair is not, ultimately, Aragorn's rejection of her love, but that, in spite of all her efforts, she cannot see an end to her tribulations. As Martinez (2003b:469) puts it, she "had never been clued into the Main Plan", meaning that she does not know about Frodo's quest and the possibility of victory; she believes that Aragorn is going to his death, and since death is coming for everyone, she would like to go, at least, in a more dignified manner. Her desperate words have lost nothing of their poignancy and relevance even in the 21st century: "All of your words are but to say: you are a woman, and your part is in the house. But when the men have died in battle and honour, you have leave to be burned in the house, for the men will need it no more" (LotR, p. 767).

Her face, as Merry notices, is that of "one that goes seeking death, having no hope" (LotR, p. 823). But her will is stronger than any depression, and her motivation to fight the Witch King is not passion, infatuation, or the desire for glory, but true filial love – that of a daughter for her father.

When she lies wounded, Aragorn knows that he is not the ultimate cause for her troubles: "Her malady begins far back before this day, does it not, Éomer?" (LotR, p. 848).

And what Éomer says to Aragorn is, to put it plainly, that he never noticed that there was something wrong with Éowyn, "until she first looked on you" (LotR, p. 848). Éomer obviously was too busy with war and 'manly' deeds and seems to have been confident that Éowyn, even "in growing fear", was content taking care of Théoden and his problems while he was, literally, riding away from them. But it is Gandalf who is able to summarize Éowyn's dilemma with penetrating insight: "You [i.e. Éomer] had horses, and deeds of arms, and the free fields; but she, born in the body of a maid, had a spirit and courage at least to match yours." Because of her "body of a maid", and nothing else, Éowyn was "doomed to wait upon and old man" falling into dotage, and "her part seemed to her more ignoble than that of the staff he leaned on" (LotR, p. 849).

Éowyn's real victory is not over the Witch King, or her uncle's order, or male-dominated society, but over her own hopelessness and fears to end up in "a cage". Her marriage to Faramir is a victory of the same sort, though, especially to modern readers, it may not seem so.

Partridge (1982:192) claims that Éowyn and Faramir's marriage is solely motivated by narrative constraints and that Tolkien generally uses marriage to tie up loose ends. Yet, in a draft of a letter to a reader, Tolkien explains that similar circumstances of life provide the basis for a deep sympathetic understanding and, later, love between Éowyn and Faramir. Both grew up in the shadow of an elder brother, both had to keep their thoughts to themselves and make concessions whenever it was necessary. Both were simultaneously overprotected and left to fend for themselves. It is only natural that he would understand Éowyn "very well" (Carpenter 2000:323). His own problems are similar to those of Éowyn, since he, as a man, is expected to act in certain ways and to adhere to certain ideals, even though he does not entirely approve of them in private: "I do not love the bright sword for its sharpness, nor the arrow for its swiftness, nor the warrior for his glory. I love only that which they defend" (LotR, p. 656).

Tolkien also says that Éowyn's feelings for Aragorn do not really change after her meeting with Faramir; she continues to love him as a young soldier would love a great captain – to use Faramir's words. After their conversation, 'young soldier' Éowyn comes to accept what she is: "No longer do I desire to be a queen" (LotR, p. 943); or, better, in Marion Zimmer Bradley's (1968:83) words: "no longer does she desire to be a *king*."

But not even Éowyn's great struggle and heroic deeds are exempt from being misinterpreted due to careless and superficial readings of the text. A girl from my hometown, who had finished reading *The Lord of the Rings* shortly before the Peter Jackson movies were released, complained (as many of us have) about the lack of female characters in the story. And she expressed her complete disappointment at the fact that Éowyn, the only woman "of any worth" (her words) in the story, ended up being *tamed* into marriage. The 'taming' is, of course, a sly reference to Shakespeare's *The Taming of the Shrew*, and many readers see Éowyn's change of heart and mind in this context. Yet it is remarkable that Éowyn herself makes a joke using the very same word: "There goes a lord who tamed a wild shieldmaiden of the North!" (LotR, p. 944).

ERENDIS

In a final chapter, I will discuss a protagonist who is probably one of the most interesting, deepest, and most realistic female characters created by Tolkien yet who is, unfortunately, one of his least-known ones: Erendis, the Mariner's wife. This character appears in Part II (The Second Age) of *Unfinished Tales* in a tale called 'Aldarion and Erendis'. The story gives the lie to most popular prejudices regarding Tolkien and women – from his seeming lack of interest in women to his alleged propagation of the 'perfect' woman.

'Aldarion and Erendis' is a bitter story that involves (at least, in the main storyline) neither perilous quests or battles nor clashes between good and evil. The centre of the tale is constituted by the deeply personal struggle between a man and a woman; as such it is a very realistic and modern tale of a marriage that crumbles under the pressure of private and political incompatibility and adversity.

In his letter to his son Michael about the relationship between men and women, Tolkien explains that men and women in love are in danger of different kinds of delusion. Men, on the one hand, look for an exaggerated true love – a love that will not be affected by the passing of years, the beginning of a family, and ordinary life. Women, on the other, although much more practical, dream of changing their loved ones. The consequences of these mutual delusions are clearly set forth in 'Aldarion and Erendis'.

Tar-Aldarion is a Númenórean prince with a passion for the sea. He learns from Círdan the art of shipbuilding and undertakes several voyages across the ocean, in spite of his father's disapproval. He and his companions found the Guild of Venturers, a good example of Lewisian male friendship as mentioned by Lewis in his *The Four Loves*. At age one hundred, still young for a Númenórean, Aldarion is seen by a beautiful, strong woman named Erendis, who falls in love with him. She has little hope of gaining the heart of a man of such elevated status, but in time she becomes close to Aldarion's mother and wins her support.

Erendis' love is not reciprocated until some years later. Aldarion is pressured (sometimes very subtly) by his parents to quit travelling, to settle down and to marry. His refusal to do so leads to a crisis and Erendis comforts him when his relationship with his family is on the brink of breaking down. They start a romance that is, however, never as blissful as that of Arwen and Aragorn, or Beren and Lúthien, for all the hardships both couples had to suffer from. While care and affection are not the problem (both Aldarion and Erendis love each other tenderly, and their relationship is approved of by their respective families), things get complicated as their different interests begin to collide. Aldarion loves the sea; Erendis wants to live among trees; he does not feel ready to commit to marriage and she, who yearns to be a mother and whose life expectancy and, thus, fertility, will not be as long as those of Aldarion, is frustrated by the delay. Besides, Aldarion and Erendis are not even free to solve their own difficulties; their families' support soon turns into another kind of pressure, and rumours of Erendis being taken advantage of begin to trouble their lives.

When, after further years of waiting, they finally get married, it is difficult to know who are they pleasing really – whether they are, at long last, fulfilling their love or whether they are just giving in to external pressure.

Tolkien says that "nearly all marriages, even happy ones, are mistakes." This one certainly is; but "life and circumstances do most of" choosing. Aldarion and Erendis begin a marriage that could have potentially been very happy, and their failing seems due to a very modern problem couples encounter: the lack of communication. As the story develops, the narrator gives us a clear picture of Aldarion and Erendis' expectations of each other and of their own lives, but we hear very little of them sharing their hopes and dreams. All we have is a single, very artificial and domestic how-was-your-day-like conversation.

Two years after their wedding, Erendis gives birth to a baby girl, Ancalimë, and hopes that her child will act as a bond to strengthen her marriage, and that Aldarion will want a male heir next. But while there is no quarrel between them, and both are still trying to please each other, their love is being neglected with neither of them realizing this.

Finally, Aldarion decides to depart one more time and promises his wife to return within two years. He is delayed against his will and does not come back until more than five years have passed. During this time, Erendis has decided that she will no longer be the ever-waiting wife of a mariner; she goes back to her family's house and secludes herself and Ancalimë in the company of female servants. Her heart grows colder as the days go by and is filled with bitterness that little by little turns into hatred. When Aldarion finally comes back from helping the elf king Gil Galad combat the newly risen Sauron, his father is too busy reproaching him for his irresponsibility towards his family to listen and understand the importance of Aldarion's news. Erendis is not willing to listen either, and the unfinished story of their relationship seems to find an end, according to Tolkien's notes, in the Númenórean equivalent of a divorce court. Erendis spends the rest of her days poisoning her own life and that of her daughter against men, and it is too late already when both she and Aldarion realize how they need each other. After the death of Aldarion, it is suggested (as a last touch of tragedy and irony) that Erendis commits suicide by drowning in the sea.

Ancalimë's life is no better. Being named the heir of her father and becoming the first of the Númenórean queens, her hatred for men does not diminish and continues after her loveless marriage; being herself miserable, Ancalimë is also jealous of other people's happiness, and, in imitation of Lady Macbeth, tries to show her power over her husband by humiliating and insulting him. The figures of Erendis and Ancalimë, even though they are driven by circumstances and with their own reasons being perfectly explained, give the lie to the claim that Tolkien is incapable of portraying women as evil. There is no difference, other than in degree, between the evil implied in destroying one life and the one destroying an entire civilization. Erendis and Ancalimë are the proof that not only all-powerful male overlords make great villains. Yet Aldarion is not blameless either, nor is he exculpated by Tolkien: it is his selfishness which started the problem.

CONCLUSION

Tolkien's views of women and women's issues are modern, though not politically correct. He is true to his vision of equality when showing his female characters not as women, but as human beings, able to be strong and weak, to succeed and to fail. Tolkien deals with women as characters, not as representatives of ideologies or as icons of the female sex seeking public approval. His stories are universal and deal with universal topics, and are not focused on any particular time or point of view, whether masculine of feminine.

LAURA MICHEL (Guadalajara, Mexico, 1971) has an undergraduate degree in applied linguistics and has completed her studies in the Master's Programme in Translation offered at the Autonomous University of Guadalajara, where she taught linguistics and literature (and a bit of Tolkien) for eleven years. *The Lord of the Rings* became her favourite book when she read it at age fourteen. She has conducted literary workshops since 1990 and edited several issues of the science-fiction and fantasy fanzine *Laberinto* (Guadalajara, 1992-99). She did most of the writing for the monograph issue on J.R.R. Tolkien of *Plan B* magazine (Mexico City, 2002) and *The Lord of the Rings* special supplement of the *Cinemania* magazine (Mexico City, 2001). Her fiction has been published in several anthologies, newspapers, and magazines.

Bibliography

Becker, Alida (ed.), 1978, *The Tolkien Scrapbook*, Philadelphia: Running Press.

Bradley, Marion Zimmer, 1968, 'Men, Halfings, and Hero Worship', in Rose A. Zimbardo and Neil D. Isaacs (eds.), 2004, *Understanding The Lord of the Rings*, New York: Houghton Mifflin, pp. 76-92.

Carpenter, Humphrey, 1990, *J.R.R. Tolkien. Una Biografía*, (translated from English by Carlos Peralta. Original title: *J.R.R. Tolkien. A Biography*, 1977), Barcelona: Ediciones Minotauro.

---, 2000, *The Letters of J.R.R. Tolkien*, (paperback edition, first published 1981), New York: Houghton Mifflin.

Challis, Erica ('Tehanu'), 2003, 'Quests, Myths and Heroines', in TheOneRing.net (eds.), 2003, *The People's Guide to J.R.R. Tolkien*, Cold Spring Harbor: Cold Spring Press, pp. 136-142.

Crowe, Edith L., 'Power in Arda: Sources, Uses and Misuses', in Patricia Reynolds and Glen H. GoodKnight (eds.), 1995, *Proceedings of the J.R.R. Tolkien Centenary Conference*, Milton Keynes and Altadena: The Tolkien Society and The Mythopoeic Society, pp. 272-277.

Ferro, Jorge N., 1996, *Leyendo a Tolkien*, Buenos Aires: Ediciones Gladius.

Gray, Patricia, 1997, *J.R.R. Tolkien's The Hobbit, A Dramatization*, (first edition 1968), Woodstock, Illinois: The Dramatic Publishing Company.

Grotta, Daniel, 1982, *Tolkien*, (translated from English by Soledad Silió. Original title: *The Biography of J.R.R. Tolkien, Architect of Middle-earth*, 1976), Barcelona: Editorial Planeta.

LeGuin, Ursula K., 1978, 'Introduction to Planet of Exile', in Ursula K. LeGuin, 1979, *The Language of the Night*, (edited by Susan Wood), New York: Perigee Books, pp. 139-143.

Lewis, C.S., 2000, *Los Cuatro Amores*, (translated from English by Pedro Antonio Urbina. Original title: *The Four Loves*, 1960), Madrid: Ediciones Rialp.

Martinez, Michael, 2003a, 'Much ado about Arwen: Elven Princess', in Michael Martinez, 2003, *Understanding Middle-Earth*, Poughkeepsie: ViviSphere Publishing, pp. 163-168.

---, 2003b, 'Guess Who's Coming to the Disaster', in Michael Martinez, 2003, *Understanding Middle-Earth*, Poughkeepsie: ViviSphere Publishing, pp. 463-473.

McLeish, Kenneth, 1982, 'The Rippingest Yarn of All', in Robert Giddings (ed.), 1984, *J.R.R. Tolkien: This Far Land*, London: Vision and Barnes & Noble, pp. 125-136.

McNew, Cynthia ('Anwyn'), 2003, 'Men are from Gondor, Women are from Lothlórien', in TheOneRing.net (eds.), 2003, *The People's Guide to J.R.R. Tolkien*, Cold Spring Harbor: Cold Spring Press, pp. 115-120.

Otty, Nick, 1984, 'The Structuralist's Guide to Middle-earth', in Robert Giddings (ed.), 1984, *J.R.R. Tolkien: This Far Land*, London: Vision and Barnes & Noble, pp. 154-178.

Partridge, Brenda, 1984, 'No Sex Please – We're Hobbits: The Construction of Female Sexuality in The Lord of the Rings', in Robert Giddings (ed.), 1984, *J.R.R. Tolkien: This Far Land*, London: Vision and Barnes & Noble, pp. 179-197.

Pearce, Joseph, 2000, *Tolkien: Hombre y Mito*, (translated from English by Estela Gutiérrez Torres. Original title: *Tolkien: Man and Myth*, 1998), Barcelona: Ediciones Minotauro.

Sayer, George, 1995, 'Recollections of J.R.R. Tolkien', in Patricia Reynolds and Glen H. GoodKnight (eds.), 1995, *Proceedings of the J.R.R. Tolkien Centenary Conference*, Milton Keynes and Altadena: The Tolkien Society and The Mythopoeic Society, pp. 21-25.

Shippey, Tom, 2004, 'Another Road to Middle-earth: Jackson's Movie Trilogy', in Rose A. Zimbardo and Neil D. Isaacs (eds.), 2004, *Understanding The Lord of the Rings*, New York: Houghton Mifflin, pp. 233-254.

Stanton, Michael N., 2001, *Hobbits, Elves, and Wizards*, New York: St. Martin's Press.

Tolkien, J.R.R., 2002, *Bilbo's Last Song*, (revised edition, first edition 1992), New York: Alfred A. Knopf.

---, 1990, *Cuentos Inconclusos de Númenor y la Tierra Media*, (translated from English by Rubén Masera. Original title: *Unfinished Tales of Númenor and Middle-Earth*, 1980), Barcelona: Ediciones Minotauro.

---, 1994, *The Lord of the Rings*, (one-volume paperback edition, first edition 1954/55), New York: Houghton Mifflin. [LotR]

---, 1979, *The Silmarillion*, (edited by Christopher Tolkien; first published 1977), New York: Ballantine Books. [Silmarillion]

J.R.R. Tolkien: A Simplicity Between the 'Truly Earthy' and the 'Absolutely Modern'[1]

BERTRAND ALLIOT

Abstract

Tolkien, during his entire life, felt affected by a fundamental loss typical of his time: that of true simplicity, transpiring through ancient languages and texts, that characterised an ancient way of being-in-the-world. This loss is linked to the appearance of the modern man, who no longer has a direct relationship with things: he is partly separated from the world and observes it through an intermediary: reason. Therefore he is no longer truly 'simple'. Nonetheless, Tolkien had his heart set on recovering this pre-modern simplicity – for instance by emphasising the values of the Hobbits or by adopting a creative process devoid of sophistication – notably because the 'evocative power' of the texts and languages of ancient times to him seemed far superior to that of modern versions. However, ultimately Tolkien would shape a new form of simplicity adapted to the present time because he knew that the original form could not be recovered. This new simplicity takes its place in the middle between what we shall call the 'truly earthy' and the 'absolutely modern'.

INTRODUCTION

The letters of J.R.R. Tolkien provide us with the premise from which we would like to once more penetrate the work of this great 20th century inventor of a world. Let us remember that his correspondence reveals the birth of *The Lord of the Rings* and of other less famous texts and also that his letters can be classified into three main groups. The first group consists of the letters sent to his children – they would be his first

---

[1] I would like in particular to thank Vincent Ferré for his thorough rereading and his numerous useful comments. Also thanks to Chantal Delsol and, for helping to edit my translation from French into English, to Nikki Funke and Hélène Beaugy.

readers – and particularly to his son Christopher. In these letters, he evokes the adventures taking place in Middle-earth and also begins a conversation that centres on the meaning of life. The second group consists of letters sent to his editor Sir Stanley Unwin and to the latter's son Rayner. They essentially deal with practical issues linked to the publication of his writings. Finally, the letters of the third group were sent to his fans or to different kinds of persons – journalists for example – with whom he discussed several questions concerning details of his writings, or the importance of certain episodes or significant facts in his work.

Linked to his fictional writings, the author's correspondence allows us to catch a glimpse of 'Tolkien's thinking'. He was, of course, first and foremost, an author of romance, even though he had a distinguished and acknowledged part to play in his field of specialisation, Philology. He therefore did not develop a 'thought', as other intellectuals of his time did. Nonetheless, by creating an imaginary world and by reflecting on his own creation, Tolkien indeed provides us with the fruit of his 'thinking' and it is the latter which will form the core of these few pages. First of all, it has the remarkable feature, compared to most other authors' 'thoughts', of having been 'offered' to and shared with millions of people throughout the world: *The Lord of the Rings* has experienced considerable success in both its literary as well as cinematographic form. It has to be said that Tolkien did not content himself with simple stories: he created a genuine secondary world with languages, legends and a mythology that constitutes an inexhaustible reservoir of questions and interests. Entering the work of Tolkien's thought is like going into a house which we realise is inhabited: each door enables us to see a bit more of its extent and wherever the eye looks, it encounters the 'presence'.

Like the majority of works that marked their time, Tolkien's carries a message of a universal nature. What is necessary here is to grasp a part of it and to understand how it was shaped. In fact, Tolkien's design is above all modest. It was little by little and without him realising it that his work was sublimated, almost in spite of himself. He elaborated his work to satisfy his most simple desires. But because he was 'from this world' and firmly anchored in it, he naturally addressed the world. Thus, technical issues are largely present in his work because he was part of the generation that experienced the advent of the era of mechanisation. However, something which will attract our attention even more is Tolkien's great devotion to simplicity – the simple, the common as opposed to the sophisticated and the cultured – which, in his own words, is greatly due to the capacity of the latter to 'ennoble' itself, in other words to surpass its mediocrity in order to produce something greater and almost divine. This eulogy of the simple is shown in the emphasis on the Hobbit people, a rural society of authentically earthy peasants whose members accept and face their destiny and history with great nobility. But what is meaningful for our time is a new form of simplicity that transpires through his work and life. It is different from the simplicity of the Hobbit, which reigned during the golden age, because it is adapted to the human being of modernity. This new simplicity as outlined by the author of *The Lord of the Rings* takes its place in the middle between what we shall call the 'truly earthy' and the 'absolutely modern'.

TOLKIEN AND NECESSITY

Tolkien was a creator of a world and thus a dreamer, a thinker. But, before being able to withdraw in peace to let his imagination have free rein, and to immerse himself in his poetic universe, he had to free himself from everyday events, from worries in his professional and family life. Thus, his correspondence reveals how heavily "vital necessities" weighed on him and how "domestic and academic troubles" (Tolkien 1981:117) slowed him down in the accomplishment of his work, the fruit of his meditation. Similarly, his letters are a succession of evocations of gruelling times inherent in every person's existence, but which seem to have had a particular importance for the author. Indeed, he seems to go through these periods – notably his wife and son's health problems and the papers he had to correct to earn a living and at which he never stopped fuming – without even for a second considering to escape them, which would no doubt be a grave temptation to many others. One feels that he conscientiously faced all tasks inherent in everyday life, that he could not free himself from necessity without having given it the attention it deserves. This inventor of a world, despite the strength of his reveries, never seemed to gaze on the concrete world with lightness. For this reason, as is evident from his correspondence, year after year one sees him bent over his literary work – over the "serious work" (Tolkien 1981:131) – after having conscientiously fulfilled the tasks he had to carry out. He seems always to have been incapable of, for instance, dedicating himself body and soul to his stories and of only scantily addressing his pressing and heavy work, or of neglecting his duties, and if he was behind in things that he should do, notably because he was busy with *The Lord of the Rings*, it was always his conscience which told him not to neglect them for too long. Tolkien resembles his fairy tale hero Niggle, a painter whose mind is engrossed in the realisation of a painting gradually taking on colossal dimensions – Tolkien himself likens this hero's situation to his own, the painting representing *The Lord of the Rings*[2]. Unfortunately, incessant 'interruptions' come to disturb his creative work, forcing him to abandon his brushes to fulfil tasks he cannot escape from, whether he thinks them duties or not, or he is compelled to do them whatever he thinks.[3] Therefore, the tale stages a character torn between two types of incompatible activities because each calls for exclusive attention to it. The hero is therefore

---

[2] See *Letters* (Tolkien 1981:257 and 320-321).
[3] See *Tree and Leaf* (Tolkien 1975:82).

obliged to alternate in space and time between a chosen activity and a necessary activity; the latter he would pass over if he was not forced to face it.

This concern for the concrete realities from here and now also appears in Tolkien's obsession for details: he says himself that he is "a pedant devoted to accuracy" (Tolkien 1981:372). It is thus that one sees him very often occupied with searching and correcting the slightest errors or incoherencies within the hundreds of pages of adventure in Middle-earth. When he realised that the movements of the moon did not fit in with the sequence and the rhythm of the scenes, he reconsidered his entire text. Thus, the immaterial pleasure he would get from building his mythology and creating a breathtaking story would always be weighed down by the necessities of a world made up of limits and rules. This is certainly the reason why the birth of *The Lord of the Rings*, from when it first started being written to when it was published, was so long and painful.

THE INSCRIPTION IN THE EARTH

Tolkien was therefore a landsman, a human being firmly attached to the concrete, like the trees he loved so much and of which the roots penetrate deeply into the ground. His work would be marked by this earthy inscription: his literary intentions were very down-to-earth as well. We have to remember that Tolkien was passionately fond of languages, words and their origins. One of his primary passions was to invent languages. However, for him a language requires "a suitable habitation" (Tolkien 1981:214): it must be inscribed in a concrete world, open itself up in a singular land. This is why he created a story for the languages of his own invention – a story steeped in a universe of myths and legends and capable of giving consistency to them. However, as the attachment to a land only has meaning in the specific and not in the general, Tolkien adapted his imaginary world to his "beloved country" that has, and it is this which he found very depressing, "no story of its own (bound up with its tongue and soil)" (Tolkien 1981:144) such as the Celtic, Roman, Germanic, Scandinavian or Finnish legends. He was not even satisfied with the Arthurian world because it is "imperfectly naturalized" and "associated with the soil of Britain but not with English" (Tolkien 1981:144)! No doubt, for Tolkien, each man is deeply rooted, even incarnated in an immaterial, cultural and social body, from which he unfolds his humanity. Tolkien liked significant spaces and raged against a world that was "getting to be all one blasted little provincial suburb" (Tolkien 1981:65). When others were delighted at the English language becoming "the biggest language group", the author called for the "curse of Babel", finding "this Americano-cosmopolitism" (Tolkien 1981:65) terrifying. Like a language, a human being has roots as a result of which they are in the world. In his letters, Tolkien states that he likes, "loves", England not because he thinks that it is above or better than another, even less because it could be a universal model, but simply because it is his and therefore its perfume inebriates him and moves him like no other. It is no doubt like this for any person regarding their relationship with their 'soil'. Also, people were evidently not allowed to speak to Tolkien about Great Britain and still less about the Commonwealth, which, one can deduce, were for him only vast spaces artificially edified above human realities and by this very fact insignificant by nature.[4] One might find his supposed contempt for the 'French mind' in his denunciation of this form of universalism "without foundation", the latter according to him therefore being unreal and hazy. It is not by accident that Tolkien became passionately fond of Old English, Anglo-Saxon dialects and old Germanic languages: the study of these idioms, which for such a long time imbued his native land, is able to reveal today what this land authentically was and what it still is in the depths of itself.

---

[4] See *Letters* (Tolkien 1981:65).

In Middle-earth, all the characters come from somewhere, are 'connected to a specific land', which explains why so many of them are suffering in exile. Their characters are the result of an alchemy between the respective contributions of their native lands, their race, their lineage and their individual personalities. Evil jostles the balance of power, dislodges creatures from their setting. Having deviated from their course, all things move concurrently and in a motion of disordered appearance slowly tend towards finding their place again and restoring the world to a point of balance: the ring is attracted to its master, the Hobbits to the Shire, the Elves to the land of the Valar and the errant king to his throne – each being to its own setting.

THE HOBBIT SIMPLICITY

One can see why Tolkien was so close to his most illustrious creatures: the Hobbits. Who are they? Peasants full of 'Englishry' to all of whom Tolkien would have given English surnames if he had done more detailed thinking and planning on the subject.[5] They are ordinary people close to nature, simple beings living in "settled home(s)" (1981:240). They have the kind of failings that all ordinary, dull-witted people who were 'born-somewhere' have, and also exhibit a spirit of parochialism. Above all, and it would be wrong to think differently, they do not much appreciate adventure: the limits of the Shire are overstepped only in the case of necessity. This is why during their quest, as Tolkien says, the Hobbits will think "first of the Shire": it is after all quite natural. Nevertheless, their dreams can sometimes take them outside of their small universe: one of Sam's grandest and simplest desires, he himself is a true hero, is "to see the Elves". Only the Frodo and Bilbo Baggins lineage has a predisposition for adventure: as if the latter ran through their veins.[6] But

---

[5] See *Letters* (Tolkien 1981:88).
[6] This is clearly explained at the beginning of *The Hobbit*.

this singular lineage is an exception. In any case, despite the mediocrity of the average Hobbit, these people have an essential quality: they have both feet firmly on the ground, which gives them a sense of reality that is particularly well developed. This good sense and ability to face life's challenges head on is no doubt at the origin of their aptitude to, when the situation requires it, transcend the mediocrity that they are usually made of. A heroic force lies dormant in each Hobbit: here we touch upon one of the main reasons that explain Tolkien's love for simplicity.

"I am in fact a Hobbit" (Tolkien 1981:288) Tolkien says in a letter to Deborah Webster in 1958. The author's 'Hobbitry' transpires throughout all of his correspondence, which is not surprising considering what has been discussed above regarding his 'earthy' anchorage. His intentions as an author of Romance remarkably reflect this character trait: in writing *The Lord of the Rings*, he wanted to give shape to a gripping story taking place in an atmosphere and a context that personally attract him. He repeatedly states the simplicity of his intentions: to let his tastes express themselves. He wrote *The Lord of the Rings* for his "personal satisfaction" (Tolkien 1981:211) and to stimulate literary pleasure, just as he had written *The Hobbit* to entertain his children. It is pointless to seek complicated explanations or to intellectualise his approach. In his letters, he never stops telling his correspondents, who sometimes see the denunciation of Stalinism, and at other times that of atomic power in his work, that he had no allegorical intention. He makes his interlocutors understand that the allegorical process is foreign to his way of thinking. Allegory is too sophisticated for his purpose, which he desires to be simpler, almost naïve. It is no doubt the symbol of the very kind of ambitious and exquisite processes he condemns all the more strongly since he used to be interested in them at a certain point in his life. In fact, he used to have the ambitious and inordinate plan to build a body of legend "high and purged of gross [...] ranging from the large and cosmogonic to the level of romantic fairy" (Tolkien

1981:144), a sort of immense and majestic painting valuable in itself because of its own artistic qualities and because of what it would be capable of inspiring in other artists who would be able to make use of its contents to 'continue' it. He quickly gave up this ambitious plan and put all of his energy into the "mere stories" (Tolkien 1981:144), those that apparently came to him from nowhere and that he spontaneously put down on paper.[7] But in reality he did not entirely discard his initial project or rather, he discarded it only as a project. It is possible for this grandiose painting to be realised, but if this is the case, it will only be through the inner force of stories. In other words, if it is to take shape, it will generate itself. It will happen spontaneously – or never – and no one can tell its shape and contents in advance, so no one can plan it. Tolkien thus adopted his character Niggle's artistic manner who paints "leaves better than trees" (Tolkien 1975:81), leaves that he carries within himself and that he paints marvellously well. The spontaneous gathering of multiple leaves soon results in the formation of a tree with numerous branches and "fantastic roots" (Tolkien 1975:81) to which a background adds itself, the whole thing becoming "Niggle's country" (Tolkien 1975:99). Tolkien was thus converted to a new kind of simplicity: from that point on he would serve this intimate 'creative surge' ready to jump out of himself and would put all his confidence in its capability to produce a painting of greater scope. Therefore, Tolkien combined the simplicity that is 'related to the land', that constitutes the basis of his stories, with a simplicity of the artistic process, that of the 'creative surge'. Nonetheless, an ambiguity remains in the real simplicity or naivety of his intentions: several writings seem to be much more thought out than he often says, as is shown in this passage in a letter to Robert Murray:

---

[7] For further information on this grandiose project, see letter No. 131 to Milton Waldman (Tolkien 1981:144).

> *The Lord of the Rings* is of course a fundamentally religious and Catholic work; unconsciously so at first, but consciously in the revision. That is why I have not put in, or have cut out, practically all references to anything like 'religion', to cults or practices, in the imaginary world. For the religious element is absorbed into the story and the symbolism.
> (Tolkien 1981:172)

The Lord of the Rings is at first glance a fundamentally Catholic work simply because it has been written by a Catholic: the author's Catholicism stands out from the text – we will soon come back to this point. Later, however, the author intentionally introduces his Catholicism: Tolkien thus proves that he could not free himself from all sophistication, from his 'reflective' capabilities. Nonetheless, this should not be a reason to call into question the sincerity of his conversion to simplicity. He was deeply 'converted' to it, yet it remains obvious, and this forms the subject of the article, that because he was a man of his time it was impossible for him to be converted to it entirely. In any case, his words stress that his writings are mostly guided by a 'non-reflective' thought.

The explanation of the fundamentally simple nature of the author's artistic process is always accompanied by the assertion of his personal simplicity. He likes to present himself as an ordinary man:

> I smoke a pipe, and like good plain food [...] but detest French cooking; I like, and even dare to wear in these dull days, ornamental waistcoats. I am fond of mushrooms (out of a field); have a very simple sense of humour (which even my appreciative critics find tiresome). (Tolkien 1981:288-289)

Thus, he delights in defending the "dull stodges": "Yorkshire's young men and women of sub-public school class and home backgrounds bookless and cultureless". He prefers, like he says to his son Christopher to

> spend [him]self on removing the 'dull' from 'stodges' [...] – a hopeful soil from which another generation with some higher intelligence could arise [...] – rather than waste effort on those of (apparently at any case) higher intelligence that have been corrupted and disintegrated by school, and the climate of our present days. (Tolkien 1981:403-404)

Tolkien is very aware of the failings of the simple, which he likes to describe and mock in his adventures. However, he likes the simple for its potential: the simple – a stodge from England, a leaf by Niggle, a fascinating story – is 'a hopeful soil' because it does not cheat, it is present in the world in the form of a primeval innocence. The relevance or power of the simple does not lie in itself but in what it is able to generate. Because it is anchored in true reality, because it is neither corrupted nor sullied, it can grow only healthy fruits. It is very uncertain whether this is possible when it comes to the products corrupted by sophistication and the artificial excess of modern society: they lack a solid and stable basis to ensure steady growth and an innate and natural sense of balance. Thus, *The Hobbit* – Tolkien realised this with hindsight – is a "study of simple ordinary man neither artistic nor noble and heroic (but not without the undeveloped seeds of these things) against a high setting – and in fact (as a critic has perceived) the tone and style change with the Hobbit's development, passing from fairy tale to the noble and high and relapsing with the [Hobbit's] return" (Tolkien 1981:159). Therefore we understand why "the inter-relation between the 'noble' and the 'simple' (or common, vulgar)" (Tolkien 1981:220) and above all the 'ennoblement of the humble' particularly move him.[8] Humble people reveal themselves through their contact with the world and history: the events that emerge and challenge them unveil their superior qualities, which

---

[8] See also *Letters* (Tolkien 1981:232 and 237).

previously lay hidden beneath their inertia. Tolkien experienced the small people's heroism and courage – he recognised these as superior to his own – in the trenches of the First World War (Carpenter 2000:180). These people do not try to defy the world, but are able to, when the situation requires it, face it with heart and an unrivalled nobility, "there is no horror conceivable that such creatures cannot surmount, by grace [...] combined with a refusal of their nature and reason at the last pinch to compromise or submit" (Tolkien 1981:120-121). For him simple and noble are closely intertwined, "without the high and noble the simple and vulgar is utterly mean; and without the simple and ordinary the noble and heroic is meaningless" (Tolkien 1981:160).

APPLICABILITY RATHER THAN ALLEGORY

According to Tolkien, the capacity of the simple to transcend itself partly explains the universal reach of his work: the sublimation of the message is a 'natural phenomenon'. This is the reason why, in their letters, many of Tolkien's correspondents misinterpret the situation, as they believe in his use of the allegorical process, though, as we have seen, their misinterpretations are not totally unfounded. The author says that he had no allegorical design, but on the other hand does not refuse the notion of 'applicability'. His story was applicable to the world he was living in because his work sprang from life: in that sense, it was impossible to "write any 'story' that is not allegorical" (Tolkien 1981:212). His story cannot be allegorical, however, because it does not support any intentional messages. Said differently, its applicability was not wished for – at least initially – even though he was well aware of the fact that "all this stuff (his creation) is mainly concerned with Fall, Mortality and the machine" (Tolkien 1981:145). As fascinating stories, which tell of the encounter between the simple and historical events, are in the process of weaving themselves, messages of universal reach are outlined and gradually take shape. The following passage from a long letter to Milton Waldman which evokes the legends of the Silmarillion, sheds light on this 'self-creating' process:

> Its centre of view and interest is not Men but 'Elves'. Men came in inevitably: after all the author is a man, and if he has an audience they will be Men and Men must come in our tales, as such, and not merely transfigured or partially represented as Elves, Dwarfs, Hobbits, etc. (Tolkien 1981:147)

Indeed, what has to 'come in' will 'come in'. Simply because the author is human, his humanity 'comes in' the narrative. Somehow, it forces its way through without announcing itself. Without the author knowing it, his work 'drinks' him or rather 'drinks' the immateriality of his person, as a piece of blotting paper would. Each stratum of Tolkien's immaterial body is in turn subjected to this absorption. Thus, in turn, he passes on his humanity to his readers – the fact that he belongs to the human race and is attached to his condition – his 'Christianity', his 'Anglicity', his 'Suffieldity' – Suffield is his mother's maiden name – and so on. Also, because the author is 'from this world' and 'of his time', the atmosphere of the age in which he lives transpires in his creation. Finally "each of us is an allegory, embodying in a particular tale and clothed in the garments of time and place, universal truth and everlasting life" (Tolkien 1981:212). Under these conditions, the work escapes from its creator and becomes autonomous, "[t]he stories arose in my mind as given things" (Tolkien 1981:267) Tolkien says. It was in re-reading his work that the author became conscious of the themes and messages that it contains. The work itself was partly unfamiliar to him and it is for this reason that he was moved to tears when writing certain passages[9] and that his interpretations of the Middle-earth adventures were given with-

---

[9] See *Letters* (Tolkien 1981:321).

out any certainty: he often writes that he 'thinks' that such or such an element has such or such a significance. In the same way as his readers, he was a spectator of his work. In order to help his fans – and himself – to understand his work, the only thing that he could do was to reveal fundamental facts that were true of him, to inform them of the 'specific'. To this end, he would, for instance, say to Deborah Webster that he was "born in 1892" and that he "lived for his early years in 'the Shire' in a pre-mechanical age" and more importantly that he is "a Christian [...] and in fact Roman Catholic" (Tolkien 1981:288).

THE TECHNICAL

The ills generated by the industrialized and modern society that would never stop worrying Tolkien are certainly at the origin of his highlighting of the simple. He was preoccupied with the hold that the technical has over the world, be it in the material or in the immaterial sphere. Technical issues constantly feature in his correspondence and lurk in the background in his books. As a "reactionary back number", he fumed against "American sanitation", "moral pep", "mass production" and the "scientific materialism" (Tolkien 1981:65) that are running off with the world. In his correspondence, Tolkien often gives the impression of a hunted man fleeing the noises and ugliness of the world and especially the internal combustion engine he seems to be relentlessly hounded by. One follows him page after page in his retrenchments and in the company of his work, sheltered from a world, which sometimes takes on characteristics of Mordor.[10] He does not really condemn the technical as such, but rather its propensity to overrun all spheres of human life and facing the spirit of the machine which is seizing the world, Tolkien only senses the obvious force of that which has stood in its simplicity from

---

[10] See letters No. 53, 58, 64, 96, 100, 102, 257 in Tolkien 1981.

time immemorial and continues to do so. From his relationship with the earth, from his presence in the world, he draws his love for the trees, for nature that in its bareness contains a force surpassing everything. This force that bears witness to the fact that "there was an Eden on this earth" (Tolkien 1981:110) would be revealed to him like nowhere else in the heart of the land bearing his lineage and which consequently saw him coming into the world, if not his birth: the land of the Suffields – his maternal ancestors. What also influenced him was his father's adoptive land, the Orange Free State's "high stony wastes" (Tolkien 1981:91) in South Africa, where he only lived for a short period of time, yet long enough for the land to pass, by capillarity, a piece of itself onto him. His thought on the technical is summed up firmly in these few words written to his son in 1944, "I especially noted your observations on the skimming martins. That touches to the heart of things, doesn't it? There is the tragedy and despair of all machinery laid bare" (Tolkien 1981:87).

The critique of the technical by the author of *The Lord of the Rings* can be linked to the thought of other 20th century authors. In fact, Tolkien's reflections on the matter often echo the thoughts of other philosophers criticising the technical and can particularly be linked to the ideas of Heidegger. In the great German intellectual's philosophy, one finds the despair of seeing calculating thought exclusively invading the being of humans. Being opposed to calculation, which inspects every single thing, he, like Tolkien, praises the simple.[11] The most powerful characteristic of the simple discloses itself when a man takes up with his origins or, like Heidegger says, when he comes back to his natal land.[12] Therefore, the philosopher shows his affection for the soil, the homeland, the national, which, sublimated, reveals a certain form of the ab-

---

[11] For instance in his short poetic text 'The Pathway' in *Philosophical and Political Writings* (Heidegger 2003).

[12] See 'Discourse on Thinking' in *Philosophical and Political Writings* (Heidegger 2003).

solute. The finite contains the infinite, the sensible contains the insensible and the spirit. Heidegger is attached to Hölderlin's poetry, which exhales this passage from earth to ether made possible through the mediation of language, speech and poetry. This speech does not reveal anything concrete but appraises that which is keeping us separated from heaven and from the eternally unknown sense it contains. Tolkien's work is marked by the same sensibility towards the world. There is obviously his love for the 'soil', the primordial place for poetry and languages, but also his interrogation of that which forever remains unanswered. Tolkien deliberately leaves us with shadowy questions, unexplained episodes in his work. These mysteries that are played out in his work echo those that remain linked to the human existence, the real existence. At the heart of these mysteries of course stands that of mortality, which is one of the major themes in his stories – "that is to say they are written by a human being", Tolkien would say. The immortal Elves call it "men's gift", a curious thing that remains unexplained by the myth, "what God has purposed for Men is hidden" (Tolkien 1981:147). It is parallel to this meditation on the world and even in opposition to it that Tolkien tends to criticize the technical and its proclivity towards fabrication (as in 'making' things), which is, in a sense, a refusal of the world and a corruption of what is most cherished within the human being.

HAVING BEEN BORN "OUT OF DUE TIME"

We now have to go further in order to understand the significance of highlighting the simple in this first and turbulent part of the 20th century, in the context of a modern and post-industrial society. In fact, the question is, "What can the significance and pertinence of the simple be in societies that are no longer simple?" Tolkien is perfectly aware of this fundamental loss that is a trait of modernity. We see modernity as a fundamental 'state' of enfranchisement in relation to the 'given' or the 'received'. Modernity has distanced itself from tradition, religion, transcendence, nature, from all things that give meaning from the outside and that give a sense of limitation. In a modern context, human existence is autonomous; it is a part set free from the whole as opposed to having been integrated before, 'taking part' in a natural or divine superior order. Modern human beings do not belong to the world as peasant society did because they embody the loss of the 'unique existence' that partly marks 'the fall'. The 'disunited' man looks at the world through a third eye, the eye of knowledge and reason, the eye that reflects the world and distances it from him, separating it completely. This is why the modern man is no longer fundamentally simple: because he has introduced a distance between himself and things, a distance filled with reason and 'reflective thought', which Tolkien refers to as the 'intelligence' of our time.

At the same time, however, this 'no longer belonging' allows the 'separated' man to see what he did not see when he was integrated in the world. It is a comfort for Tolkien, "[o]therwise we should not know, or so much love, what we do love. I imagine the fish out of water is the only fish to have an inkling of water" (Tolkien 1981:64). Like any 'separated man', Tolkien appreciates the simple, the beauty of the martins, because he is no longer really a simple being, but an 'after the fall' man. The truly simple man would not appreciate the simple but would merely content himself with being thus. He would thus be unable to praise the simple, as Tolkien does, because he lacks the indispensable detachment which this kind of process requires.

In spite of this consolation, Tolkien cannot rid himself of the feeling of having been born "out of due time" (Tolkien 1981:64), because the new situation that modern men have ended up in and that opens new prospects, at the same time alters their relation with the world. This alteration is of the same nature as that which takes place when an individual passes from childhood to adulthood. In his text *On*

Fairy Stories, in which he talks about his boyhood, he starts a particular sentence as follows: "In that (I nearly wrote 'happy' or 'golden', it was really a sad and troublesome) time I liked ..." (Tolkien 1975:42). In spite of the sorrowful memories of his childhood, the first word that comes to his mind when describing this period is 'happy'. This hesitation demonstrates that the state of ignorance which characterizes childhood shelters man from a type of knowledge that disrupts the 'peaceful' course of existence. Pre-modern times were also plunged into such a state of ignorance that the ones being 'born out of due time' are deprived of: gaining knowledge also means seeing one's misfortune. This misfortune is that of one's condition not that of one's daily life. All beings – like the young Tolkien – have a sense of their own daily misfortunes but not all are able to perceive the misfortune of their condition with the same accuracy – the young Tolkien, unlike the mature Tolkien, is still ignorant of this. The alteration of modern man's relationship with the world – compared to that of the childhood of humanity – certainly comes partly from the loss of ignorance, as ignorance used to mask the misfortune of the human condition.

In the present time, other signs that accompany the new high consciousness of what makes the misfortune of the human condition can be testimonies of this alteration. Tolkien realises for instance that values such as honour and fidelity have not passed from heroic times to the present without having been damaged. Luckily they have not disappeared; yet they have been corrupted by the atmosphere of the present, simply because their validity can be, at every moment, reconsidered, discussed and put into question by the reason of the man who, from now on, is outside the world. These values are vested with infinitely less conviction because humans have distanced themselves from everything and thus their way of being in the world is not authentic anymore. Tolkien's poem *The Man in the Moon Came Down Too Soon* from *The*

Adventures of Tom Bombadil partly seems to be an account of the great emptiness which the Oxford professor felt as a modern man:

> At plenilune in his argent moon
> in his heart he longed for fire:
> Not the limpid lights of man selenites;
> for red was his desire.
> For crimson and rose and ember-glows,
> for flame with burning tongue,
> For the scarlet skies in a swift sunrise
> when a stormy day is young.
>
> He'd have seas of blues, and the living hues
> of forest green and fen;
> And he yarned for the mirth of the populous earth
> and the sanguine blood of men.
> He coveted song, and laughter long,
> and viands hot, and wine,
> Eating pearly cakes of light snowflakes
> and drinking thin moonshine.
> (Tolkien 1995:38)

The character in the poem is outside the world: he does not live on earth but on the moon. His lunar every-day environment, marked by inconsistency, leaves him in an unsatisfied state. He lives in a world which is as pure, beautiful and limpid as it is elusive, vaporous and insipid: pearly cakes, snowflakes and moonshine. Dreaming of hearty meals, he is only being served light snacks. Then, he is eager to come down to earth as this is for him the place of tangible realities. Down there, he could meet the 'firmness' and rough reality with which he wants to feed and fulfil himself: he dreams of viands, of sanguine blood, of laughter long. Therefore, he would like to exchange the coldness for heat, the limpid lights for ember-glows, the barren moon for the nourishing earth. In a sense, he wants to become 'consubstantial' to the world, penetrate its substance and feed himself with it until he is pleasantly full. This desire will, of course, remain unsatisfied. Like other 'poets of modernity' such as Rimbaud, Tolkien here seems to put into verse the gap that modern men are confronted with: they are constrained to inhabit a dimension disconnected from the genuine world which leaves them in a permanent state of 'disunion' and puts them in a situation where they are only able to exist "at the surface of things"[13] (Bonnefoy 1992:12).

This assertion of 'division' that gives Tolkien the strong feeling of being born 'out of due time' is reinforced by the effect that ancient languages and texts have on him. He is seized by something like a clamour coming from the depths of time and earth. A clamour – or a song – with singular tones which his own epoch has not been able to produce and which seem to be made of a higher essence. Where does this tenacious impression come from? No doubt from the fact that the ancient languages and texts that are the substance of this clamour, rather than talking about the world as it is seen through the objective and critical eye, make the world speak through them. They utter the world's 'heartfelt cry'. It is by means of this cry torn from the world that the latter shows itself in the Truth. The world exists through its cry and not only through what science and reason can explain to us about it. The author's vocation for philology lies in the discovery – or rediscovery – of this earthy heartfelt cry and in his will to re-engage with that which has made it possible.

Apart from the literal power of ancient languages and texts, the 'superiority' of the pre-modern simplicity or authenticity also seems to be strengthened by its ability to properly face the grim realities of this world. Today, as shown for instance by the products of the technical, calculation and 'reflectivity' are dragged into a permanent re-evaluation or re-invention of the world that veil what it truly is. Excessive intelli-

---

[13] Personal translation of the French poet Yves Bonnefoy's words, in *L'Arrière Pays*.

gence and reason, when investigating the real, end up 'mis-evaluating' it or rather – and this amounts to much the same – evaluating it too harshly: this makes it unnecessarily complicated and results in the presentation of an 'uninhabited' real. The world is full of difficulties, hardness, dangers; its realities call for quick, sensible, adapted responses. However, the sophistication of structures and thoughts complicates the development of responses, weighs down the efficiency of reactions and ultimately jeopardizes the societies from which these originate. This conviction of Tolkien's is probably derived from his encounter with history; he experienced its most symptomatic manifestation: war. In the face of this kind of recurrent event, he was able to conclude that the attitude of the simple people – the only ones who conserve qualities from the heroic period in the present time – was best adapted to face the agitation of the world and therefore to guarantee the preservation of favourable conditions for happiness. One particular question would haunt him for a considerable part of his life, "Would we have survived had we solely been armed with the 'intelligence' of our time, without the contribution of simplicity?" Stated otherwise, "Has progress made a decisive contribution to improve our relationship with reality?" According to him, this has not been the case.

Therefore, Tolkien was torn between two antinomical convictions. The first is that the pre-modern way of being-in-the-world, thanks to its simplicity or its authenticity, is superior to the modern way in terms of at least two aspects: the reach of its artistic productions and its ability to propose answers that are 'opposable' to the 'real'. The second is the fundamental and irremediable distancing of the majority of men from this authentic form of simplicity. From this time onwards, all of his thinking would be committed to solving this equation: recovering, without denying the new situation of the modern age, a more authentic way of being-in-the-world to enable one to give appropriate answers to the concerns of daily life and reviving, within the artistic sphere, the world's heartfelt cry. In order to solve this equation within this new context, a redeployment of simplicity is needed. In fact, Tolkien's eulogy of the simple, which we have tried to describe here, is not a purely gratuitous act with the sole aim of stressing what contemporary men have definitely lost, contributing to their misfortune. Humans have lost true simplicity but can adopt a new form of simplicity which has been adapted to the present time.

GUARDING AGAINST THE 'ABSOLUTELY MODERN'

The uncompleted fall

Our time is marked by the feeling that Eden has been lost and by the certitude – for every reasonable being – that it will never be recovered, but also by the sensation that it is sometimes possible to perceive its lightness; "[w]e all long for it (Eden), and we are constantly glimpsing it: our whole nature at its best and least corrupted, its gentlest and most human, is still soaked with the sense of 'exile'" (Tolkien 1981:110). As Tolkien says, we may "recover something like it" but in a peculiar way, we are "just as [...] the converted urban get[ing] more out of the country than the mere yokel, but [who] can not become a real landsman" being "both more and in a way less (less truly earthy anyway)" (Tolkien 1981:110). We are no longer truly earthy, we no longer belong to the world in the same way, even if we still belong to it. Being simple, for a modern man, is already admitting that he no longer truly is so: this is the first lesson that can be drawn from Tolkien's thought and the first draft of a new kind of simplicity. Being simple means accepting the evidence that we are fallen and that we cannot fill the emptiness that results from this. It is precisely what men seem not to accept. Tolkien feels – and that is here where his critique of the excessive nature of all things technical originates – that "the whole human race" is carrying out "the fall to its bitter bottom" (Tolkien 1981:110) and in a way putting the finishing touches to the latter's work. He argues that with the aid of tools like the machine and scientific materialism, humans are throwing themselves wholeheartedly into the illusory and unhealthy project of world reification.[14]

The continuation of the fall is the attempt to accomplish absolute modernity: the recovery of Eden not by going back to the golden age or the truly earthy but by means of the temptation of constructing it. The modern plan, we have said, is founded on the autonomy of men and individuals in relation to nature, tradition and religion. Thanks to the development of knowledge and the instrument of reason, they have the ability to construct new from old and to free human beings from certain contingencies and determinations. Absolute modernity, which is the most successful form of this ability, pushing the latter's logic to its height, aims to finally reach the 'genuine life', a form of the absolute. This form of the absolute therefore is the result of a wilful act which is in opposition to the 'genuine life' waiting for humans after death, that in the garden of Eden which has been given or created but not constructed. The temptation of the 'absolutely modern' comes from the incomplete character of mere modernity that leaves humanity in the middle of the ford, burdened by an uncompleted, therefore unsatisfying, existence.

Tolkien's words on the fall emphasize the necessity of not going beyond the first stage of modernity. Humanity – at least a part of it – has been dragged down. The setting in motion of this movement has opened up a new perspective from which it is possible to envision the realisation of all 'possibilities'. But the promises of such a transformation of the world are largely the fruits of an illusion. Of course, following this direction may well bring about a profound change in life and the world, but it is vain to think that happiness can be perfected. Even worse, this attitude can keep humans separated from what is most 'cher-

---

[14] See *Letters* (Tolkien 1981:110).

ishable': the beauty of the world as it has been given to us, the one revealed to us after the fall. Therefore, Tolkien pleads first for a human being capable of accepting this place in the 'middle', which has been allocated through the uncompleted fall.

The humility before the 'given'
In the face of the temptation of absolute modernity the author promotes this new form of simplicity, which is based on the acceptance of the definite loss of authentic simplicity. In order to continue this primeval acceptance, being simple means, first and foremost, not rejecting what comes naturally from oneself: sometimes, one has to *be* without looking back on oneself with hindsight. Thus, the fact that Tolkien says that he likes wearing ornamental waistcoats is not a way of being falsely simple, but rather of revealing, in a somewhat theatrical way, what in him is the simple. Similarly, the author saying that he detests French cooking probably does not relate to the latter's lack of gustative delights. Besides, a simple 'being' would not 'detest' French cooking. With this remark, he most likely intends denouncing the sophistication and excessive and conventional ecstasy that are sometimes provoked by the refinements of French culture. We also understand that this particular way of campaigning for simplicity shows that Tolkien himself was not an 'authentic' simple being like the 'dull stodges' or genuine Hobbits are. For him, simplicity cannot be anything but imperfect – as shown by his ambiguous relation to allegory – because conspicuously wanting to be simple or authentic already means not truly being so.

To be simple today is also to accept a part of oneself, somewhat less anecdotal than what has been discussed above, that links each individual to their culture and that is 'irreducibly' attached to each human being. This acceptance was unfailingly anchored in Tolkien. It was not the result of a deliberate choice or of a conscious act, but the testimony of an immaterial heritage which formed an integral part of his person in the same way his 'carnate' body did. Having been born English, he naturally liked England and that which makes up the country's character and identity. He did not seek to be rid of his historical and cultural heritage, to deny it just because it had not consciously been chosen. He took it as an inalienable context through which he could delve into the heart of things and, no doubt, into his own heart as well. This is where his passion for 'languages rooted in the land' – such as Anglo-Saxon and Middle English dialects and also Icelandic, which over the centuries has retained a true authenticity – came from. One notes on that subject that he was not interested in the important French language influence on English – he did not like French. French, introduced by the Normans, was the literary language, that of the nobility. It came from the top and was artificially imposed on a pre-existing base that was in no way related to it. In those days the languages spoken by the common (native Saxon) man were the English dialects, which Tolkien would never stop loving.

Thus, through his eulogy of the simple pleasures of existence and through showing his attachment to his cultural identity, Tolkien went against the stream of dominant thought. He was opposed to a strong tendency of his time – and ours – which Tom Shippey (2000:11) refers to as that of the "cosmopolitan intelligentsia" that likes "re-inventing" itself and adopting "glamorous pose". He remained distanced from this kind of pretence and never thought of denying his middle class English roots. Thus Tolkien did not contemplate breaking with what preceded and surpassed him. He would try to hold on to this humility in the presence of the 'givens' of life, even if they seemed, on the outside, most insignificant.

A distrust of creative activity
Tolkien's concern for simplicity ultimately took on the shape of a distrust of literary work. In fact, as we have already mentioned, one of his major preoccupations was to remain sensitive towards the realities of

this world. However, his creative work was prone to keep him distanced from it. He warned himself against the pride and passivity of the Elves, which he criticises in his tales and which originates from their almost exclusive vocation for creating the aesthetic, an activity that does not require them to be aware of the real. Thus Tolkien – like anyone else – had to know how to silence his Elvish part; by means of making a concerted effort, he had to constantly remind himself of the real and answer to its 'demands'. It is here that we find the explanation for the author's focus on 'necessity', as described in the introduction of this essay, but also for his servitude to the 'creative surge'.

In fact, by first relating his daily worries to his correspondents before turning to a discussion on his stories and mythology, he seems to give thanks to the world. Also, he often mocks – or apologises for – the serious way he talks about his histories and creation. He always relativises the importance of his literary work that may take him away from the real. In doing so, he lets his interlocutors know and reminds himself that the only thing that deserves substantial attention, for the time being and as long as we are on earth, is the concrete world and that it has to be cherished for what it is and not for what we believe it to be or would like it to be.

Afterwards, he attempts, within the creative realm, not to speak about the world, but as an heir of the authors of heroic times, to make the world speak through him. The process of creating *The Lord of the Rings* is penetrated by his willingness to let himself be carried away by what we have called the 'creative surge'. His most determined wish, according to his letters, was to free his work from any kind of sophistication and from too much 'reflective' thinking, as these were suspected of transferring the power of reason to the immaterial artistic realm, reason, under the control of the technical, already being prevalent in the material or physical spheres. Sophistication in the artistic sphere is an added sign of the omnipotent tendency of calculation to overrun human existence: it is for this reason that when writing his creative works Tolkien suppressed his vague desire to make use of allegory. His insistence on tirelessly repeating that his work is not allegorical was due to his intentionally preventing himself from making use of allegory. And if he did so intentionally, it is because allegory threatened to introduce itself into his work at any time. Thus, his irritation when encountering allegorical interpretations of his work was matched only by his determination to oppose allegory as such. This emphasises again what makes modern writers radically different from those of ancient times: the latter sang of the world naturally, their 'creative surge' was not impeded by any kind of 'reflection'. Today, to utter again the heartfelt cry discussed above, or something close to it, the 'creative surge' has to clear a path for itself among numerous obstacles; this path can only come into existence through a preceding intervention of the will. This is the author's will to revive simplicity, to be 'incarnated' into the world and its realities that have shaped the great 'Tolkienian' poem. The latter is also – which partly explains its success – a heartfelt cry: that of a world jeopardised by an excess of reason and calculation that needs to be balanced out by an equivalent amount of song and poetry.

Through various aspects, Tolkien's tale *Leaf by Niggle* sums up all of the author's morality, as studied in the last pages, that aims to enable the co-habitation of the desire for sub-creation and concern for the real. Niggle, like Tolkien – the allegory is obvious even if the author tries to minimise his intention – is an artist who spends most of his time painting a picture by using the 'creative surge method'. This is the reason why its dimensions never seem to stop growing. Niggle would like to devote himself entirely to this work of the spirit but is regularly interrupted by calls from the outside world. Thus, Niggle's neighbour, Parish, often comes to disturb his creative work because he needs help from him – for instance to repair his roof – or because he feels that he ought to tell Niggle to make more of an effort to maintain his garden, which is overrun with weeds – as Niggle clearly has better things to do. Evidently Parish represents the truly earthy man, who does not understand the first thing about why Niggle is spending so much of his time on this painting. In response, Niggle tries to answer as best he can – without any bad will but also without any peculiar fervour – to these solicitations coming from the outside world. This is how Niggle's life progresses until the day when he is judged by his 'voices' in what seems to be the purgatory at the end of the journey that has been promised him since the beginning of the tale and that is representative of death.[15] On what basis is Niggle judged? On the importance he has accorded to the tangible realities of this world, which his judges refer to as 'laws'. For instance, maintaining one's garden is prescribed by such a law, so is giving greater importance to helping one's neighbour repair his roof rather than to spend time on an artistic activity. Niggle is clearly being reproached for his involvement in an activity that is evidently useless. However, two things finally save him in the eyes of his judges. Firstly, he was disposed to painting, thus by engaging in this activity he has responded to a call of nature – which in itself is a kind of law – and has also not accorded it any real significance since "he never thought that that made him important" (Tolkien 1975:91). Therefore he remains humble before his creative work. Secondly, he has not totally neglected the 'prescriptions of law' and the call from the outside world. He tries as best he can to respond to them though he is reproached for calling them 'interruptions'. And perhaps one of the decisive points for the judges is that he has never pretended "even to himself that" his commitment for painting "excused his neglect of things ordered by law" (Tolkien 1975:91): here probably lies the final reason why the voices apparently show leniency towards him. There is no doubt that Tolkien imagined the course of his own last judgement in a similar fashion and that some simple rules

---

[15] For a detailed analysis of *Leaf, by Niggle* see Shippey (2000:266-277).

stated in the tale guided his decisions and actions throughout his life: keep, as far as possible, a constant focus on the realities of this world, respect the 'laws' that have been imposed on us, give priority to the tangible rather than the abstract, give priority to facing the real rather than escaping with the help of thought or imagination.[16] Here again, we notice the new role that a strong will can play: for Parish bowing before the real is a natural act, as the real is all that he is aware of, but for a man 'separated' from the world, sophisticated, like Niggle, doing so is a duty and thus an act of will. Such an act is the only way, in a modern context, of preventing human beings from trying to construct an illusory 'elsewhere' for themselves.

ACCEPTING THE LOSS OF THE 'TRULY EARTHY'

Ultimately Tolkien gives out another lesson: just as it is illusory to attempt to construct a heavenly 'elsewhere' during one's terrestrial sojourn, the desire to rediscover it here on earth is equally pointless. In other words, we cannot go back to the earth – or to the truly simple – without at the same time betraying the authenticity of the act of doing so. We cannot recover the primeval innocence, the primeval simplicity; this is only outwardly possible through the intervention of pretence, because the loss of this innocence and simplicity has become a given of contemporary existence. Tolkien could have gone back and settled on the Suffields' land or in another area resembling it. We have to remember that according to him this is the Shire. Thus he could have fled the combustion engine he hated, as well as the factories, power stations and big flat modern buildings. But he did nothing like this. To the amazement of many, because this fact apparently contrasted with the evocative power of his work, he led "an ordinary suburban life […] bringing up

---

[16] On the idea of 'escape' see *On Fairy Stories*, the part about 'Recovery, escape, consolation'.

his children and tending his garden" (Carpenter 2000:118). He lived in a modest suburban house that W.H. Auden described as "hideous", exactly like the pictures on the walls (Tolkien 1981:373). He probably never thought of going back to the 'Shire' because he could no longer 'be' in it authentically: like the city dweller we mentioned earlier, he is aware of no longer being 'truly earthy'. Returning to the native land to live in the Shire, for an after-the-fall man like himself would be betraying the new simple, which accepts the definite loss of the simplicity of primeval men. This process of going back can today only be the result of a reflective and sophisticated act not related to the reality of the present time, which assigns humans a new and uncomfortable position. The temptation of the truly simple like that of the absolutely modern does not give any answers: like the former it is a refusal to accept our condition and the world as it is.

This lesson also lies in the conclusion of *The Lord of the Rings*. At the end of their adventure, the ring bearers can no longer stay within the confines of the Shire: they cannot be "one and whole" (Tolkien 1993:309) in it anymore. They have reached a condition similar to that of modern men: they are 'divided' and have experienced the fall. It is evident that of all the races inhabiting Middle-earth, that of the Hobbits is the one that is not yet 'fallen'. The Hobbits are still innocent and ignorant, 'one and whole'; they have remained sheltered from the primeval fall. The exception, no doubt, is the lineage of Frodo and Bilbo that has been differentiating itself from the rest of the Hobbits even before the ring saga begins: Bilbo has already encountered the 'vast world' and because he wants to leave, knows that he no longer really belongs to the land of the Hobbits. The arrival of the ring in this sense only increases the motion of the fall that has already begun. Frodo goes a step further in experiencing the fall, as he is entrusted with the burden: he is forced to encounter the vast world and to face it, while also being tempted with access to evil and power. He is compelled to leave the 'space-time' of the Shire, where the unchanging and cyclical simple life has thus far 'enshrined' him in sufficiency. As he faces his destiny alone and finds himself for the first time in an unknown world without the possibility of holding on to a 'paternal' figure – unlike Sam – he inexorably heads for the point of no return. He can no longer return to the time and place where he could be without seeing and knowing and where he used to be truly simple. Frodo cannot go back in order to live again in the happiness and unity of yesteryear. With Bilbo, he will leave for the Grey Havens – a paradise usually unreachable for mortals – for "a period of reflection and peace" (Tolkien 1981:328) where they will be cared for until it is time for them to die. Only Sam can remain in the Shire – though this will only be for a short period of time – to live there as a simple man. This is because during the entire adventure he does not focus on the ring – except for a short period of time that will finally prove to have been too long after all – but on serving Frodo. His love for his master and the trust he puts in him protects him: his true devotion keeps him from seeing the ring. He is only the bearer of the ring bearer. The latter has been sacrificed for a greater purpose. This is what lies in the Sam and Frodo exchange at the end of *The Lord of the Rings*:

> 'But,' said Sam, and tears started in his eyes, 'I thought you were going to enjoy the Shire, too, for years and years, after all you have done.'
> 'So I thought too, once. But I have been too deeply hurt, Sam. I tried to save the Shire, and it has been saved, but not for me. (Tolkien 1993:309)

The Shire has recovered its lustre of yesteryear but those who have lost the truly earthy at the same time have lost the ability of enjoying it. Frodo is a man who is changed, differentiated, separated and who cannot step in the same river again even if its course has been restored. Frodo is like his creator and a modern man: he is condemned to wander between 'two waters', the water of childhood where the truly simple man baths and the boiling bathwater of the 'absolutely modern'.

CONCLUSION

Tolkien's entire work is marked by this duty to simplicity or humility in the context of this fundamental and constitutive loss of his time: the loss of true simplicity which is linked to the loss of the unity of existence. It is the testimony of an author who engages in an inner search and who longs to make this new feature of the human condition his own. As Tom Shippey says, Tolkien's tales contain many anachronisms: mixing the ancient and the modern, the Christian and the pagan, the civilised and the savage. This reflects the life of the great Oxford professor, who went back and forth between the heroic pre-Christian age he visited on a daily basis when studying ancient languages and texts and the modern age he happened to live in. His closeness to the ancient time would allow him to become aware of the original qualities of the time he had been born in as well as the discomfort imposed on those living in it. This is where his regret comes from of not having been born in 'due time'. Still, he knows his regret to be irreducible despite the ultra-modern logic that does not lead to an absolute but to world destruction. Thus, we have to accept this uncomfortable position of being between two waters or being 'out of the water'. Of course, while we are on earth, we can set up artificial 'space-times' that are like many theatrical stages where the hammer and the anvil clumsily work the truly earthy or the absolutely modern. However, these two extremes cannot be constructed; they can either be lived or regretted. The second option is the one assigned to us, but would this mean that 'genuine life' is absent? No, 'genuine life' is the one which has been given to us, which intervenes 'in between': let us have the humility and simplicity to acknowledge it.

Tolkien was never a globetrotter, a tourist taking in exotic attractions: he did not travel a lot. Nor did he purchase a cottage in the country in order to cultivate an *art de vivre* which had disappeared or which had possibly never even existed. He managed to protect himself, thereby going against the general current of his time, against leading a life made up of illusions. He remained aloof from the ludicrous *mises en scène* that, due to the inappropriateness of their casting, reflected nothing of real life. He lived humbly in the suburbs of his time without either consuming the present time or attempting to construct a new one. Thanks to the Christian faith and his innate sense of creation or 'subcreation', as he preferred to call it, he managed to keep himself at a distance from the mirages that caught the attention of his contemporaries. He created an immaterial artistic work, the fruit of his thought. He cultivated the artistic, aesthetic and purely scientific aspects of human nature and like the Elves had a "devoted love of the physical world, and the desire to observe and understand it for its own and as other – i.e. as a reality derived from God [...] – not as a material for use or as power-platform" (Tolkien 1981:236).

Tolkien's work, the myths he created, are significant for the present time and might be better adapted to it than those written by authors before him. Some have criticised *The Lord of the Rings* because "all the good boys came home safe and everyone was happy ever after". This demonstrates how many critical analysts have a simplistic view of Tolkien's work: they see it as a classical confrontation between good and evil. This confrontation is omnipresent in his work and its main aim is to stimulate literary pleasure. Any sophisticated convolutions used to realise this aim are useless. Besides, does complexity better reflect the order of the world than simplicity? Has good not been confronting evil on the chessboard of the world since time immemorial? Simplicity is not necessarily simplistic: in Tolkien it is deep and detailed. However, as we now know, there is more than this in the Oxford professor's work. Unfortunately – since his tales are applicable to the world – the good boys do not come home safe and sound. They have to adopt this land, in reality unchanged but new for them, a land that is both foreign and familiar, close to them and distant. They have to learn how to love, Middle-earth.

BERTRAND ALLIOT University of Marne-la-Vallée, France. Doctoral candidate specialising in Political Science whose thesis focuses on the idea of nature within Western civilisation.

Bibliography

Bonnefoy, Yves, 1992, *L'Arrière Pays*, (first edition 1972), Paris: Poésie/Gallimard.

Carpenter, Humphrey, 2000, *J.R.R. Tolkien: A Biography*, (first edition 1977), London: Unwin Hyman.

Heidegger, Martin, 2003, *Philosophical and Political Writings*, (edited by Manfred Stassen), New York: Continuum.

Shippey, Tom A., 2000, *J.R.R. Tolkien: Author of the Century*, Boston: Houghton Mifflin.

Tolkien, John Ronald Reuel, 1975, *Tree and Leaf*, London: George Allen and Unwin.

---, 1981, *The Letters of J.R.R. Tolkien* (edited by Humphrey Carpenter, with the assistance of Christopher Tolkien), London: George Allen and Unwin.

---, 1987, *The Hobbit*, (first edition 1937), London: George Allen and Unwin.

---, 1993, *The Return of the King*, (second edition; first edition 1955), Boston: Houghton Mifflin Company.

---, 1995, *The Adventures of Tom Bombadil*, (first edition 1962), London: HarperCollins.

The Maker's Will ... Fulfilled?

JESSICA BURKE & ANTHONY BURDGE

Abstract

Tolkien, the Inklings and writers of fantasy post WW II set a standard by utilizing fantasy as a means to convey moral, religious, spiritual thoughts and 'truths' of our primary world. Tolkien's 'On Fairy Stories' best details his thought process concerning how this is accomplished. Through successful 'sub-creation' we are fulfilling the Maker's will by imitating Creation and creating in the image of which we were created. As sub-creator, we can provide a successful escape through the means of fantasy, creating a believable secondary world, in which we can learn as we were meant to, i.e. through communion with beast and bird, and experience the reality of nature as opposed to machine. A believable secondary world was created in the same fashion as the Creator, through word and language.

Since Tolkien's time and the establishment of this thought, modern society and culture has warped and perverted, consciously or unconsciously, the tasks, clearly spoken about by Tolkien, the Maker has set before us. Fantasy and escape is now a means of detachment from, rather than a communion with, our world. Has our world sought to enrich creation through fantasy? Are machines and industry now more 'real?' Are Tolkien's insights only contained within academic and artistic circles? Are we fulfilling the Maker's will by creating with words and language, or are we perverting words and language for gain, greed through commercialism, and materialism? Are we any further along to uncovering truths or becoming a harmonic whole, or have we fallen further?

Tolkien, in his fiction and critical papers, shared his insights regarding Creation, sub-creating, the will of the Maker, the tasks of man, the Fall of Man, and where our modern world stands in all of this during his time. This paper seeks to find out whether modern society and culture has succeeded in furthering the tasks and will of the Maker, as well as Tolkien's insights, or has indeed fallen further from accomplishing them.

> [Grundtvig and Tolkien] believed that Man, made in the image and likeness of a Maker, fulfilled that Maker's will by creating with words, thereby helping him gain a better understanding of his existence and uncovering underlying truth. (Agøy 1995:34)

In a paper contrasting Tolkien with Danish theological poet N.F.S. Grundtvig, Nils Ivar Agøy sheds new light and perspectives on Tolkien's legendarium. Agøy postulates the potential of Grundtvig's influence upon Tolkien's theory of sub-creation. Tom Shippey has explored the correlation between Grundtvig and Tolkien, yet nowhere within Tolkien' *Letters*[1] is there mention of any influence by Grundtvig on Tolkien (Flieger 2005:148). From an early age, Tolkien read and loved fairy stories. With his "life long urge to create," he was moved to write his own (Flieger 2005:15). This urge, a talent toward creativity, was further explored and extended upon by his scholarship, ultimately being fueled by his wartime experiences (Flieger 2005:15). Tolkien's 'On Fairy Stories' is his refutation of earlier scholarship, which presented misconceptions regarding their source, structure, history and purpose. This paper aims to understand what the 'Maker's will' is according to Tolkien, how it is fulfilled, and if we continue to make use of it as a modern people in order to have a more complete understanding of the truth to our life and existence.

During the past several years, especially in a world post Peter Jackson's film interpretation of *LotR*,[2] it has become apparent to the writers of this piece that – for the most part – the mainstream Western World of today has little or no interest in digging deep, getting to the roots, finding truths, exploring the depths of our being, or using our

---

[1] *The Letters of J.R.R Tolkien*, edited by Humphrey Carpenter, will be abbreviated as *Letters*. For complete bibliographic information, see the bibliography.

[2] *The Lord of the Rings* will be abbreviated as *LotR*.

talents as sub-creators. Tolkien's work inspires and invigorates our sense of the sacred, opening the doorways to exploration. In an age where production companies and studios manipulate the film market for the perfect fan[3] – which leaves most consumers unable to see past the images on screen – there is a separation between those who find beauty in the depths of Tolkien's original work and those who are satisfied with a surface reading as interpreted by an egotistical third-party. In our work, both in the realms of Tolkien Studies and education, we have observed a disparagement arising, or being rediscovered, a reluctance in getting to the source of things. This is not to say that everyone finds exploration, both personal and creative, meaningless. Nor are we trying to say that every person born to live and breathe is required to examine the truths in life. The hardest task is looking in the mirror. But all too often in the Americanization of the world, we have found that the notions of Creation and enchantment have been relegated to a tiny corner of the bookshelf, left to stagnate, and be forgotten especially in our consumer world of progress and mega-marketing.

The playwright, Tom Stoppard, through the device of comedy conveys just how enchantment – and the fantastical imagination – in all its various forms, shapes, and modes of existence has been treated in the Western world of today:

> A man breaking his journey between one place and another at a third place of no name, character, population or significance, sees a unicorn cross his path and disappear. That in itself is startling, but there are precedents for mystical encounters of various kinds, or to be less extreme, a choice of persuasions to put it down to fancy; until – "My God," says a second man, "I must be dreaming, I thought I saw a unicorn." At

---

[3] For more about the construction of the 'perfect fan' see Murray 2004.

> which point, a dimension is added that makes the experience as alarming as it will ever be. A third witness, you understand, adds no further dimension but only spreads it thinner, and a fourth thinner still, and the more witnesses there are the thinner it gets and the more reasonable it becomes until it is as thin as reality, the name we give to the common experience [...] "Look, look!" recites the crowd. "A horse with an arrow in its forehead! It must have been mistaken for a deer." (Stoppard 1991:21)

Enchantment is the horse mistaken for a deer. It is the hideous recollection from childhood of the Ringling Brothers and Barnum & Bailey 'unicorn' which was nothing more than a surgically molested baby goat. Seeing that poor creature was scarring to so many children during the 1980s: many were left thinking that this ill-used beast was the real thing. Yet some knew it could not be. It did not speak to that essence of enchantment harbored within a select few willing to search for the truth of Creation – the Maker's Will. Very much like Stoppard's unicorn, the experience brought a sense of alarm and horror rather than delight. But the horror did not come from the notion of the unicorn, it came from what modern man did to the sense of enchantment, combined with an almost total lack of comprehension or desire to comprehend the Will of any Maker.

To the uninitiated, uninformed, and uninterested, those unable to comprehend myth or fantasy, Tolkien is a stodgy British 'amateur' who wrote a fortuitous blockbuster while living the life of tweed in the Oxford countryside. Not to mention the fact that he was a conservative and highly devout Roman Catholic. To the 'enlightened' – otherwise known as Tolkien enthusiasts or Tolkien scholars – Tolkien was a man before his time, a man in touch with something greater than himself, a man in tune with the ebb and flow of the universe. One way this harmony manifested in Tolkien's life and work can be seen in his treatment of nature. Throughout his life, Tolkien revered nature. In each of his works – both his fiction and in many of his expository essays – by touting his own faith in the natural world, nature's order, and the utter mystery of life, he re-invigorates a sense of the sacred in nature and our world, and in so doing he also sets a standard for us all. For the most part, his works can stand the tides against "corporate culture's ubiquitous distractions, religion's alienation from and negativity toward nature, along with the mindset of scientific materialism [...]" all of which have "effectively destroyed our sense of community and kinship with the cosmos" (Fox 2004:7). In his 'Spiritual Problem of Modern Man' Jung, in exploring faith and religion, touches on this creative lack of faith, as well as how Tolkien in fact heralded the notion of 'modernity' and his disappointment in our world:[4]

> Many modern people call themselves modern – especially the pseudo-moderns. Therefore the really modern man is often to be found among those who call themselves old-fashioned. They did this firstly in order to make amends for their guilty break with tradition by laying all the more emphasis on the past, and secondly in order to avoid the misfortune of being taken for pseudo-moderns. Every good quality has its bad side, and nothing good can come into the world without at once producing a corresponding evil. This painful fact renders illusory the feeling of elation that so often goes with consciousness of the present – the feeling that we are the culmination of the whole history of mankind, the fulfillment and end-product of countless generations. At best it should be a proud

---

[4] Tolkien time and again throughout the *Letters* makes disparaging remarks about Mankind's state of affairs. One interesting letter, number 96, goes on to discuss "the forgotten beauty" of the Eden myth. He also says that the modern world is unable to recover the idyllic sense of peace from Eden – we are incapable of doing so (*Letters* 109-111).

> admission of our poverty: we are also the disappointment of the hopes and expectations of the ages. Think of nearly two thousand years of Christian Idealism followed, not by the return of the Messiah and the heavenly millennium, but the World War among Christian nations with its barbed wire and poison gas. What a catastrophe in heaven and on earth! [...] I believe I am not exaggerating when I say that modern man has suffered an almost fatal shock, psychologically speaking, and as a result has fallen into profound uncertainty. (Jung 1976:459-465)

How has this uncertainty manifested in our world? By this lack of faith and a neglect of creative well-being. As Jung continues to pinpoint the crises facing our world today, he says: "So long as all goes well and all our psychic energies find an outlet in adequate and well-regulated ways, we are disturbed by nothing from within" (Jung 1976:463). For our purpose, this can be translated to mean that the general populace neither continues to discover the sparks of truth, nor does it uncover the signposts hidden within the unconsciousness of humanity and the natural world. Alternatively, the fear arises that Tolkien's mythology will only continue to remain more the property of academic syllabi than of popular audience (Flieger 2005:x). In his scholarship and sub-creative literary work, Tolkien challenges not only scholars but also his readers. He sets the standard for his contemporaries, seekers and writers who would come after him: for the sub-creative act, and fantasy itself, are inherently tied to one another, which furthers the thought that modern society tends to separate the two.

In his essay 'On Fairy Stories', Tolkien concisely lays out the function of fantasy and its legitimacy as a "natural human activity" (143-144):

> To many, Fantasy, this sub-creative art which plays strange tricks with the world and all that is in it, com-

bining nouns and redistributing adjectives, has seemed suspect, if not illegitimate. To some it has seemed at least a childish folly, a thing only for peoples or for persons in their youth. As for legitimacy I will say no more than to quote a brief passage from a letter I once wrote to a man who described myth and fairy-story as 'lies'; though to do him justice he was kind enough and confused enough to call fairy-story making 'Breathing a lie through Silver'.

> 'Dear Sir,' I said – 'Although now long estranged,
> Man is not wholly lost nor wholly changed,
> Dis-graced he may be, yet is not de-throned,
> and keeps the rags of lordship once he owned:
> Man, Sub-creator, the refracted Light
> through whom is splintered from a single White
> to many hues, and endlessly combined
> in living shapes that move from mind to mind.
> Though all the crannies of the world we filled
> with Elves and Goblins, though we dared to build
> Gods and their houses out of dark and light,
> and sowed the seed of dragons – 'twas our right
> (used or misused). That right has not decayed:
> we make still by the law in which we're made.

Fantasy is a natural human activity. It certainly does not destroy or even insult Reason; and it does not either blunt the appetite for, nor obscure the perception of, scientific verity. On the contrary. The keener and the clearer is the reason, the better the fantasy will it make. If men were ever in a state in which they did not want to know or could not perceive truth (facts and evidence), then Fantasy would languish until they were cured. If they ever get into that state (it would not seem at all impossible), Fantasy will perish, and become Morbid Delusion.

It is this world of "Morbid Delusion" that we all live in – or in which we, as modern men and women, are born into (Campbell 1972:388; Jung 1976:465-466). At once our society has no singular, all-encompassing myth, and in having no myth, we have – in all essence – no faith.[5] In *The Power of Myth*, Campbell denotes the loss of the biblical root of faith, Occidental literature (Campbell 1988:4), and Jung likewise remarks that "the various forms of religion no longer appear to come from within [...] they seem more like items from the inventory of the outside world" (Jung 1976:466).

Agøy states that Tolkien "referred to Man's gift of Fantasy as his symbol of kingship over the rest of creation" (Agøy 1995:33). Tolkien "agreed that the gift was used most effectively when describing those things that could not be directly observed in the primary world" (Agøy 1995:34). Has fantasy been carried to excess and Man's gifts from the Maker ignored? Has the written word of the modern popular audience found itself further from the truths set forth by Tolkien, thereby causing us all to spiral further into an already Fallen state of being? Does humanity continue to exercise this gift? Or does it abuse the Word and language for selfish gain? At this point, the answers to some of these questions may only be speculated.

For the popular audience, Tolkien's methods and theories for accessing the Maker's will, and accessing the divine, may be impossible. The term 'impossible' is not fact. It is merely the opinion of the authors of this piece. This impossibility is a response to humanity's lack of courage to harness the fuel that fires our spirit. Perhaps this is why the multi-layered, interconnectedness of Tolkien's legendarium is not

---

[5] The Western World, being a so-called 'melting pot' of culture and faith, has no all-pervasive myth. All too often there is an assumption that this 'all-pervasive' myth is Christian. For many this is true, but this belief neglects the myriad of other faiths, beliefs, or disciplines that permeate the Western World. Because of this 'melting pot' approach, any notion of a singular myth has been negated. Secular myths are from a wholly different view and are not included in this statement.

readily apparent to most readers and is thought to remain solely the stuff of academia.

What are the gifts and subsequent duties endowed to humanity by the Maker, gifts which we are expected to fulfill through the beauty of words? As explored by Tolkien, in 'On Fairy Stories' – evidenced in his letters and later criticism – humanity is viewed as the ultimate sub-creator, co-workers of our Creator. By the use of language, as well as the Mythopoeic and fantastical imagination, we reflect divinity in the creative process. The sub-creator – the artist under the Great Maker – primarily utilizes words to give tribute to the Creator, by creating and utilizing those methods and channels of which we know to have been used already in our making (Carpenter 1979:188). A sub-creator like Tolkien, having mastered these methods, 'ceases to invent', and thus a successful Secondary World is revealed. A spirit – or the Spirit, which is other than ego – possesses the sub-creator. This poetic psychology has reverberations back to Plato; however, it is not until shortly after the Renaissance that 'genius' becomes a function of individuality rather than spirit (Barfield 1967:77). The ability to reach a rich vein of such material and to translate it effectively into philosophy, literature, music, or scientific discovery is one of the hallmarks of what is commonly called genius (Jung 1964:25). It was said someone 'had' genius, (a spirit, being possessed of or influenced by, inspiring, like a Muse, the poet/artist) rather than so-and-so 'is' a genius. The super-individual, a poet/artist who is inspired by spirit, or possessed of Spirit, has made the modern day transition into a cult of the individual. Tolkien resurrects the earlier 'genius' notion and balances between the poles of individuality and divine inspiration. Tolkien supports this by stating that though his purpose was largely literary, in relation to the spirit, body and the flow of story he said that parts were "rather revealed through me than by me" (Carpenter 1979:189).

How are these gifts found? First by silencing the everyday sensory overload we tend to take for granted in modern life. It is the stillness within, the source of artistic expression, where the words are found and pour forth. This can be done in a variety of ways, through the Sacraments and Eucharist (as cited by Tolkien), meditation, prayer, theological dedication and communion with nature, which are methods modern petitioners of faith and religion tend to forget. Yet these 'methods and channels' are very much open and accessible to those who are not petitioners of a particular faith and religion. These 'truths' and 'signposts' are discovered via the telling of the story rather than the study of methodology. Tolkien struggled between his dedication to his faith, as cited by Verlyn Flieger,[6] and writing a story applicable to people of all faiths and backgrounds. Judeo-Christian religious belief tends to see nature as an object outside of us, further separating humanity from its deep connection to the world. This was not always the case, for "people living in pre-industrial societies, nature is not something that is distant from and external to us – rather, it is something that interacts with us all the time" (Smith 2006:14). Tolkien, inspired by Barfield's thoughts on language, felt this separation was due to the gradual change from our use of language. "The further we distance ourselves from nature, the more fragmented language becomes. In its origin language was at one with the world (i.e., sound and meaning were united) but over time it has become more and more subjective and symbolic" (Smith 2006:12). This is another way his creative process tends to differ from his struggle with faith.

Tolkien's thoughts and processes were very radical for his time and continue to be so for ours. Applicability is one of the most deep-seated and fundamental pieces to the Tolkien puzzle – and is so often

---

[6] 'Past, History and Memory', a paper presented by Professor Flieger at the Tolkien 2006 Conference at the University of Vermont, April 2006.

shunted to the wayside for more comfortable readings that shy away from the deeper meaning of personal applicability, and the revealing of personal truths. "I cordially dislike allegory in all its manifestations, and always have done so since I grew old and wary enough to detect its presence. *I much prefer history, true or feigned, with its varied applicability to the thought and experience of readers*"[7] (*LotR* 11). As cited by Tolkien, applicability is within the thought and experience of the reader. The reader is able to uncover aspects of his or herself, to wipe clean the lens so to speak, and see the enchantment within our world. The natural enchanted world, through the applicability of Tolkien's work, appears sentient, thereby allowing humanity to feel re-connected to our living universe and less alone. Tolkien felt that fairy-story or myth should reflect or contain certain elements of moral and religious truth, yet they should not be explicit enough in the form known and utilized in the primary 'real' world (Carpenter 1979:144). In contrast to Lewis, and some of Tolkien's contemporaries, this method of applicability is not a 'prescribed stream of thought' fed directly into the weaving of stories. The author, by incorporating this prearranged stream of consciousness in the story, tells the reader what to think or do – therefore the allegorical tale is born. These are the forms of the primary 'real' world spurned by Tolkien, and by so ignoring these threads of allegorical realism, he allowed the reader to reach personal conclusions and achieve individual growth through the work. The allegorical method is not conducive to allowing the reader's unconsciousness to flower for itself. The sub-creator knows and feels the potential works within himself or herself, having tapped into the "master currents below the surface" or "the spiritual in man" the sub-creator is privy to that "which lies *on the other side* of our natural consciousness" (Barfield 1967:82-83).

---

[7] The stress on the latter sentence is ours.

Fantasy, a sub-creative art that Tolkien tells us is a "natural human activity" (Tolkien 1997:144), utilizing the 'stuff' of the Primary World, which guides us to an understanding of the unseen. Through these means it is the fulfillment of Truth or the Maker's Will, which utilizes our 'natural human' activities, and gifts, endowed to us by our Creator. For modern day, Fantasy is a childish and irrelevant, detached endeavor we play with in youth.

> [...] in our daily experience, we need to state things as accurately as possible, and we have learned to discard the trimmings of fantasy both in our language and in our thoughts – thus losing a quality that is still characteristic of the primitive mind. Most of us have consigned to the unconscious all the fantastic psychic associations that every object or idea possesses. The primitive, on the other hand, is still aware of these psychic properties; he endows animals, plants, or stones with powers that we find strange and acceptable. (Jung 1964:30)

Jung's usage here of the primitive is key. He refers to cultures before modern day, whether Native or Aboriginal, that are the inhabitants of our pre-industrial world – a world where Middle-earth is its primitive prehistory, and the enchantment, or the fantastical that ensues from it. The people and world of Middle-earth are endowed with Jung's "fantastic psychic association" and "psychic properties". Tolkien utilizes another similar term to define it: enchantment. Tolkien's use of fantasy informs the reader of our planet's growing health concerns (for example those affecting nature and humanity) and his work is a response to it.

True fantasy is difficult to achieve. At times it becomes a failure by becoming mere decoration or a distortion of universal truth. If the stories of fantasy, of Faërie the Perilous Realm, and the inhabitants of these fantastical worlds, primarily elves, are all invention of the mind of

Men, then they are true in the sense that they reflect universal truth (Tolkien 1997:113). As Tolkien tells us, Fantasy, the "making or glimpsing of Other-worlds, was the heart and desire of Faërie" (Tolkien 1997:135), which he felt was a "human art" only best expressed in words and literature (Tolkien 1997:140). Within Faërie, the traveller is to know and be connected to a world that has, up until this point of entry, remained unseen, which seen by an enchanted mind's eye (the star upon our brow), the lens is then cleansed of the primary world's chaos, modern disbelief and 'fallen nature'. For the serious reader, via academia or general audience, to truly understand Tolkien's methodology, his analysis of the "true nature and appropriate uses of fantasy" 'On Fairy Stories' is required reading (Flieger 2005:18).

In the fantasy world we see things as are we were meant to see them (Tolkien 1997:155). What does Tolkien imply in this – to see things as we were meant to see them? First, as we read the stories and absorb their words, the gifts and unconscious tools are activated. This means in the Primary world we are capable of seeing and understanding the mysteries that surround us:

> For in the primitive's world things do not have the same sharp boundaries they do in our "rational" societies. What psychologists call psychic identity, or "mystical participation," has been stripped off our world of things. But it is exactly this halo of unconscious associations that gives a colorful and fantastic aspect to the primitive's world. We have lost it to such a degree that we do not recognize it when we meet it again. With us such things are kept below the threshold; when they occasionally reappear, we even insist that something is wrong.
> (Jung 1964:31)

The normally unseen forces of the divine creation are thus revealed, which enriches our involvement in the created world about us. As we know Tolkien wished to dedicate his mythology to his home, England. Yet what is again at play here is its applicability. The beauty and power of Tolkien's work is worldwide, affecting any of his readers who are surrounded by the natural world. Even with limited exposure to the natural world in major cities, readers are able to become more aware and appreciate its enchantment regardless of their level of study. This aspect of the unconscious mind will awaken, allowing the reader a renewed awareness of the Primary World, which is not only the draw – or 'magic' – of the work, but an underlying reason for its continued appeal. This 'magic' not only opens the doors of perception, cleansing the lens so to speak to see the underlying enchantment and beauty but also allows us to view the horrors of our world that suffocates it. The power and enchantment of Faërie gives us the ability to survey space and time, to hold communion with other living things (bird, beast, tree, plant) and gain knowledge and understanding of the inner workings of our universe and world about us. Fantasy becomes the vehicle for awakening the dormant, unconscious second sight, which enchants and assists in our connection to a living Primary Universe. Without this vehicle for seeing our Primary World "as we were meant to see it" we remain a prisoner in a world of shadows. Although these aspects remain wholly unseen and hidden to skeptics, i.e. those who need tangibility as proof, they are not any less real. When one chooses to stay a prisoner within a shadow world it does not make the experience of the adventurous any less 'real' or believable. These human capabilities have lain dormant in our everyday waking lives. This state of being is not easily achieved and is perilous for some. It becomes "independent of imagined wonder and the mind that conceives it" (Tolkien 1997:116). Why is this state not already apparent to our world? For it is the modern mechanized mind of men, which has made the streetcar, lamppost and technology more readily believable than the song of the bird, the unicorn, and the realms of natural wonder. We become further disconnected from ourselves, and our universe as our dependence upon technology has increased. For hundreds of years the mind's eye was the theatre of imagination; now the dizzying images of television and its addictive nature, for some, have overwhelmed modern (wo-)men's senses. The images within their mind are no longer their own. These images have been spoon-fed by agencies and media that create the silly sit-coms and reality crazes that seek to humiliate in ways never imagined in the gladiatorial arena. All of which does not allow any room for the viewers' own creative spirit and imagination.

The snobbery of Tolkien's critics and detractors have helped, and in some ways succeeded, in furthering Tolkien's work from the view of it being an anti-modernist sub-creative work of art. As technology and commercialism has done, the 'literati' or 'marketing elite' have separated works that are not a part of their pre-fabricated, soulless and cynical modern framework. The modern critic arrogantly dismisses works, such as Tolkien's, whose views differ radically from his own. This 'grown-up literary guard' is unable to appreciate a good fantasy novel, created in one of the most key forms of literary creation, which holds dear the values of a pre-modern world. Patrick Curry could not have captured this notion better concerning the values of Tolkien's work:

> They are just the values whose jeopardy we most now feel: relationships of respect with each other, and nature, and (for want of a better word) the spirit, which have not been stripped of personal integrity and responsibility and decanted into a soulless calculus of financial profit-and-loss. Wisdom in Middle-earth is not a matter of economic, scientific or technological expertise, but a practical and ethical wisdom.
> (Curry 2004:131)

In perusing bookseller chain stores, for example Barnes and Noble or Borders, we noticed that Tolkien's *The Hobbit* or *The Lord of the Rings* and at times volumes of *The History of Middle-earth*, have been shelved in the children's section. Has society come away so far from Tolkien's thoughts concerning his work for it to be shelved entirely in the children's area, when in 1955 he felt the 'fairy-story' to be a genre for adults (Carpenter 1979:209)? This marketing scheme solidifies, and returns society's mentality to Andrew Lang's misconception, which Tolkien refuted with 'On Fairy Stories', that in a "post-childhood or modern world fairy tales would only – indeed could only – be enjoyed by children" (Flieger 2005:22). Where does this leave Tolkien, who felt that the so-called 'fairy-story' was one of the highest forms of literature and quite erroneously associated with children (Carpenter 1979:220). Tolkien has said explicitly that *LotR* was "*not* written for children", he was very pleased to hear children from the age of ten upwards had read *LotR*, but felt it was stuffed with words that they would be unlikely to understand. He had hoped it would, however, serve to increase their vocabularies (Carpenter 1979:310). Yet, the marketing schemes surrounding the merchandising of the *LotR* films have made it very hard to actualize these statements, especially when these films have been entirely geared toward children and the young adult. But not only that: they have been geared for a mindless audience, an audience unable to think for themselves, an audience bred on humiliation, violence, gore and the grotesqueries of Western entertainment. And in so doing, the filmmakers have totally disregarded Tolkien, and completely reworked his original text. This dismissal and compartmentalizing of Tolkien furthers the notion that his work need not be considered true literature. Such underestimation and compartmentalisation of Tolkien as 'non-literature' for 'non-adults' can be seen in Edmund Wilson's diatribe against fantasy as literature, 'Oo, Those Awful Orcs', and Burton Raffel's postmortem approach to *LotR* in '*The Lord of the Rings* as Literature'. Wilson's critique links his deep-seated dislike for the fantastic with a personal distaste for any literature remotely connected with childhood (Wilson 1989:51). Raffel takes a different but equally branded approach.

Raffel fails to recognise the nuances in Tolkien's language, fails to make the connection to epic and romance, and admittedly prefers D.H. Lawrence to J.R.R. Tolkien (Raffel 2000:20). These critiques colored the public's reading of Tolkien for years to come. Until the likes of Jane Chance, Randel Helms, and Jared Lobdell in the 1970s and 1980s, no one dared to rage against this prescribed stream of thought, this prefabricated mold that categorized Tolkien as an unworthy 'other.'

An interesting and modern twist to the tired approach of pigeonholing Tolkien, and in connection to the Tolkien fan, lies in the methods of New Line Cinema and the marketing behind the *LotR* films. In "Celebrating the Story the Way It Is:' Cultural Studies, Corporate Media, and the Contested Utility of Fandom' Simone Murray adeptly outlines the marketing schemes implemented by New Line Cinema, Peter Jackson, and the production team behind the *LotR* films. New Line Cinema sought to collaborate with the Tolkien fan rather than segregate, and in so doing New Line engineered a new breed of fandom. The genetically bred fan in turn has become a creature antithetical to Tolkien's prescribed audience. New Line and their marketing elite programmed their target audience's frame of mind with a prescribed stream of thought. In seeking to control the perception of Jackson's interpretation of Tolkien, New Line fed the existing fan-base prefabricated sentiments in a "steady drip-feed of [...] information" and in so doing created a fan unable, and in many ways unwilling, to think independently (Murray 2004:19). To use a Trekkie comparison: Tolkien fans after the Jackson films are analogous to the Borg, with PJ and New Line as the center of the hive.

Our world is one of 'molds' and 'labels'. The end result is a society that no longer has the right to think, neither for itself nor outside the proverbial box. We apply a label to ourselves, anything to do with religion, profession, sexuality; we can dig deeper and see molds arising, and movements sprouting forth – so-called modernist, post-modernist, neoconservative, liberal, hippie, yuppie, yippy, neo-apocalyptic post colonial scholars. The label, mold, or movement predetermines our thoughts. For his critics, Tolkien's work remains outside this narrow definition of literature, therefore taking an uncomfortable stance as a thing "unclassified" (Curry 2004:138).

Another unclassifiable quantity that makes Tolkien so very awkward for those seeking to remain living within the box of their labelled humanity is language. Humanity's form of verbal articulation, the ability to write and 'speak one's mind', to describe the world about us transcends. Language is the spark that brings us back to the divine.

> Man uses the spoken or written word to express meaning of what he wants to convey. His language is full of symbols, but he also often employs signs or images that are not strictly descriptive. What we call a symbol is a term, a name, or even a picture that may be familiar in daily life, yet that possesses specific connotations in addition to its conventional and obvious meaning. It implies something vague, unknown or hidden from us. (Jung 1967:3)

Tolkien, similar to how a composer seeks to provoke certain reactions in the listener's mind with music, used the combination of specific phonemes (Smith 2006:11). The art of the word form, the articulation of sound and meaning through the spoken word, once capable of giving pleasure to poetic societies, has been lost to the modern pursuits of employers, self-advancement and the cult of the individual. Tolkien felt that language was indeed rooted in the landscape, and inseparable from it. It was rooted in human consciousness and also inextricably bound up with our condition as human beings – a natural product of our humanity, the ability to express and communicate (Smith 2006:12). The world has now progressed from its roots of interconnectivity with nature, where language was once one with it, consciousness and culture existing within nature, to fragmentation, subjectivity, symbolism and detachment. Our change in the use of language has further detached us from nature. In humanity's attempt to become 'free and independent', language has become more fragmented as this detachment has occurred.

Tolkien's languages of Quenya, Sindarin, and the other tongues of Middle-earth have been labeled as 'fake' or 'made-up' by the 'unenlightened'. The work of Tolkien linguistic scholarship has proven these affirmations otherwise. Our society's use of language, has changed, subsequently affecting human consciousness. The further we get away from our natural world and continue to define Tolkien's work as mere fantasy and cast it aside, the less our society is able to grasp the importance and complexities of his work. From ancient to medieval scholars, from Aristotle to Aquinas, belief was that in language – expressing the spark of the divine spirit – was an implicit function of society. Tolkien "was before his time in seeing language as a part of man's participation in nature, something both internal and external, flowing in both directions, a notion that has become relatively popular only in the last few years when we have started to ask why we have turned our backs on the natural world with such devastating consequences" (Smith 2006:17). Language is no longer from the very depths of the natural 'sensory world', it is now derived from the sensations, the pleasures of the flesh and external gratification (Smith 2006:15). We live in an industrial society where the focus is a prefabricated sensory world which programs the consumer into the language of the product. One of society's most destructive tools, television and our cult of visual aids, creates a new language of consumerism no longer in tune with our landscape. This artificial creation marches not to the beat of the Maker's Will, but to designer clothes, technology, machines, beauty ads and 'reality shows'. This hungry, ever changing machine is in turn called 'progress' by society. For most, education and attending school is just a tedious aspect of life one must do before joining the 'real world'. It is a general sentiment that there comes a time when you must go out and work and not worry of school any longer, thus becoming a part of the industrial world, working nine to five and never allowing yourself to grow past being a cog in the vast machine of society.

The once latent linguistic faculty in children, allied with a higher art, has fallen from its earlier development (Tolkien 1997:202). A child's first exposure to language is no longer through art, poetry and education – as was so often the case during Tolkien's time – but now children are first exposed to language through cartoons, toys, commercials, and pop music, which stunts the growth and fruition of their linguistic faculties. In most schools, language appears as a fixed system. There is no invention, nor investigation into its expansion, which is detrimental to their understanding of story and its relation to language. In speaking of language construction and its function Tolkien (1997:210) states:

> [F]or perfect construction of an art-language it is found necessary to construct at least in outline a mythology concomitant. Not solely because some pieces of verse will inevitably be a part of the (more or less) completed structure, but because the making of language and mythology are related functions; to give your language an individual flavour, it must have woven into it the threads of an individual mythology, individual while working within the scheme of natural human mythopoeia, as your word-form may be individual while working within the hackneyed limits of human, even European, phonetics. The converse is true, your language construction will *breed* a mythology.

In this Tolkien shines through as the true sub-creator citing how both the world, its mythology and language are dependent upon one another. Each aspect is functioning in relation to the other. Tolkien's work also brings to light how these ideals and practices fall apart, how we were once one people, or many invested in the fruition of creativity and nature. *The Silmarillion* is an example of Tolkien's investigation into how culture and language has fragmented. It is humanity's separation, individualization, compartmentalization, and our incessant dependence upon industry that continues to detach us from the natural world. In our world, "the individual is the only reality" (Jung 1964:45).

> The further we move away from the individual toward abstract ideas about *homo sapiens,* the more likely we are to fall into error. In these times of social upheaval and rapid change, it is desirable to know much more than we do about the individual human being, for so much depends upon his mental and moral qualities. But if we are to see things in their right perspective, we need to understand the past of man as well as his present. That is why an understanding of myths and symbols is of essential importance.
> (Jung 1964:45)

If Tolkien's work is continued to be viewed by those outside the university as a 'great film', but too long of a book, or relegated to the same shelf as Dungeons and Dragons, then the true message of reunification for our world with our Maker is lost.

JESSICA BURKE (co-chairman Heren Istarion: The North East Tolkien Society, editor-in-chief of *Parma Nölé*) was born in 1974 in Brooklyn, New York. A graduate of The City University of New York, Ms. Burke has studied anthropology, folklore, medieval literature, mysticism, 19th-century literature, Arthuriana, and Judeo-Christian theology. She has written extensively on the legends of Arthur, the poetry of Edmund Spenser, and, of course, Tolkien. Ms. Burke is an aspiring author of medieval fantasy, much influenced by the works of J.R.R Tolkien. Her first experience with his writing came after an excursion to the N.Y. Public Library at the age of five, where she borrowed a recording of Professor Tolkien reading the chapter 'Riddles in the Dark' from *The Hobbit*.

ANTHONY SCOTT BURDGE (founder, co-chairman and webmaster of Heren Istarion: The North East Tolkien Society), who has walked the paths of Middle-earth since an early age, is an independent scholar. Mr. Burdge's studies range includes Norse mythology, medieval literature, native American literature & culture, and Judeo-Christian ideology and text. His interest in Tolkien grew from the age of eight, when he received his first copy of *The Hobbit*. Over the last decade Mr. Burdge has delved into the mythological world while studying the works of J.R.R. Tolkien. He is an aspiring writer and a contributor to the *Encyclopedia of Children's Literature* by Oxford University Press, *The J.R.R. Tolkien Encyclopedia* by Routledge and has spoken at numerous universities and conferences. For a more complete list of publications for both Mr. Burdge & Ms. Burke please visit: www.herenistarion.org.

Bibliography

Agøy, Nils Ivar, 1995, '*Quid Hinieldus cum Christo?* – New Perspectives on Tolkien's Theological Dilemma & his Sub-Creation Theory', in Patricia Reynolds and Glen H. GoodKnight (eds.), *Proceedings of the J.R.R. Tolkien Centenary Conference*, California: Mythopoeic Press, 1995, pp. 31-38.

Barfield, Owen, 1967, *Speaker's Meaning*, Middletown, Connecticut: Wesleyan University Press.

Carpenter, Humphrey, 1979, *The Inklings: C.S. Lewis, J.R.R. Tolkien, Charles Williams and their Friends*, Boston: Houghton Mifflin.

--- (ed.), 2001, *The Letters of J.R.R. Tolkien*, Boston: Houghton Mifflin.

Campbell, Joseph, 1972, *The Hero with a Thousand Faces*, New Jersey: Princeton University Press.

---, 1988, *The Power of Myth*, (edited by Betty Sue Flowers), New York: Doubleday.

Curry, Patrick, 2004, *Defending Middle-earth Tolkien: Myth and Modernity*, Boston: Houghton Mifflin.

Flieger, Verlyn, 2005, *Interrupted Music. The Making of Tolkien's Mythology*, Kent and London: The Kent State University Press.

---, 2006, 'Past, History and Memory', (paper presented at the Tolkien 2006 Conference at the University of Vermont, April 2006).

Fox, Matthew, 2004, 'Reflections on the Sacred Mirrors', *COSM: Journal of Visionary Culture* 1, 2004, pp. 6-8.

Jung, Carl Gustav, 1976, *The Portable Jung*, (edited by Joseph Campbell), New York; Viking Press.

---, 1964, *Man and His Symbols*, New York: Dell Publishing.

Murray, Simone, 2004, 'Celebrating the Story the Way it Is: Cultural Studies, Corporate Media and the Contested Utility of Fandom', *Continuum: Journal of Media & Cultural Studies* 18.1, 2004, pp. 7-25.

Raffel, Burton, 2000, 'The Lord of the Rings as Literature', in Harold Bloom (ed.), *Modern Critical Interpretations: J.R.R. Tolkien's The Lord of the Rings*, Philadelphia: Chelsea House Publishers, 2000, pp. 17-35.

Smith, Ross, 2006, 'Fitting Sense to Sound: Linguistic Aesthetics and Phonosemantics in the Work of J.R.R. Tolkien', *Tolkien Studies* 3, 2006, pp. 1-20.

Stoppard, Tom, 1991, *Rosencrantz & Guildenstern Are Dead*, New York: Grove Press.

Tolkien, J.R.R. 1991, *The Lord of the Rings*, (illustrated Centenary edition), Boston: Houghton Mifflin.

---, 1997, *The Monsters & the Critics and Other Essays*, (edited by Christopher Tolkien), London: HarperCollins.

Wilson, Edmund, 1989, 'Oo, Those Awful Orcs', in Alida Becher (ed.), *A Tolkien Treasury*, Philadelphia: Running Press, 1989, pp. 50-55.

Brief Considerations on Determinism in Reality and Fiction

FRANK WEINREICH

Abstract

Determinism plays a crucial role in considerations on ethics and free will. This is true for the real world as well as for invented worlds like Middle-earth. This paper discusses the issue of determinism and non-determinism in reality and fiction on a basic level and in conclusion shows how free will might very well exist as a fact in the invented world of Middle-earth.

> *"Well, if one knew what the future held, say, defeat or even victory, would he try less hard, or instead more so, depending on what he knew? And if he changed his conduct because of knowing, and thereby changed the outcome, would he not thwart Destiny, and thus perhaps upset the balance of all?"*
> *Alain fell silent and looked 'round the table at pondering faces. Then he reached out and laid his hand atop Camille's and grinned, saying, "Besides, instead of knowing the future; I'd much rather be surprised."*
> Dennis L. McKiernan, *Once Upon a Winter's Night*

Why might determinism be a problem in reasoning about J.R.R. Tolkien's fictional work? It is because the question of determinism plays a crucial role in every ethical discussion of free will, regardless whether it turns up as a topic in reality or in fiction.[1] If one assumes (or refutes)

---

[1] The world in which we are living, the third planet of a certain sun in one arm of the spiral galaxy, called the Milky Way by the inhabitants of the said planet, and the galaxy it is part of, and also the universe in which this arrangement is placed, are hereby referred to as *reality*. *Fiction*, for the purposes of these considerations, are stories *invented* by the inhabitants of said planet. I am aware that the assumption that there exists a certain reality outside the thinking of individuals is disputed by

the existence of free will and therefore responsibility for one's actions as well as one's omissions, this assumption depends on one's understanding of determinism and on the exact nature of determinism. If, on the one hand, one has to conclude that binding determinism rules everything that is happening or undertaken, than no one can be singled out and given responsibility for the results of certain undertakings or omissions. If, on the other hand, one argues that determinism is not given or that its reach does not cover completely the outcome of the reasonings of sentient beings, then persons can be blamed or praised for their actions. This is true for both reality – or the Primary World, as Tolkien would have said –, and for fiction – the Secondary, or Subcreated Worlds. Thus, considerations on free will and, consequently, also on determinism play an important role in the interpretation of Tolkien's works – the stories and lays of Middle-earth being what they are: reports on the struggle between good and evil carried out by or on the backs of free or enslaved Valar, Maiar, Elves, Orcs, Hobbits, Trolls, Dwarves, Dragons and Men.

---

some philosophers and quite a few intellectuals of various professions. This is not the place to discuss the underlying world views that feed these doubts about reality (see Sandkühler 1999a for a brief summary of this problem). It shall only be made explicit that the following reasoning about reality is founded on the "axiomatic assumption" (Mayr 2000:61) that there is a reality; that it is, in its existence as well as in its properties, independent from human reasoning and recognition (Sandkühler 1999b:1042), yet which people consciously as well as unconsciously take for granted. This is proven by the fact that they do take part in discussions, a fact which would be pointless without the assumption of some practical reality, for which Nikolaus Knoepfler coined the term "practical realism" (see below and Knoepfler 1997:112f.).

DETERMINISM IN THE PRIMARY WORLD[2]

Physical and physiological processes, including the observable[3] processes inside the brain which, as far as science can say, lead to every deliberate action of sentient beings, are part of a chain of causes and effects which does not allow for any freedom in the sense of breaking out of said chain. It was this chain of cause and effect that back in 1812 made the French physicist Pierre-Simon Laplace claim that he could describe the exact state of the universe at any point in the future, if only he had sufficient means to calculate the data. While this was a slight exaggeration, Laplace was right in principle. Everything is part of cause and effect relations and therefore computable in principle, at least as long as the world is seen as monistic.[4] And every speculation on metaphysical constructs or beliefs are just this – speculative.

The consequence of this seems to be that the world is deterministic. This is even true in the light of quantum mechanics, as Nikolaus Knoepfler has pointed out. Even if on a subatomic level nondeterminism might be a fact, which is not proven (1997:103), there exists no necessary conclusion that nondeterminism on the micro level leads to nondeterminism on the observable macro level – and even if it did, random subatomic processes would still determine the processes on the macro

---

[2] The terminology of one Primary and many Secondary Worlds is based on Tolkien's writings. In his famous essay 'On Fairy Stories' Tolkien calls the world in which we live the "Primary World" and, for invented worlds like Middle-earth or those of other authors, he coins the term "Secondary World[s]". Both kind of worlds are created, the real world by God and the Secondary Worlds by their narrators – a process he defined as *sub-creation*, created after God's creation and, for the Catholic Tolkien, of course, in an inferior manner.

[3] "Observable" through certain technical picture producing methods like positron emission tomography and other noninvasive or invasive procedures.

[4] Even dualistic world views usually assume cause and effect scenarios, especially in ethical considerations. But since under dualistic or nonmaterialistic beliefs an entity of a different matter, often referred to as the soul, is part of the discussion, it poses no problem to describe this otherworldly matter as free in principle, which on the other hand means that the bearer of this soul is responsible for her actions.

level, which does not lead to freedom and free will of sentient beings (103). Again, even considering the quantum level, determinism rules the universe as long as one does not take refuge in dualistic world views.

But does this observation really constitute such a problem in ethical reasonings? It does! But then, does it really lead to the dreaded anarchy of ubiquitous non-responsibility? At first sight, determinism is very problematic indeed. Yet if one takes a closer look first at the difference between determinism and predictability and, secondly, at the life people actually lead, the loopholes for evil doers, claiming they could not act otherwise than they had, for "I couldn't help myself, Sir", can be plugged.

The important difference between predictability and determinism gets confused sometimes. Chaos Theory might provide a good picture of this. One of the main realizations of Chaos Theory[5] is the unpredictability of everything. Seemingly minimal events can have immense effects. Often the famous butterfly wing in the South American rain forest is mentioned as an example: the beating of one butterfly wing is said to cause a minimal irritation of currents in the warm jungle air that, by means of various amplifying confluences, cause a hurricane in Florida. Of course, one would hardly think of that when enjoying the beautiful play of sunlight on the blue wings of *Morpho peleides* while vacating in Brazil. And that is exactly the point of it. If one would catch the butterfly the moment before it makes its fateful fluttering, one could save lives and properties. Is the person to blame who does not do so? Only in the case if she knew what would occur ... and that she can never know, because, as Chaos Theory states correctly, that is simply not predictable. And yet it was the wing of the butterfly that determined the outbreak of the storm. For ethical reasonings this means that, though there is a

---

[5] See Gleick 1987 for an introduction to Chaos Theory.

deterministic flow of causes and effects, people are still obliged to do what is *probably* right[6] at the moment they consider a certain action.

If people started to catch every butterfly they could lay hands on, it would most likely not result in peaceful weather all around the world. But to stick a knife between someone's shoulder blades would most probably affect that person negatively. For practical purposes, common sense and the jurisdiction correctly assume that there is so much freedom in people's behaviour that choices between doing something and omitting that something are given.[7] The point in the discussion of unpredictability and determinism is that though everything in the material world is embedded in a chain of cause and effect, the actions of people are free in so far as human beings can predict the consequences of their actions in most ethical relevant cases to such an extent that one can act according to this outlook, and in consequence can be held responsible for one's deeds.[8]

This assumption is also called "practical realism" ("praktischer Realismus", Knoepfler 1997:112): "Our whole life is witness to the assumption that we think our lives are, within certain limits, at our disposal" (114).[9] This realism earns the label 'practical' since it integrates

---

[6] This is not the place to dwell on what 'right' means in this context, since this an abstract line of thought that in (moral) reality depends on the situation and the options at hand.

[7] And where they are not given, as for example in the case of mental illness, or not totally given, as for example in the case of extreme poverty of thieves, the determining causes for morally and legally wrong behaviour are usually taken into account, at least in modern and democratic jurisdictions.

[8] The problem of responsibility increases with the complexity of situations. While it is not hard to determine that violent behaviour against people who cannot defend themselves is not right, it might be hard to judge whether participating in genetic research on gene manipulation is right or wrong in the sense of whether said research may prove beneficial or harmful in the end. But even informed considerations, which, for example, put the benefit of patients above economical interests of the commercial sponsors of that research, can draw sufficient guidelines to morally correct choices for or against the participation in complex issues.

[9] "[U]nsere ganze Praxis legt davon Zeugnis ab, daß wir in bestimmten Grenzen über unser Leben zu verfügen meinen" (Knoepfler 1997:114).

the scientific realization of determinism with the daily experience of freedom, thus admitting a practical (and morally as well as legally binding!) form of free will and indeterminism. Although everything is determined (in a monistic weltanschauung, and science can provide no other), man, the human personality, as a result of billions of forming (determining) influences, is an acting entity in its own right that has the capability of making responsible decisions – everything else would be an incapacitation totally incongruent with the daily experience of living in a society.

DETERMINISM IN THE SECONDARY WORLD[10]

The same chain of cause and effect which rules everything in the primary world is also observable in most invented worlds, if only for the sake of allowing the reader to follow the story. Stories which would constantly neglect the patterns of cause and effect would probably be no longer comprehensible. However, it would be possible for an author to break out of the jail of deterministic laws of the Primary World and invent new rules, at least for a part or some aspects of her creation.

But it seems that for Middle-earth, its sub-creator J.R.R. Tolkien does not claim this freedom of the story-teller[11]: "The country of the book, Middle-earth, is a land much like our own, as mythical, but no more so. [...] It is a world [...] subject to natural law" (Beagle 1966:X). Hence Middle-earth is a world in which the principles of determinism rule. And it is a created world, a fact that for the primary world, in which we live, can only be speculated upon. So is everything set on its

---

[10] See footnote 2 for an explanation of the nomenclature of counting different worlds.

[11] I am not going speculate on the reasons why the author is not using this freedom, but explanations, which take into account Tolkien's obsession with the 'historical truth' of Middle-earth, which can only resemble 'truth' in reality if the history and makeup of Middle-earth also follow cause and effect-chains, seem to point in the right direction.

predetermined way? That might well be so, but it need not necessarily be so. At least two nondeterministic explanations are possible.

The first one questions the extent of determination on a macro level in Middle-earth. The world is created in a deliberate act of will by a supreme being: Iluvatar. Iluvatar uses music for bringing this universe of His into physical being. The accords of this music follow patterns which, in the end, lead to an unavoidable outcome not unlike Judgement Day, which people of Christian faith believe in. It remains unclear whether every detail in the history of Middle-earth is foretold by Iluvatar, and, in consequence, unavoidable, or whether only the general outcome of salvational bliss is determined,[12] while the way to this end may just as well tumble along the extremes of unpredictable catastrophes and periods of well being and righteousness through the Ages. It is, for example, possible that the Third Age could have ended with Sauron's triumph (after all, it was a very close call), followed by thousands of years of utter despair for Middle-earth's inhabitants. If so, then the concept of sentient beings, as devised by their Maker, might just as well be sufficient to *guarantee* that at some time in the future of a dark Fourth Age enough purehearted people would arise to thwart Morgoth's servant and allow for a Fifth Age (and possible further ages) until the music is reunited in the last and lasting theme.

The second explanation refers to the fact that Middle-earth is not placed in a monistic universe. The cosmos of Middle-earth is a dualistic one consisting of a material plane (including Valinor) and a spiritual plane, i.e. the nondescript place where Iluvatar resides. At least humans, who do not reach the halls of Mandos after their demise, seem to have a

---

[12] The questionability of the amount of determinism is only one point. Another point can be made by discussing the difference between foresight and determinism. Might it not be that Illuvatar has 'only' foreseen what would come? That he was omniscient but not almighty? That the happy ending of the Middle-earthian universe was due to most of its inhabitants being 'good' on a very basic level, so that evil could not persist? Other points could be made ...

spiritual spark – a soul – and this soul might just as well be free of the restraints of cause and effect, and thus in itself a powerful new movens introduced to the Secondary World.

Alternatively, men also might have been thrown into a macrodeterministic world in which the victory for Morgoth and Sauron is impossible, just as Iluvatar had prophesied. But even then men still could fail and be judged accordingly – indeed, all of Middle-earth could be a testing place for men. Frodo could have failed and could have claimed the Ring for himself while still walking in The Shire. Fate (Iluvatar) may then have chosen a worthier Hobbit. Under slightly different circumstances, Denethor might have withstood the mental onslaughts of Sauron through the Palantír, but incidents would still have followed nearly the same pattern on the Pelennor, before the Black Gate and at Mount Doom. In a dualistic cosmos these and other scenarios are possible and are not marred by logical faults that might occur within a different setting.

CONCLUSION

Empirically based scientific reasoning regarding determinism in the Primary World leads to only one realization – we live in a deterministic universe where every incident is embedded in a chain of cause and effect. That incidents are totally unpredictable and, on a quantum level, might just as well be governed by random subatomic processes, does not change this realization one bit. But people live their lives on an 'as if'-basis, acting 'as if' they had a freedom of choice. And, for all practical purposes, the sane mind does indeed have this freedom of choice at her disposal and is able to choose a course of action at her own will. Fictitious worlds, like Middle-earth, follow only the design of their creator and can be deterministic, nondeterministic, or something in-between. Middle-earth, as Tolkien has pointed out, resembles in its makeup the Primary World. Hence it is deterministic on a materialistic level. And even on the spiritual level that is superimposed on the material level of Arda determinism seems to be the dominant concept.

But although Middle-earth seems to be governed by Iluvatar's will, the efforts of the heroes of the Ring are heroic and testify to a stern will to do the right thing. They testify to a will that would have had the freedom to refuse the tasks of the members of the fellowship at the beginning, at least as far as they know.[13] The heroes might lead a deterministic life in the same sense of determinism that we do. But it would also still have been their admirable free choice to endure – the same way someone in the Primary World acts heroic. Yet this Secondary World is not only materialistic; and even though Middle-earth is dualistic, there is still no proof that Iluvatar's – in principle unalterable – design would not have allowed for freedom and free will in a limited way, as I have tried to point out in the second section of this paper: the determinism may not be absolute, or, alternatively, some of the beings in Arda have been created free. One just cannot *say* ... but I *believe* that Tolkien meant his creatures to possess free will, else their individual salvations and damnations would lack any meaning.

FRANK WEINREICH studied philosophy, communication sciences and politics in the early Nineties and holds a PhD in philosophy from the University of Vechta. He is working as independent scholar, freelance author and editor in Bochum, Germany since 2001. His interests focus on ethics, bioethics, media ethics, technology assessment, education, new media, fantasy and science fiction and, of course, on Tolkien's works. He has published numerous books, articles and essays and is co-editor of *Hither Shore*, the Scholarly Journal of the German Tolkien Society and co-editor of *Stein und Baum*, a German source for fantasy literature and works on fantasy. He may most easily be contacted through his professional homepage www.textarbeiten.com or via his private Tolkien-Site which at the moment carries nearly forty articles, essays and stories on Tolkien and Middle-earth: www.polyoinos.de/tolk_stuff.

---

[13] At least the Four Hobbits do not seem to have a very clear idea of the spiritual nature of Middle-earth (see Weinreich 2005 for a discussion of their ethical motivations).

Bibliography

Beagle, Peter S., 1966, 'Tolkien's Magical Ring', in J.R.R. Tolkien, *The Tolkien Reader. Stories, Poems and Commentary by the Author of The Hobbit and The Lord of the Rings*, New York: Ballantine Books, pp. IX-XVI.

Gleick, James, 1987, *Chaos. Making a New Science*, London, New York: Penguin.

Honegger, Thomas, Andrew James Johnston, Friedhelm Schneidewind, Frank Weinreich, 2005, *Eine Grammatik der Ethik*, Saarbrücken: Edition Stein und Baum.

Knoepfler, Nikolaus, 1997, 'Das Leib-Seele-Problem und der Determinismus', *Philosophisches Jahrbuch* 104, pp. 103-116.

Laplace, Pierre-Simon, 1995, *Théorie analytique des probabilités*, (reprint of the first edition, Paris 1847), Paris: Gabay.

Mayr, Ernst, 2000, *Das ist Biologie. Die Wissenschaft des Lebens*, Heidelberg, Berlin: Spektrum Verlag.

McKiernan, Dennis L., 2001, *Once Upon a Winter's Night*, New York: RoC.

Sandkühler, Hans-Jörg (ed.), 1999, *Enzyklopädie Philosophie*, two volumes, Hamburg: Meiner.

Sandkühler, Hans-Jörg, 1999a, 'Realismus', in Hans-Jörg Sandkühler (ed.), *Enzyklopädie Philosophie II*, pp. 1346 – 1350.

Sandkühler, Hans-Jörg, 1999b, 'Erkenntnistheorie/Erkenntnis', in Hans-Jörg Sandkühler (ed.), *Enzyklopädie Philosophie II*, pp. 1039-1059.

Tolkien, John Ronald Reuel, 1988, *Tree and Leaf*, London: Grafton.

---, 1988a, 'On Fairy Stories', in J.R.R. Tolkien, *Tree and Leaf*, pp. 9-73.

Weinreich, Frank, 2005, 'Ethos in Arda', in Thomas Honegger et al., *Eine Grammatik der Ethik*, Saarbrücken: Edition Stein und Baum, pp. 111-134.

"Man does as he is when he may do as he wishes"
The Perennial Modernity of Free Will

JASON FISHER

Man is condemned to be free.
Jean-Paul Sartre

Abstract

J.R.R. Tolkien was certainly no modernist; rather, he was what we might call a traditionalist – some might even have called him a Luddite. But this does not mean that his magnum opus, *The Lord of the Rings*, as well as its various satellite works, fails to exhibit some of the qualities of modernity. Indeed, one reason for Tolkien's unabated popularity can be ascribed to the fact that his works concern themselves with perennial problems of the Human Condition. Among these are good and evil, life and death and – the subject of this chapter – free will and destiny. I will argue that, whether or not the question of free will can ever be finally settled in the Primary World, Tolkien nevertheless believed in it and endowed his own creations with it. In order to establish this, I will trace the relevant history of free will as a matter for philosophical and religious debate, examine the marks the subject has left in the works of the Inklings in general and of Tolkien in particular, and then trace free will (and its partner, providence) through Tolkien's fictive Secondary World of Middle-earth.

INTRODUCTION

In a very real sense, Tolkien's works will always be 'modern',[1] insofar as they confront questions of perennial importance to all human beings: free will, good and evil, life and death, and so forth. Indeed, one can make a defensible argument – much as Tom Shippey has done in *J.R.R.*

---

[1] That there is a very real difference between 'modernism' and 'modernity' may be taken as a given; as it is off the main point, I will not take the time to offer detailed definitions or explain their distinctions here.

Tolkien: Author of the Century (2000:ix) – that a large part of the unabated appeal of Tolkien's works lies in their preoccupation with those same perennial questions of such great importance to us all. The 20th century, a unique point in time, and one now distinctly of the past tense, provided the crucible in which Tolkien pondered these problems for himself. But because he uniquely separated Middle-earth from our own world in time, it is both familiar and yet different enough to serve as a timeless proxy in which to contemplate these recurrent, ever-relevant matters for ourselves. In the pages that follow, I would like to zero in on one of these in particular: the question of free will. Even today, in the opening years of the 21st century, we human beings continue to fiercely defend an ancient and fundamental claim to free will, despite all 'modern evidence' (causality, reductionism, and so forth) to the contrary. But that claim itself, whether and to what degree it is tenable or not, is enduringly human and 'modern' in its own right.

In another of his books, Tom Shippey (2003:137) reminds us of the Anglo-Saxon proverb from which I have taken a part of my title: "*Man deþ swá hé byþ þonne hé mót swá hé wile*, 'Man does as he is when he may do as he wishes,' or more colloquially, 'You show what you're like when you can do what you like.'" For my purposes, what this really means is that a man (one thinks of Faramir) may show his quality – either good or evil – in his actions, and may take the blame or the credit for those actions, only when he is *free* to act in the first place. Without that freedom, a man would act without intent, and he would be owed neither praise nor censure for the outcome of those actions. He would, in effect, be no more than a puppet.

Bringing the point back to Tolkien's fictive world as a special stage on which this premise can be tested, the notion of free will plainly pervades *The Hobbit* and *The Lord of the Rings*. Frodo's choice to spare Gollum proves critical to the destruction of the Ring. Bilbo's similar decision, years earlier, likewise would come to "rule the fate of many"

(Tolkien 1965a:69). Still earlier, Bilbo's choice to accompany the Dwarves on their adventure leads to his finding the Ring in the first place. Indeed, in abandoning Gollum, the Ring itself appears to demonstrate its own free will (diabolical though its actions may be).[2] But while it is tempting to trace these seemingly causal relationships backward through time and to derive some kind of deterministic rubric from them,[3] in reality, these decisions are quintessential exercises of free will in a demonstrably teleological universe. Were they not, the actors in Tolkien's great morality play would be freed from all consequences and responsibility, merely reciting lines long written, and Frodo's sacrifice – like a badly-acted stage death – would become hollow and wholly unsatisfying to us as readers.

Likewise, Tolkien's Creation Myth, the Ainulindalë, tempts readers into the assumption of a deterministic worldview. The Ainulindalë does imply a (partial) awareness of the future, certainly; however, to conclude that mere knowledge of the future somehow precludes the free will of its participants is a fallacious presumption – a point to which I will return a little later. Indeed, Ilúvatar only 'shows forth' a part of the Music, and its complex harmonies merely instigate and catalyze, rather than predetermine, future events; they need not and *do* not entail determinism. Indeed, Melkor's actions during – and after – the Music characterize perhaps the most egregious abuse of free will possible. Yet, like Satan or like Adam, he must be free to act – though he must also accept the consequences of his actions.

Whether free will exists in the Primary World is a different, but related, question. It is one we should consider; however, it would be inappropriate to superimpose the results of our analysis on Tolkien

---

[2] Whether the Ring's *apparent* will actually represents a free will of its own or merely the will of its Master is a matter for debate.

[3] As Pierre-Simon Laplace would no doubt have approved.

himself.[4] Rather, they will inform the discussion without dictating its final destination. Indeed, whether 'right' or 'wrong', we must give equal weight to Tolkien's views on free will as they undergird the entire length and breadth of his fictional universe. By setting Tolkien's views in the context of his personal religious beliefs, we can situate his notions of free will within the larger context of the entire human argument on free will and then determine where this leaves us. But as I indicated above, merely to engage in the debate is itself inherently 'modern'; human beings have always done so and likely always will. In some ways, the more unanswerable the question, the longer it will shadow our footsteps into the future – carrying works of great philosophical and moral depth like *The Lord of the Rings* with us.

To lay the necessary groundwork for the discussion to follow, it is essential to begin with the concept of free will itself – and with the other face of this philosophical Janus, determinism. Boiled down to their essential natures, these notions entail, on the one hand, freedom, and on the other, the lack of it. Not surprisingly, then, these concepts are generally taken to be the two diametric poles of a single philosophical dichotomy, and are usually deemed to be in mutual, irreconcilable exclusion of one another. But is that really true? As I hope to show in the ensuing discussion, the truth of the matter may rather be that free will and determinism, instead of lying at opposite poles, are rather more of a continuum, a tense balance whose center may shift over time and with circumstance. Indeed, I think this is very much what Tolkien believed. But in order to get to the heart of what Tolkien thought about these questions, insofar as it is possible to determine, we need to examine the fertile soil from which his ideas would have sprung. That is, we

---

[4] See Weinreich's contribution on determination in reality and fiction in this volume.

have to trace the origins of the concept of free will in general and of the Catholic perspective on it in particular.

A SHORT HISTORY OF FREE WILL

A full history of the human debate on free will would easily fill an entire volume by itself, and the perennial importance of this question to human beings can be glimpsed in the fact that virtually every major philosopher, from the pre-Socratics all the way up to Bertrand Russell (an atheist who did not believe in free will) and Daniel Dennett (an atheist who *does* believe in free will),[5] have taken the time to grapple with the matter and weigh in with an opinion. But despite the substantial history involved, we cannot attempt to extrapolate Tolkien's own views on the subject without first establishing at least a rough history of those aspects of the debate that would have been relevant to Tolkien's education and background. During the process, we will hit just the high points that would have been important in seeding Tolkien's opinions – and which would ultimately go on to bear fruit in his fiction.

For our purposes, the idea begins with the Greeks. Why don't we begin with the Bible? To do so would be problematic at best and very likely inconclusive, as what the Bible has to say about free will is notoriously ambiguous – a fact easily explainable by its many writers, working over many periods. Therefore, our short history of free will begins with the efforts of the pre-Socratics', and in particular with the Atomists', efforts to explain causation in terms of a system of essential elements, of which they deemed the universe to be made.[6] This desire to explain

---

[5] The atheism of both Russell and Dennett would be grounds enough for Tolkien to have discounted their opinions on the matter entirely. Still, interested readers are referred to Russell's *Why I Am Not a Christian* and Dennett's *Consciousness Explained*.

[6] This atomistic / elemental philosophy is echoed in *The Silmarillion*, where we have the pantheon of the Valar, each with his or her own elemental specialization.

observable phenomena in terms of deducible causes, together with the perceived power the Gods exerted over Man, led to a philosophical structure largely skewed in the direction of what we would call determinism. But at the same time, even the rational-minded pre-Socratics were evidently uncomfortable with the idea of discarding the perceived (or perhaps it was only wished for) freedom of man to act as he would; and this anxiety is evidenced by a quite noticeable vacillation between determinism and chance (or choice). We find a representative example of the push and pull between these two poles in Empedocles. Simplicius quotes him as saying, on the one hand, "There is an oracle of necessity, an ancient decree of the gods, / eternal, sealed with broad oaths," while on the other hand, "There by the will of chance all things think" (Barnes 2001:136, 138). A similar tension between the idea of freedom and the idea of necessity (usually divine, but sometimes cast in terms of what would later become the causality of the natural sciences) was voiced by Leucippus, Democritus, Heraclitus, Parmenides, Anaxagoras, and others of the pre-Socratics.[7] Finally, Aristotle, through his doctrine of the four causes, would carry the debate the furthest, bringing it all the way into the Middle Ages.

The next major player of importance to us is Augustine of Hippo, the so-called Saint Augustine of Roman Catholicism.[8] During the 4th and 5th centuries, Augustine wrote extensively on matters of religious philosophy, which made him a progenitor of many of the religious movements and reformations that would follow. Among these writings was his important 'Letter on Grace and Free Will'. In it, and in other related

---

[7] In actuality, the term 'pre-Socratic' is something of a misnomer. As Barnes (2001:xii) points out, "Socrates was born in 470 and died in 399, so that many of the 'Presocratic' philosophers were contemporaries of Socrates."

[8] For a lengthier discussion of St. Augustine in specific relation to Tolkien, see Matthew Fisher's 'Working at the Crossroads: Tolkien, St. Augustine, and the Beowulf-poet'.

letters,[9] he offered his own interpretations of free will in response to the arguments and positions of the Manichaeans and Pelagians. Pelagius, indeed, went so far as to accuse Augustine of a fatalistic and deterministic view on free will. In his own tract, 'On Free Will' (which unfortunately has been lost), he charged Augustine with falling under the (wrong, in his view) influence of the Manichaeans in the debate on predestination. But in his own writings, Augustine clarified his position as one in which free will was very real and very much alive, but only so far as it was permitted and ultimately circumscribed by God. In essence, Augustine felt that *unlimited* free will ran counter to the idea of divine grace, in which he believed as or even more strongly.

This brings us to another luminary in the darkness of the Middle Ages: Anicius Manlius Severinus Boethius.[10] His final work, *De Consolatione Philosophiae (The Consolation of Philosophy)*, would become one of the most influential philosophical dialogues of the Middle Ages, the Renaissance, the Enlightenment, and beyond – and its influence is still felt today. Tolkien would certainly have been very well acquainted with this work, as would any Edwardian scholar educated in the Classics. His fellow Inkling, C.S. Lewis, wrote about Boethius in his delightfully illuminating *Studies in Words*, as well as in his introduction to Medieval and Renaissance Literature, *The Discarded Image* (in which Boethius rightfully has his own full chapter). In fact, I could refer interested readers to no better introduction to the context and works of Boethius, as well as to their place in the collective bosom of the Inklings, than Lewis's chapter in *The Discarded Image*.

---

[9] Most notably, the letters, 'On Rebuke and Grace' and 'Against Two Letters of the Pelagians', *inter alia*.

[10] For a closer look at the influences of Boethius on Tolkien, readers are referred to Kathleen Dubs's 'Providence, Fate, and Chance: Boethian Philosophy in *The Lord of the Rings*'.

Of key importance for the thread of my argument here is Book V of *The Consolation of Philosophy*, 'Free Will And God's Foreknowledge'. The argument of that fifth and final book, for Lewis at least, "underlies every later treatment of the problem of freedom" (Lewis 2005:88). At its heart, Boethius expounds the view that "Man has a measure of freedom, though a less perfect freedom than divine natures" (Boethius, Book V, Summary); that is, once again, Boethius speaks for a kind of tense balance between freedom of the personal human will within and only as allowed by the greater divine will. We also see in Book V a direct confrontation of what has by now become a *de rigueur* objection to free will: that it is in direct contradiction to divine foreknowledge, which is supposed in the Christian tradition to be infinite. I am going to table that objection for the moment so as to proceed with my contextual history on the philosophical treatment of free will – but I will be returning to that issue shortly.

By this point in our short history, moral consequences and a code of derived ethics begin to come into the picture in much more obvious ways. For example, we have Peter Lombard's exposition on the *liberum arbitrium*, which in Latin is as good a translation of 'free will' as one could reasonably expect. In his *Libri Quattuor Sententiarum* of 1150, he writes:

> *Liberum arbitrium* is a faculty of reason and will, by which good is chosen with the assistance of grace, or evil, when grace is not there to assist. And it is called 'liberum' with respect to the will, which can be turned toward either [good or bad], while [it is called] 'arbitrium' with respect to reason, as it has to do with that power or faculty to which the discerning between good and evil belongs.

In essence, then, we see here the emergence of a more 'modern' idea of free will – a human faculty involving the discernment of good versus evil as well as a conscious choice between them. And moreover, looking back to St. Augustine, Lombard's definition also relies on the mediation of grace as the facilitator of free will.

Our next stop as we close in on the present day is Thomas Aquinas.[11] Aptly enough, G.K. Chesterton, a forefather to the Inklings, summarized Aquinas's views on the subject of free will very clearly in his biography of the theologian:

> [Aquinas's position] is plainer still in more popular problems like Free Will. If St. Thomas stands for one thing more than another, it is what may be called subordinate sovereignties or autonomies. He was, if the flippancy may be used, a strong Home Ruler. We might even say he was always defending the independence of dependent things. He insisted that such a thing could have its own rights in its own region. [...] And in exactly this sense he emphasised a certain dignity in Man, which was sometimes rather swallowed up in the purely theistic generalisations about God. Nobody would say he wanted to divide Man from God; but he did want to distinguish Man from God. [...] But let us not forget that its upshot was that very Free Will, or moral responsibility of Man, which so many modern liberals would deny. Upon this sublime and perilous liberty hang heaven and hell, and all the mysterious drama of the soul. It is distinction and not division; but a man *can* divide himself from God, which, in a certain aspect, is the greatest distinction of all. (Chesterton 2001:19-20)

---

[11] For a more detailed look at Aquinas in relation to Tolkien than I have time to pursue in these pages, see 'Thomas Aquinas' in *The J.R.R. Tolkien Encyclopedia: Scholarship and Critical Assessment*.

And thus once more, we see the tense balance of which I have been speaking: man indeed has free will – up to a point.

This brings us to 16th century Saxony and into the midst of that famous and prolonged debate between Desiderius Erasmus and Martin Luther. Various personal, religious, and philosophical disagreements between them led ultimately to Erasmus's 1524 tract, *De Libero Arbitrio*, in which he makes the case for free will; which was followed the next year by Luther's *De Servo Arbitrio*, which is half an argument for the bondage of the will and half a personal attack on Erasmus. In 1526, Erasmus took up the cudgel again and offered his final word in the feud with Luther in the appropriately (and impressively) titled *Hyperaspistes diatribe adversus servum arbitrium M. Lutheri*. Divested of their character assassinations and boiled down to their essential theological arguments, Luther believed that Man's will was not free, that it was dominated and bound by Satan, and that only the exercise of a higher power (God) *could* free it. Erasmus, on the other hand, felt much as did Aquinas and Augustine before him, that Man is, in his nature, essentially free to perform good or evil, within the confines of divine omnipotence.

The remaining three centuries leading up to Tolkien's own time were largely focused on the emergence of science and reason (so-called), in which we began to see the first naturalistic theories on free will. Thinkers such as David Hume, Spinoza, Pierre-Simon Laplace, William James, Sigmund Freud, Friedrich Nietzsche – and a whole catalog of others cut from the same cloth – began to engage in the debate that free will might be merely an illusion, and that all Man's actions are bound by precedent causes. Such naturalistic explanations, antithetical to his own Roman Catholic views, would, for the most part, have been discarded by Tolkien outright.[12] Rather, Tolkien's opinions on the nature of Man's

---

[12] Although the majority of 20th century theories of free will either concluded that it is merely the illusion of ignorance or else allow for free will at the cost of the idea of God, there are a minority of opinions that propound both free will and God, and

will – free or otherwise – would have been predominantly dictated by his Catholicism. His own views, as a result, would have found their direct ancestors in the beliefs of Augustine, Boethius, and Aquinas. Zeroing in on the direct influence of these and other views, including the vagueries the Bible has to offer on the subject, I would like to turn next to what he we can determine about Tolkien and the Inklings' own views, in their own words.

TOLKIEN, THE INKLINGS AND FREE WILL

I have already alluded more than once to what I have been calling the 'tense balance' between Man's free will and God's omnipotent ability to circumscribe the exercise of that will. Augustine, Boethius, Aquinas, and Erasmus all seem to have held fairly similar views, differing only in the particulars of exactly how much freedom Man can exercise, when he can exercise it, and in what degree and by what means (e.g. grace) that exercise is bounded or facilitated from above. As these views informed the development of Roman Catholicism over the course of the centuries in question, it's perfectly reasonable to surmise that Tolkien would have subscribed to much the same views himself. But I believe we can do a little better than merely to surmise.

Among the Inklings (and actually far beyond that circle), C.S. Lewis became well known as the most prolific Christian apologist the group produced – with Dorothy Sayers probably the closest second. He wrote numerous books on many and various aspects of his religious belief system. He differed from Tolkien only in the details: while Tolkien was

---

do so, moreover, within the rigors of modern science and mathematics. Perhaps the most notable such theory can be found in Frank Tipler's *The Physics of Immortality*. It is, of course, quite an understatement when Tipler (1994:2) says, "[t]hat we have free will, that God exists, and that He will one day resurrect each and every one of us is not what one expects to be the message of physics, to say the least". For discussion of the theory as it pertains to free will in particular, see Tipler (1994:159-160, 186-187, 201-202).

a Roman Catholic, Lewis was an Anglican. And as he did on so many topics, Lewis weighed in on free will on more than one occasion. In *Mere Christianity*, for instance, he wrote from a perspective that clearly took free will as a given: "If God thinks this state of war in the universe a price worth paying for free will [...] then we may take it, it is worth paying" (Lewis 1958:48). He goes on to address the question of freedom more directly, writing:

> The idea was that, just as all bodies are governed by the law of gravitation and organisms by biological laws, so the creature called man also had *his* law – with this great difference, that a body could not choose whether it obeyed the law of gravitation or not, but a man could choose either to obey the Law of Human Nature or to disobey it.
>
> We may put this in another way. Each man is at every moment subjected to several sets of law but there is only one of these which he is free to disobey. (Lewis 1958:4)

In *The Problem of Pain*, Lewis drills down even deeper into his conception of the fundamental nature of free will. The so-called problem of pain, as defined by Lewis (2001a:16), runs like this: "If God were good, He would wish to make His creatures perfectly happy, and if God were almighty He would be able to do what He wished. But the creatures are not happy. Therefore God lacks either goodness, or power, or both" And what is Lewis's answer to this thorny conundrum? Boiled down, his answer is that Man's exercise of his free will – endowed to him by God – for evil is the source of pain. Insofar as Man exercises his will for good, he will be happy; for evil, he will not. In Lewis's (2001a:24-25) own words:

> We can, perhaps, conceive of a world in which God corrected the results of [abuses] of free will by His

creatures at every moment: so that a wooden beam became soft as grass when used as a weapon, and the air refused to obey me if I attempted to set up in it the soundwaves that carry lies or insults. But such a world would be one in which wrong actions were impossible, and in which, therefore, freedom of the will would be void; nay, if the principle were carried out to its logical conclusion, evil thoughts would be impossible, for the cerebral matter which we use in thinking would refuse its task when we attempted to frame them. [...] Try to exclude the possibility of suffering which the order of nature and the existence of free will involve, and you find that you have excluded life itself.

Essentially, then, God allows pain in order to preserve free will. For Lewis, the solution to the problem of pain goes to the heart of the doctrine of free will. If humans are truly free to choose good or evil, he reasons, then evil must be a real possibility. An omnipotent God could surely prevent evil, but he could only do so at the cost of human freedom. Human freedom, Lewis would contend, is better than a world without suffering because it makes real love and real goodness possible. Such discussions were common fodder for the Inklings in their weekly meetings. Moreover, as a close friend of Tolkien, Lewis would certainly have had some influence on his thinking; and in fact, their friendship was strengthened by their common religious views.[13]

---

[13] In addition to Lewis, Dorothy Sayers also wrote about free will. She was a Roman Catholic, like Tolkien; however, she was not quite a member of the Inklings. Rather, she was – shall we say – kept on the outer circle of the group. For lengthy discussion of Dorothy Sayers vis-à-vis the Inklings, I refer curious readers to Candice Fredrick and Sam McBride's *Women Among the Inklings*. For Sayers' own discussion of free will, in both the Primary and Secondary Worlds, see *The Mind of the Maker*, Chapter 5, 'Free Will and Miracle'.

But to return to Tolkien himself, can we determine whether his views were in accord with Lewis's? I think we can, and we should begin by taking a look at his letters. Unlike his friend C.S. Lewis or *his* friend, Dorothy Sayers, Tolkien failed to leave us much in the way of personal theology. He did not write the kinds of apologetics and expositions on the subject that either Lewis or Sayers did, so we are left to conclude what we may from the most personal nonfiction he did leave us: his letters. It is clear even from very early on that Tolkien accepts the idea of free will as a matter of course, relevant to his own actions in his own life. In 1944, he wrote in two different letters to his son Christopher, away in the RAF in World War II, first that "[a]s souls with free-will we are, as it were, so placed as to face (or to be able to face) God. But God is (so to speak) also behind us, supporting, nourishing us (as being creatures)" (Tolkien 1981:66); and later, that "[p]robable under God that we shall meet again, 'in hale and in unity', before very long, dearest, and certain that we have some special bond to last beyond this life – subject of course always to the mystery of free will, by which either of us could throw away 'salvation'" (Tolkien 1981:76).

And what of the idea of the 'tense balance' between free will and the ultimate power of God to curtail it when he deems necessary? The next year, in 1945, Tolkien again wrote to Christopher, this time saying, "Of course, I suppose that, *subject to the permission of God*, the whole human race (as each individual) is free not to rise again but to go to perdition and carry out the Fall to its bitter bottom (as each individual can singulariter)" (Tolkien 1981:110, emphasis mine). A decade or so later, Tolkien further hinted at his acceptance of this uneasy compromise in a pair of letters to Naomi Mitchison. He was speaking about *The Lord of the Rings*; however, I think his quotes may be taken as representative of his personal theology.[14] In the first case he writes: "The story

---

[14] Some might question the validity of this assumption; however, I base it on Tolkien's assertion that *"The Lord of the Rings* is of course a fundamentally

is cast in terms of a good side, and a bad side, beauty against ruthless ugliness, tyranny against kingship, *moderated freedom with consent* against compulsion that has long lost any object save mere power, and so on; [...]" (Tolkien 1981:178-179, emphasis mine). In the second case, he says that "the supremely bad motive is (for this tale, since it is specially about it) domination of other 'free' wills" (Tolkien 1981:200). Here, Tolkien's use of quotation marks is very telling, with its unspoken suggestion that there are limits to the freedom of man's will. Below the level of God, certainly, man's will may be regarded as free; however, Tolkien clearly believed that God ultimately reserves the right to act on the fundamental nature of the world, to carry out miracles, and to reach within it from outside, as it were, to curb man's freedoms when it suits his design. To put this in the terms of Tolkien's fictive world, for example, Ilúvatar makes Melkor free to act as he chooses in Middle-earth, yet Ilúvatar can always step in and overrule him, as he does in the War of Wrath, changing the shape of the world and thrusting Melkor beyond the Gates of Night and out into the Void.

At the same time, though, how do we reconcile this idea with the apparent predestination of the Music of the Ainur? Indeed, the foreknowledge of the Valar in general as well as Mandos' frequent prophecies in particular, seem to tempt us into a rather more deterministic worldview. Where is Man's (or Elf's) free will in all of this? As you will recall, I alluded to this problem earlier when talking about Boethius and Book V of *The Consolation of Philosophy*. As it happens, there are at least two ways to approach the problem without sacrificing free will. And in any case, remember that we have established that, for Tolkien, man's will, while predominantly free, is not *perfectly* free – this is our 'tense

---

religious and Catholic work; unconsciously so at first, but consciously in the revision" (Tolkien 1981:172). Given this explicit statement, it would seem perfectly valid to extrapolate aspects of Tolkien's Catholicism from comments he made about an avowedly Catholic work.

balance'. Lewis, in *The Discarded Image*, analyzes Boethius's position on the issue quite effectively, defusing the objection in this way:

> Eternity is quite distinct from perpetuity, from mere endless continuance in time. Perpetuity is only the attainment of an endless series of moments, each lost as soon as it is attained. Eternity is the actual and timeless fruition of illimitable life. Time, even endless time, is only an image, almost a parody, of that plenitude; a hopeless attempt to compensate for the transitoriness of its 'presents' by infinitely multiplying them. [...] And God is eternal, not perpetual. Strictly speaking, He never *fore*sees; He simply sees. Your 'future' is only an area [...] of His infinite Now [...] I am none the less free to act as I choose in the future because God, in that future (His present) watches me acting. (Lewis 2005:89)

That Lewis himself believes this and is not merely summarizing Boethius only, we can determine by referring to one of the Screwtape Letters. In fact, Lewis even mentions Boethius in the letter, and it is clear that he accepts the tenor of the argument. He writes:

> But you must remember that [Man] takes Time for an ultimate reality. He supposes that [God], like himself, sees some things as present, remembers others as past, and anticipates others as future. [...] If you tried to explain to him that men's prayers today are one of the innumerable coordinates with which [He] harmonises the weather of tomorrow, he would reply that then [God] always knew men were going to make those prayers and, if so, they did not pray freely but were predestined to do so. And he would add that the weather on a given day can be traced back through its causes to the original creation of matter itself – so that the whole thing, both on the human and on the

> material side, is given "from the word go." What he ought to say, of course, is obvious to us; that the problem of adapting the particular weather to the particular prayers is merely the appearance, at two points in his temporal mode of perception, of the total problem of adapting the whole spiritual universe to the whole corporeal universe; that creation in its entirety operates at every point of space and time, or rather that their kind of consciousness forces them to encounter the whole, self-consistent creative act as a series of successive events. Why that creative act leaves room for their free will is the problem of problems. [...] How it does so is no problem at all; for [God] does not foresee the humans making their free contributions in a future, but sees them doing so in His unbounded Now. And obviously to watch a man doing something is not to make him do it.
> (Lewis 2001b:149-150)

And this last statement, of course, brings us to the second common argument against free will: that divine foreknowledge causes action, and therefore precludes free will. But of course, as we have just seen in Lewis, this argument hardly holds water. As early as Milton, the flaw in its assumptions had been laid bare.[15] The upshot of this is that the foreknowledge of the Valar – and even the prophecies of Mandos – do nothing in themselves to mitigate free will. And Tolkien confirms this supposition in a 1954 letter to Father Robert Murray, where he wrote that "[Gandalf] has no more (if no less) certitudes, or freedoms, than say a living

---

[15] See Book III (ll. 114-119) of *Paradise Lost* (Milton 1971:301):
As if Predestination over-rul'd
This will, dispos'd by absolute Decree
Or high foreknowledge; they themselves decreed
Their own revolt, not I: if I foreknew,
Foreknowledge had no influence on their fault,
Which had no less prov'd certain unforeknown.

theologian. In any case none of my 'angelic' persons are represented as knowing the future completely, or indeed at all where other wills are concerned. Hence their constant temptation to do, or try to do, what is for them wrong (and disastrous): to force lesser wills by power: by awe if not by actual fear, or physical constraint" (Tolkien 1981:203). Therefore, it seems clear that Tolkien neither intended the Valar's awareness of the future to be complete nor to influence the free will of the Children of Ilúvatar.

At this point, we are beginning to converge on the traces of free will Tolkien has embedded into his Secondary World, so I will conclude this section by summing up. It seems clear, both from evidence in the views and writings of his friends and fellow Inklings (particularly Lewis, but also Dorothy Sayers, Charles Williams, and Owen Barfield – a full consideration of which space does not allow me) as well as from his own letters, that Tolkien both believed in the free will of man as well as in God's ability to moderate it when necessary. This is, essentially, the same tense balance between having total free will and having a will that is free only to a certain point, that I tried to show in my discussion of Augustine, Boethius, Aquinas, and Erasmus – and indeed which traces its roots back to the vacillations of pre-Socratics like Empedocles. At this point, I'd like to take a much closer look at free will in the fictive Secondary World of Tolkien's Middle-earth.

FREE WILL IN TOLKIEN'S SECONDARY WORLD

Probably the most logical point at which to begin a discussion of free will in Tolkien's fictive Secondary World is with the Ainulindalë, the Creation Myth in which the world – and everything and everyone in it – is first sung into being. Some have claimed that the Ainur may not, in fact, have had their own independent wills at all. They were, after all, directly and purposely created by Ilúvatar and were "the offspring of his thought" (Tolkien 1977:15). Moreover, while they sang to Ilúvatar, we are told that "they sang only each alone, or but few together, while the rest hearkened; for each comprehended only that part of the mind of Ilúvatar from which he came, and in the understanding of their brethren they grew but slowly" (Tolkien 1977:15). This could suggest that they were, in fact, without their own wills but that rather each Ainu was merely acting out a part of Ilúvatar's greater will – much the way Ilúvatar explains to Aulë, of his unauthorized creations, the Dwarves, "Thou hast from me as a gift thy own being only, and no more; and therefore the creatures of thy hand and mind can live only by that being, moving when thou thinkest to move them, and if thy thought be elsewhere, standing idle" (Tolkien 1977:43).

Yet this argument, when pursued, loses steam fairly quickly. Taking the last example, that of Aulë, we need only turn to Tolkien's letters for an answer. In October 1958, Tolkien began drafting the continuation of a letter to Rhona Beare, in which he addressed various of her questions regarding the (then unpublished) legends of the Elder Days. Toward the end of the draft (and perhaps the reasons it was abandoned), Tolkien found himself lapsing from the composition of a letter and into the construction of new, actual fiction. There, he wrote:

> The One rebuked Aulë, saying that he had tried to usurp the Creator's power; but he could not give independent life to his makings. He had only one life, his own derived from the One, and could at most only distribute it. 'Behold' said the One: *'these creatures of thine have only thy will*, and thy movement. Though you have devised a language for them, they can only report to thee thine own thought. This is a mockery of me.'
>
> Then Aulë in grief and repentance humbled himself and asked for pardon. And he said: 'I will destroy these images of my presumption, *and wait upon thy will.*' And he took a great hammer, raising it to

> smite the eldest of his images; but it flinched and cowered from him. And as he withheld his stroke, astonished, he heard the laughter of Ilúvatar.
>
> 'Do you wonder at this?' he said. 'Behold! thy creatures now live, *free from thy will*! For I have seen thy humility, and taken pity on your impatience. Thy making I have taken up into my design.'
> (Tolkien 1981:287, emphasis mine)

I believe it is very clear from this passage that Tolkien's intent was for the Ainur to have free wills of their own. Indeed, Aulë's actions represent just such an act of freedom; were his will *not* free, how could he have possibly departed from the will of Ilúvatar and created the Dwarves in the first place?

Another example should suffice to drive home the point. Returning to the passage I quoted earlier, at the outset of the Ainulindalë, "it came to pass that Ilúvatar called together all the Ainur and declared to them a mighty theme. [...] Then Ilúvatar said to them: 'Of the theme that I have declared to you, *I will now* that ye make in harmony together a Great Music. And since I have kindled you with the Flame Imperishable, ye shall show forth your powers in adorning this theme, each with his own thoughts and devices, *if he will*. But I will sit and hearken, and be glad that through you great beauty has been wakened into song'" (Tolkien 1977:15, emphasis mine). In my view, the two uses of "will" here are very telling. In the first case, Ilúvatar *wills* – that is, he instructs or directs – that the Ainur should take up the theme and elaborate upon it; while in the second, he acknowledges the freedom of each Ainu to choose not to do so – "*if* he will." To me, the two – the powerful directive of Ilúvatar's will and the choice allowed the Ainur – sum up and once again reinforce the same 'tense balance' between free will and providence that I have alluded to previously. And in the Ainulindalë, the Ainur do, in fact, take up the task and produce a great and wondrous music; but one of them, Melkor, takes his own free will a little too far – with far-reaching consequences.

This act of rebellion, moreover, should serve as yet more convincing evidence that the Ainur possess their own independent, free wills. Assuming for a moment that the Ainur do *not* have their own free wills but are rather merely performing a deterministic sequence of actions as willed directly by Ilúvatar alone, what implications would this have for Melkor's behavior? It would imply that Ilúvatar *intended* Melkor to rebel, and that Melkor, indeed, had no choice in the matter. But this cannot be what Tolkien meant us to think. To believe this would require us to fully exonerate Melkor of all wrongdoing, since a lack of free will entails a lack of responsibility. But Tolkien's moralistic worldview is at complete odds with such a utilitarian interpretation. Tolkien is all about choices freely made and the acceptance of the consequences of them. Melkor must, in fact, be free to act, because Tolkien means him to act as his Lucifer – his fall and transformation into Morgoth to echo Lucifer's fall and transformation into Satan. In this sense, Melkor not only has free will, his use of it to rebel against Ilúvatar constitutes the most egregious abuse possible of the gift of that freedom. Yet – and this is where we see providence again – despite his efforts to mar the music and to overmaster the work of his brethren, the limit of Melkor's freedom is nevertheless itself circumscribed by the greater will of his Creator, who explains that

> Mighty are the Ainur, and mightiest among them is Melkor; but that he may know, and all the Ainur, that I am Ilúvatar, those things that ye have sung, I will show them forth, that ye may see what ye have done. And thou, Melkor, shalt see that no theme may be played that hath not its uttermost source in me, nor can any alter the music in my despite. For he that attempteth this shall prove but mine instrument in

> the devising of things more wonderful, which he himself hath not imagined. (Tolkien 1977:17)

Melkor, like all the Ainur, is free; however, that freedom is bounded by the permission of Ilúvatar. Putting it another way: Melkor is free to move his pieces in the great game that is the struggle for dominion over Middle-earth, but Ilúvatar made – and can change, if he wishes – the rules of that game.

So, I think it is reasonably safe to say that the Ainur exhibit free will. What about the Children of Ilúvatar, Elves and Men? Should we allow them the same freedom? Or are they merely the pawns of greater powers? To decide the questions of the Elves, we need look no further than Fëanor, whose very name means "Spirit of Fire" (Tolkien 1977:63).[16] In the *Quenta Silmarillion*, we read that "Fëanor grew swiftly, as if a secret fire were kindled within him. He was tall, and fair of face, and masterful, his eyes piercingly bright and his hair raven-dark; in the pursuit of all his purposes eager and steadfast. Few ever changed his courses by counsel, none by force. He became of all the Noldor, then or after, the most subtle in mind and the most skilled in hand" (Tolkien 1977:64). We are also told that "Fëanor was driven by the fire of his own heart only" (Tolkien 1977:66). It scarcely seems possible that this description could apply to an automaton, devoid of its own will. Moreover, Fëanor's ill will (the word is deliberately chosen) toward his half-brothers, Fingolfin and Finarfin, is telling. And then there is the making of the Silmarils.

This act of subcreation, much like those of Aulë (unauthorized, but accepted through mercy) and Melkor (a twisted mockery, rejected utterly), takes place only within the confines of higher providential will.

---

[16] For a discussion of free will in specific relation to Fëanor and Frodo – arguably the key figures of *The Silmarillion* and *The Lord of the Rings*, respectively, see Richard Purtill's *J.R.R. Tolkien: Myth, Morality, and Religion*, Chapter 9, 'Frodo, Fëanor, and Free Will'.

Fëanor creates the Silmarils, but their light came from the Two Trees of Valinor, which were created by Yavanna, who herself was created by Ilúvatar directly. Had Fëanor repented, like Aulë, his work would have turned to good, but he *chose*, through the empowerment of his own free will, to take the path of his enemy, Melkor, and descend into rebellion and ruin. Fëanor exhibits his own freedom in creating the Silmarils, though we may see providence peeking in – "it may be that some shadow of foreknowledge came to him of the doom that drew near [to the Two Trees]" (Tolkien 1977:67) – but he exhibits just as much freedom in withholding them from the Ainur after the death of the Two Trees. Given the opportunity of permitting Yavanna to restore life to the Trees, at the cost of destroying the Silmarils, Fëanor exclaims, "This thing I will not do of *free will*. But if the Valar will constrain me, then shall I know indeed that Melkor is of their kindred" (Tolkien 1977:79, emphasis mine). And of course, the Valar do not (and probably *cannot*) constrain him, leading to the ensuing exile and grief of the Noldor. Fëanor, determined to "carry out [his] Fall to its bitter bottom" (Tolkien 1981:110), continues to act in accordance with his own (albeit misguided) will, in defiance of all council or better judgment – first, speaking the blasphemous Oath of Fëanor; then, leading the Noldor from Tirion; then, committing the treacherous kinslaying at Alqualondë; and finally, returning to Middle-earth to wage war on Morgoth for the recovery of the Silmarils. All of these actions come with consequences, for which, ultimately, Fëanor – and not some deterministic puppet-master – must be held responsible.

Space does not permit – nor does the argument require – a full reckoning of every other Elf and Man in *The Silmarillion* who exhibits independent freedom of will. But a few other examples may be given without elaboration. Beren, for instance, chooses to attempt the recovery of one of the Silmarils from Morgoth's iron crown out of his love for Lúthien. Lúthien, in her turn, chooses a mortal life and the kinship of Men over Elves out of her love for Beren – a freely made choice which Arwen would later echo out of her love for Aragorn. Indeed, Lúthien follows Beren to the Halls of Mandos and sings for his life. Thingol, her father, withholds the Silmaril from the Sons of Fëanor, who "vowed openly to slay Thingol and destroy his people, if they came victorious from war, and the jewel were not surrendered of free will" (Tolkien 1977:189). And still later, Eärendil, by an act of free will, dares to sail into the Uttermost West, seeking the succor of the Valar in the travails of Elves and Men with the evil of Morgoth. And here again, I would suggest that we see free will circumscribed by the providence of a greater will: Eärendil's action, though freely chosen, should have resulted in immediate failure; however,

> the wise have said that *it was by reason of the power of that holy jewel* that they came in time to waters that no vessels save those of the Teleri had known; and they came to the Enchanted Isles and escaped their enchantment; and they came into the Shadowy Seas and passed their shadows, and they looked upon Tol Eressëa the Lonely Isle, but tarried not; and at the last they cast anchor in the Bay of Eldamar, and the Teleri saw the coming of that ship out of the East and they were amazed, gazing from afar upon the light of the Silmaril, and it was very great. Then Eärendil, first of living Men, landed on the immortal shores. (Tolkien 1977:247-248)

In *The Hobbit* and *The Lord of the Rings*, the point – and consequences – of free will are even more pronounced. So many of the strings of seeming coincidences that propel the action of the story hinge upon such free choices. For example, that Sméagol chose to murder Déagol and take the ring; that the Ring later 'chose' to abandon him in the caves under the Misty Mountains (I will return to the idea of the Ring's own free will shortly); that Bilbo would choose to keep it secret from

Gollum; and so many others. I would like to examine a couple of these points of freedom a little more closely.

When Bilbo decides to leave the Shire, Gandalf prevails upon him to leave the Ring to Frodo, and although he has great difficulty in actually doing it, "he gave it up in the end of his own accord: an important point" (Tolkien 1965a:58). This is in direct conflict with the apparent will of the Ring itself – the will to betray any but its Master, and the drive to return to its Master's black hand. In fact, as the Ring gains control over its bearer, one might wonder whether it is not, in fact, actually leeching its will from the bearer; and as the bearer becomes more and more enthralled to the lure of the Ring, the Ring itself grows stronger and stronger to work its (or perhaps we should say its Master's) will through that agent. This is an interesting embellishment on the more basic idea of individual versus greater will.

More importantly, as Bilbo freely chose to lay aside the Ring, Frodo chooses freely to bear it. Frodo's choice is made nowhere more clear than in the Council of Elrond, where he accepts the burden of the Ring – with all concomitant hardships of that decision – and agrees to bear it on the mission of its destruction. Yet at the same time, once again, the presence of providence – of a larger will than that of the individual – is present. Though Tolkien never uses the word 'providence', his intention is nevertheless clear when he writes: "At last with an effort he [Frodo] spoke, and wondered to hear his own words, as if *some other will* was using his small voice. 'I will take the Ring,' he said, 'though I do not know the way'" (Tolkien 1965a:284, emphasis mine). It may be tempting here, once again, to ascribe a kind of determinism to "some other will", as if Frodo, in fact, had no choice at all; yet this would be a mistake. Indeed, in his reply to Frodo, Elrond brings together this tense balance between the free will of the individual and the larger will of God when he says: "I think that this task is appointed for you, Frodo. [...] But it is a heavy burden. So heavy that none could lay it on another. I do not lay it on you. But if you take it *freely*, I will say that *your choice* is right" (1965a:284, emphasis mine).

This is a pivotal scene. Here, we see that Frodo is free to choose whether to take the Ring or to leave it behind for others to worry about. At the same time, it is hinted that some larger (one might daresay 'divine') design *intends* for Frodo to bear the burden. Gandalf hints at much the same thing when he refers to Frodo that there is "something else at work, beyond any design of the Ring-maker. I can put it no plainer than by saying that Bilbo was *meant* to find the Ring, and *not* by its maker. In which case you also were *meant* to have it. And that may be an encouraging thought" (Tolkien 1965a:65). Of the scene at the Council of Elrond, Wayne Hammond and Christina Scull (2005:259) write in their *The Lord of the Rings: A Reader's Companion*:

> Frodo has been chosen, that he is fated to bear the Ring; but Frodo nonetheless has free will, and may choose whether or not to accept his fate. In his draft letter to Eileen Elgar, September 1963, Tolkien calls Frodo 'an instrument of Providence' (p. 326), and makes it clear that his quest succeeded in the end, despite his failure himself to put the Ring into the Fire, because he undertook it with free will, with humility and out of love for the world he knew.

And while Frodo freely chose the Ring, many others who could have taken it from him by force freely chose not to do so. Among these are Gandalf – "Do not tempt me! I dare not take it, not even to keep it safe, unused" (Tolkien 1965a:71); Elrond – "I fear to take the Ring to hide it. I will not take the Ring to wield it" (Tolkien 1965a:281); Aragorn – "If I was after the Ring, I could have it – NOW! [...] But I *am* the real Strider, fortunately [...] I am Aragorn son of Arathorn; and if by life or death I can save you, I will" (Tolkien 1965a:183); Galadriel – "I pass the test [...] I will diminish, and go into the West and remain

Galadriel" (Tolkien 1965a:381); and Faramir – "But fear no more! I would not take this thing, if it lay by the highway. Not were Minas Tirith falling in ruin and I alone could save her, so, using the weapon of the Dark Lord for her good and my glory" (Tolkien 1965b:280). And Samwise, of course, is a special case. He both takes the Ring and relinquishes it out of loyalty to his master, Frodo, and he stands firm against the deceptions of the Ring in its own country:

> Already the Ring tempted him, gnawing at his will and reason. Wild fantasies arose in his mind; and he saw Samwise the Strong, Hero of the Age, striding with a flaming sword across the darkened land, and armies flocking to his call as he marched to the overthrow of Barad-dûr. And then all the clouds rolled away, and the white sun shone, and at his command the vale of Gorgoroth became a garden of flowers and trees and brought forth fruit. He had only to put on the Ring and claim it for his own, and all this could be.
> In that hour of trial it was the love of his master that helped most to hold him firm; but also deep down in him lived still unconquered his plain hobbit-sense: he knew in the core of his heart that he was not large enough to bear such a burden, even if such visions were not a mere cheat to betray him. The one small garden of a free gardener was all his need and due, not a garden swollen to a realm; his own hands to use, not the hands of others to command.
> (Tolkien 1965c:177)

Others, however, are overmastered by their lust for the Ring or for the power it might provide. Among these, Boromir and Gollum are the most obvious examples. But even the Ring represents only one of many fulcrums on which the question and consequences of free will balance. The Palantír, for example, is an equal temptation, testing both the mighty and the meek. Saruman, Denethor, and Pippin all fall prey to its allure. And still weaker, meaner people – such as Gríma Wormtongue – make their choices out of lust or envy or the desire to elevate their position in the social order. Yet the Ring, of course, remains the single strongest artifact of temptation – in some ways, it is the equivalent to the Silmarils in the *Quenta Silmarillion*. But in the end, each individual person has a choice to make: they may either resist its call or give in; they may either choose the difficult way or the easy; the right or the wrong. And while fate (or providence or grace – whatever one calls the finger of the divine reaching down into each person's life) may help to set the rules of the game, the individual moves are up to the players. And whether they win or lose in the end is partly up to them.

CONCLUDING REMARKS

Elves, Dwarves, Men – and Hobbits – are called "the Free Peoples" (Tolkien 1965a:289) precisely for the reason that they *are* free: free to defy evil or to join with it – or to hide from the conflict, taking neither side. We know that Tolkien himself believed very strongly in both free will and in the divine intercession of providence in the Primary World. And in building his Secondary World as a subcreative homage to the work of that greater Creator, God, he would certainly have transferred that belief into Middle-earth. Whichever way we lean in the philosophical debates of the 20th and 21st centuries, and whether or not we decide that free will genuinely exists or is merely an illusion, Tolkien nevertheless was convinced of its truth. We must therefore accept it as true for Middle-earth, whether true or false in the Primary World.

To look at it from another angle, Tolkien's fiction centers on sacrifice and courage in the face of insurmountable opposition. To aver that free will is merely an illusion, then, would be to imply that Bilbo, Frodo, Gandalf, and all the rest, made no real choices at all, and that their actions were predetermined from the beginning. This cannot be what Tolkien intended, as it would destroy all sense of meaning in the cathartic sacrifices of the Free Peoples – just as it would render Sauron, Saruman, the Nazgûl, and the Ring blameless for all of their actions. No, free will within Middle-earth must be accepted as the clear intention of its author. Indeed, writing of Elves and Men, Tolkien makes the point very explicitly in a draft letter to Michael Straight: "they were rational creatures of *free will in regard to God*, of the same historical rank as the Valar, though of far smaller spiritual and intellectual power and status" (Tolkien 1981:236, emphasis mine). Yet that freedom is still subject ("in regard to") to the greater will of God, whom Tolkien conceived of as the only completely free being. Verlyn Flieger (2002:129) summarized the relationship between these two elements very well, writing that,

> The interactions of Men and Elves, then, are to involve and embody the interplay of free will and destiny. Tolkien clearly intended both to be powerful albeit not always complementary forces in his world and may well have envisioned each as the necessary function of the other.

And the mere fact that we continue to debate and puzzle over whether we are truly free or enslaved by causality – or whether reality is somewhere in between – testifies to the perennial importance of such questions. That Tolkien has taken a comforting stand on the question may help to account for his continuous popularity. And so long as readers feel the question is an important one, Tolkien's fictive Secondary World will provide a satisfying microcosm in which to explore its consequences to the lives of free beings.

JASON FISHER, an independent scholar from Dallas, TX, was educated at Texas A&M University in English, Philosophy, and Psychology. Most recently, Jason has written a series of articles for *The J.R.R. Tolkien Encyclopedia: Scholarship and Critical Assessment* (edited by Michael Drout and forthcoming from Routledge in 2006). He is also currently at work on a contribution for another Walking Tree Publications project celebrating the thirtieth anniversary of the publication of *The Silmarillion* (edited by Allan Turner). In addition, Jason has presented papers on J.R.R. Tolkien and the Inklings in a variety of academic settings.

Bibliography

Barnes, Jonathan, 2001, *Early Greek Philosophy*, (2nd revised edition), London: Penguin Books.

Boethius, *The Consolation of Philosophy*, (translated by H.R. James), London: Elliot Stock, 1897. Accessed at http://www.gutenberg.org/files/14328/14328-h/14328-h.htm.

Chesterton, G.K., 2001, *Saint Thomas Aquinas*, New York: Image Books (Doubleday).

Dubs, Kathleen E., 2004, 'Providence, Fate, and Chance: Boethian Philosophy in *The Lord of the Rings*', in Jane Chance (ed.), 2004, *Tolkien and the Invention of Myth: A Reader*, Lexington (KY): University Press of Kentucky, pp. 133-144.

Fisher, Matthew A., 2006, 'Working at the Crossroads: Tolkien, St. Augustine, and the Beowulf-poet', in Wayne G. Hammond and Christina Scull (eds.), 2006, *The Lord of the Rings 1954–2004: Scholarship in Honor of Richard E. Blackwelder*, Milwaukee (WI): Marquette University Press, pp. 217-230.

Flieger, Verlyn, 2002, *Splintered Light: Logos and Language in Tolkien's World*, Kent (OH): Kent State University Press.

Fredrick, Candice and Sam McBride, 2001, *Women Among the Inklings: Gender, C.S. Lewis, J.R.R. Tolkien, and Charles Williams*, Westport (CT): Greenwood Press.

Hammond, Wayne G. and Christina Scull, 2005, *The Lord of the Rings: A Reader's Companion*, London: HarperCollins.

Lewis, C.S., 1958, *Mere Christianity*, (revised and enlarged edition), New York: Macmillan.

---, 2001a, *The Problem of Pain*, San Francisco: HarperSanFrancisco.

---, 2001b, *The Screwtape Letters*, San Francisco: HarperSanFrancisco.

---, 2002, *Studies in Words*, (2nd Canto edition), Cambridge: Cambridge University Press.

---, 2005, *The Discarded Image: An Introduction to Medieval and Renaissance Literature*, (Canto editon), Cambridge: Cambridge University Press.

Milton, John, 1971, *The Complete Poetry of John Milton*, (edited by John T. Shawcross; revised edition), New York: Doubleday.

Purtill, Richard, 2003, *J.R.R. Tolkien: Myth, Morality, and Religion*, San Francisco: Ignatius Press.

Sayers, Dorothy, 1987, *The Mind of the Maker*, San Francisco: HarperSanFrancisco.

Shippey, Tom, 2000, *J.R.R. Tolkien: Author of the Century*, Boston: Houghton Mifflin.

---, 2003, *The Road to Middle-earth: How J.R.R. Tolkien Created a New Mythology*, (revised and expanded edition), Boston: Houghton Mifflin.

Tipler, Frank, 1994, *The Physics of Immortality: Modern Cosmology, God, and the Resurrection of the Dead*, New York: Doubleday.

Tolkien, J.R.R., 1965a, *The Fellowship of the Ring*, (2nd edition), Boston: Houghton Mifflin.

---, 1965b, *The Two Towers*, (2nd edition), Boston: Houghton Mifflin.

---, 1965c, *The Return of the King*, (2nd edition), Boston: Houghton Mifflin.

---, 1977, *The Silmarillion*, Boston: Houghton Mifflin.

---, 1981, *The Letters of J.R.R. Tolkien*, (selected and edited by Humphrey Carpenter), Boston: Houghton Mifflin.

Freedom and Providence as Anti-Modern Elements?[1]

THOMAS FORNET-PONSE

Abstract

The question of freedom and determination is a very actual and important question in our modern societies. From a theological viewpoint, it is combined with the question about divine providence and Gods acting in history. This seems to contradict modern concepts of freedom.

In this article, I consider whether the depiction of freedom and providence in Tolkien's fictional works (especially Middle-earth) can be understood in the context of Catholic theology as well as Tolkien's time as an anti-modern element in his work or rather as a contribution to combine Christian theology and modern concepts. Therefore, I am dealing with free will, freedom of choice and freedom of action in Middle-earth as characteristic features of the created beings in Middle-earth as well as the acting of Ilúvatar throughout history. Subsequently I analyse the patterns of determination and providence in Middle-earth and the way this is combined with the individual freedom.

INTRODUCTION

The question of freedom and determination is a very real and important question in our modern societies. Some neurophysiologists like Wolf Singer or Gerhard Roth state on the basis of their experiments that freedom of will is an illusion as human actions are determined by neural processes (cf. Singer 2004, Geyer 2004).[2] If this were true, it would have enormous consequences for the possibility of moral responsibility and

---

[1] Many thanks to Layra Varnam for carefully correcting this article.
[2] Dickerson (2003:14ff) quotes Bertrand Russell with his absolute denial of the existence of human free will and states a sharp contrast to Tolkien's view. Dickerson's book is not wholly unproblematic since he presupposes an understanding of Tolkien's "Christian beliefs as tremendously important to understanding his works" (219f.) which limits the applicability of the text.

for the theory of criminal law, undermine the most important convictions of most religions, and contradict the main aspects of human societies and their experience of free will. While it is not the aim of this article to enter into this discussion, these debates do highlight the significance of human freedom for modern societies. Combined with the emphasis on individuality and the weakening of institutions and collectives, freedom is one of the most important features of modern everyman's anthropology (cf. Nida-Rümelin 2005:26-43).

It is small wonder that the theological concept of divine providence and God's acting in history does not harmonize simply with this modern understanding, as it is understood as a limitation of human freedom. Furthermore, natural disasters and social catastrophes undermine the belief in a divine government and conservation of the world. Link (2005:414, my translation) explains this problem:

> The belief in providence offers an interpretation of our life and furthermore, history as a whole; it offers an overlapping connection of sense, embracing past and future, which we can combine without difficulty neither with our experience (e.g. of freedom to resistance against violence) nor with biblical evidence of God.

The relationship between human freedom, divine omnipotence, and providence is a widely discussed subject in the three monotheistic religions Christianity, Judaism and Islam. While they differ in their emphasis on human freedom and God's omnipotence, they all – disregarding extreme positions – stress the existence of both. Since diverse modern concepts of freedom are opposed to or even contradict the monotheistic concept of providence and freedom held by these religions, and the denial of God as subject of/in history is part of modern claims at the beginning of the last century, a further question arises. Is a reconciliation between these poles necessary and possible or does the theological concept of providence fundamentally contradict the modern view of freedom?

Since J.R.R. Tolkien is regarded e.g. by Shippey (2001:viif), Flieger (1997:2) and Curry as an author of the 20th century whose work was influenced by his time, which they suggest provides an explanation for his continuing attraction for today's reader, a closer look at the concept(s) of freedom present in *The Lord of the Rings* and Tolkien's *Legendarium* may be interesting. After all, the existence of Ilúvatar and of the *Ainulindalë* as influencing or determining the progress of history are facts in Middle-earth. Dickerson (2003:14) describes the difference between Tolkien's views and the view of his time as follows:

> Tolkien's basic philosophical beliefs were also in contradiction to the prevailing materialist presuppositions of modernism as well as the relativism of postmodernism, especially with respect to his views on human free will and objective morality.

Purtill (2003:165) refers to the question of the proper use of free will as a point of disagreement between Tolkien and modern critics. Combined with the theological question about the relationship between human freedom and divine providence it is worth considering whether Tolkien's depiction of freedom and providence should be understood in the context of Catholic theology as well as Tolkien's time as an antimodern element in his work. If Tolkien's views were so at odds with the view of his readers, one cannot easily explain his success.

FREE WILL, FREEDOM OF CHOICE AND FREEDOM OF ACTION IN MIDDLE-EARTH AS CHARACTERISTIC FEATURES OF THE CREATED BEINGS IN MIDDLE-EARTH

The first text in *The Silmarillion*, the *Ainulindalë*, is concerned with the creation of Eä and is of the uttermost importance for addressing the question of freedom and determination.[3] Since I analyzed this text in detail elsewhere (Fornet-Ponse 2005:158-166), it is not necessary to repeat my whole argument. In brief, I argued that although the Ainur's remembrance of their part in the music may lead to a far-reaching, if not complete determination of events with a limitation of freedom of choice and freedom of action, it is by no means necessary to assume a complete determination. Firstly, the knowledge of the Ainur is limited by Ilúvatar's freedom, for he has not revealed everything to them:

> Yet some things there are that they cannot see [...]; for to none but himself has Ilúvatar revealed all that he has in store, and in every age there come forth things that are new and have no foretelling, for they do not proceed from the past. And so it was that as this vision of the World was played before them, the Ainur saw that it contained things which they had not thought. (Sil:18)

Secondly, the Vision of the Ainur did not show the complete history: "for the history was incomplete and the circles of time not full-wrought when the vision was taken away." (Sil:20)[4]

Furthermore, it is important to refer to the difference between prescience and determination, for a knowledge which is outside of time

---

[3] In this article, I use the version in *The Silmarillion* and not the various different versions in *History of Middle-earth* since they do not differ significantly in the relevant passages.

[4] Cf. Finrod's argument against Andreth in *The Athrabeth Finrod ah Andreth* with his emphasis on Ilúvatar's freedom and the 'open end' of the Music (*Morgoth's Ring* [MR]:318f).

does not determine events in time; it does not constitute a causal connection.

> For the Great Music had been but the growth and flowering of thought in the Timeless Halls, and the Vision only a foreshowing; but now they had entered in at the beginning of Time, and the Valar perceived that the World had been but foreshadowed and foresung, and they must achieve it. (Sil:20)

The authorship of Eru instead of the Valar is emphasized by Tolkien in his letter to Waldman: "Their power and wisdom is derived from their Knowledge of the cosmogonical drama, which they perceived first as a drama (that is as in a fashion we perceive a story composed by some-one else), and later as a 'reality'." (Letters:146) Moreover, Ilúvatar expresses his absolute sovereignty over the *Ainulindalë*:

> And thou, Melkor, shalt see that no theme may be played that hath not its uttermost source in me, nor can any alter the music in my despite. For he that attempteth this shall prove but mine instrument in the devising of things more wonderful, which he himself hath not imagined. (Sil:17)

This seems to diminish Melkor's freedom and responsibility, but since his freedom is emphasized throughout the work (and is the basis of evil in Tolkien's *Legendarium*), this sentence reflects rather the opinion of, for example, Thomas Aquinas, who argues that God can bring good out of evil. If Melkor, the Valar and the Eruhíni are not responsible for their deeds, then the whole *Quenta Silmarillion* (and *The Lord of the Rings*) is rather pointless. Eru's sovereignty and his *creatio continua* is expressed in the renewing of the Vision to Manwë after Yavanna's request for help for the *kelvar* and *olvar* where "he saw that all was upheld by the hand of Ilúvatar; and the hand entered in, and from it came forth many wonders that had until then been hidden from him in the hearts of the Ainur." (Sil:41)

Thus, combining both Eru's freedom and sovereignty and the freedom of the Ainur (and the Children of Eru) as expressing God's plan and the fulfilment of this plan by individuals, it becomes clear that in *The Silmarillion* there is a providential pattern which reflects main points of a sound Christian account of providence (cf. Deuser 2003). Providence can be understood within the context of soteriology or questions of God and creation, and means that God's effective will leads free creatures to participation in his inner-trinitarian life. A Christian understanding of providence emphasizes on the one hand God's sovereignty and acting in history and on the other hand human freedom. In some theological opinions God binds himself to human freedom, he does not force Man to salvation, but attempts everything within his power to enable Man to freely agree to salvation. Even though Christians cannot be sure that all Men will be redeemed, they have (!) to hope that it will occur. This hope expresses both the belief in God's providential power and human freedom.

Additionally, the prescience of the Ainur is limited by other wills (cf. Letters:203 and 285) and it is important to mention Tolkien's reflection on prophecy in *Ósanwe-Kenta* [OK] that a mind placed in time cannot see the future but "can learn of the future only from another mind which has seen it. But that means only from Eru ultimately, or mediately from some mind that has seen in Eru some part of His purpose." (OK:31) In this text, Tolkien stresses the freedom of Eru and the importance of individual will in a communication of thought.

Concerning human and Elvish freedom, it is important to emphasize that Elves and Men are conceived by Eru alone. "None of the Ainur had part in their making. Therefore when they beheld them, the more did they love them, being things other than themselves, strange and free." (Sil:18) The making of the dwarves by Aulë and their adoption by

Ilúvatar, who gave them life of their own, is another evidence of the freedom of the Children of Ilúvatar.

The first chapter of the *Quenta Silmarillion* mentions a fundamental difference between Elves and Men as a result of the Gift of Ilúvatar. Men "should have a virtue to shape their life, amid the powers and chances of the world, beyond the Music of the Ainur, which is as fate to all things else" (Sil:41). This is combined with death as leaving of the circles of the world. This passage can be understood as expressing human freedom and an Elvish determination by the Music of the Ainur. But in my opinion, this is not a valid interpretation since it contradicts the whole structure of *The Silmarillion* with its emphasis on free choices and deeds.

Besides the limitation of the knowledge of the Ainur by other wills, another argument against a determination of Elves and Men by the *Ainulindalë* as result of the Ainur is the incomplete understanding of the

> theme by which the Children entered into the Music [...]. For which reason the Valar are to these kindreds rather their elders and their chieftains than their masters; and if ever in their dealings with Elves and Men the Ainur have endeavoured to force them when they would not be guided, seldom has this turned to good, howsoever good the intent. (Sil:41)

Regarding the emphasized freedom of Men beyond the Music of the Ainur, Flieger (2002:128) distinguishes strictly between Elves and Men: "While Elves are bound by the pattern of the Music – not necessarily within themselves but in the external events of their lives – Men are not." The Elvish freedom is limited to "internal choices", Elves "may have power over their own natures, though not over external happenings" (52f). This assumption leads to problems not only in the interpretation of Elvish (free) decisions which have great significance in the course of history, such as many of Fëanor's decisions[5] (the Kinslaying, the siege of Angband, etc., of Ulmo's warnings to Turgon and Orodreth and their (free) response to it), but also in the interpretation of contacts between Men and Elves. If Men are not determined by the Music of the Ainur and play a relevant part in the history of Arda, how can Elves be determined? What about the marriage of Beren and Lúthien, and Lúthien's help in fulfilling the Quest? What about Túrin's influence in Nargothrond and the statement that the tale of his fate "is woven with the fate of the Silmarils and of the Elves" (Sil:199)? What about the explicit statement that Morgoth's army won the Nirnaeth Arnoediad only because of Men's treachery (cf. Sil:192)? Since Flieger's view does not sufficiently explain this questions, Dickerson's view (2003:109f) seems more appropriate, "the Elves do indeed have free will, even though all their choices will ultimately lead to the fulfillment of what has already been seen."

The free will of the Elves is mentioned explicitly in *Laws and Customs among the Eldar*. At first concerning the marriage between Elves: "The Eldar wedded once only in life, and for love or at the least by free will upon either part." (MR:210) The freedom of each *fëa* is mentioned by some Valar as cause for a non-returned love, other Valar mention the marring of Arda. Concerning the relationship between *hröa* and *fëa*, an Elvish *fëa* 'consumes' his body, but "its fate was to inhabit Arda to its end." (MR:219) A houseless *fëa* is open to direct instruction

---

[5] I disagree with her view that if Fëanor could have freely given up the Silmarils "[s]ubsequent events or deeds would not be externally different, but the motives behind them could be different, as could his attitudes toward himself, the Silmarils, and the peoples whose lives are intertwined with his" (Flieger 2002:114). In my opinion, the statement that "yet had he said yea at the first, before the tidings came from Formenos, it may be that his after deeds would have been other than they were" (Sil:79) is not an 'odd' one but is based on Fëanor's free will and his possibility to act freely in given circumstances and therefore influence these circumstances.

of the Valar, it is summoned to Mandos, "and the summons proceeds from just authority, and is imperative; yet it may be refused." (MR:223) Another aspect of Elvish Freedom is the possibility to die by their will, "as for example because of great grief or bereavement, or because of the frustration of their dominant desires and purposes." (MR:341)

In my opinion, the causal nexus between mortality and freedom of the circles of the world is the central clue to understanding the difference between Elves and Man. It does not mean that Elves are determined while Men are not, but that Elves are bound to the world and its end while Men are not. The *Ainulindalë* does not determine all events in Arda but only the pattern in which freedom of will and freedom of action is possible. I agree with Weinreich (2004:81f) that Ilúvatar can allow discordances and unforeseeable interludes without endangering the final result. But this is in accordance with the theological conviction that providence does not determine Man but challenges his freedom (cf. Ratzinger 2000:44). The Music of the Ainur does not determine all (or most) events in Arda but only the main lines of history – as the concluding sentences of the *Quenta Silmarillion* hint at:

> Here ends the SILMARILLION. If it has passed from the high and the beautiful to darkness and ruin, that was of old the fate of Arda Marred; and if any change shall come and the Marring be amended, Manwë and Varda may know; but they have not revealed it, and it is not declared in the dooms of Mandos." (Sil:255)

Thus, I agree with Dickerson, Weinreich et. al. in arguing for the freedom of will and freedom of action of Ainur, Elves, Dwarves and Men. This freedom is not wholly identical in all 'races', since it is connected to mortality, but there is a fundamental freedom of Ainur and Elves in regard to Eru and (some) external events. Even Orcs can to some extent be regarded as free, but concerning their emergence Tolkien himself was undecided (cf. MR:409-423). It is certain that "Melkor could not 'create' living 'creatures' of independent wills" (MR:413) and Orcs are therefore a corruption either of Men or of Elves. But their independent will is suppressed nearly completely by Melkor (and later Sauron).

The protagonist's moral responsibility and free will is important throughout the whole of *The Lord of the Rings*. Since this has been recognised by many critics, and since Dickerson (2003) has dealt with this extensively, it is sufficient to refer to the different important choices of Aragorn after the breaking of the Fellowship, the choices of Frodo to take the Ring, of Samwise, of Faramir, etc. The Elvish freedom is expressed in Elrond's and Galadriel's refusal of the Ring.

THE ACTING OF ILÚVATAR THROUGHOUT HISTORY

Having dealt with the freedom of the created beings in Eä, we can now turn to a further aspect of our problem, the acting of Ilúvatar throughout history. Firstly, it is important to mention a difference between Ilúvatar's relationship to Eä and the God of Judaism, Christianity and Islam: for Ilúvatar is much more remote. While the conviction of *creatio continua* is the consensus amongst the three aforementioned monotheistic religions and expresses the lasting preoccupation of God with the world created by him – without it, the world would cease to be –, Ilúvatar entrusts Arda to the Ainur and acts only in a few events. This is in accordance with the *Ainulindalë*, in which Ilúvatar only declared first one theme, then a second and a third, but not the whole music. The theme declared by Ilúvatar leaves room for the free interpretation of this theme by the Ainur. By declaring the second and third theme, Ilúvatar can integrate the patterns introduced by Melkor and this shows that the final result of the music cannot be altered. Tolkien wrote in drafts to Straight (1956):

> There is no embodiment of the One, of God, who indeed remains remote, outside the World, and only di-

> rectly accessible to the Valar or Rulers. These take the place of the 'gods', but are created spirits, or those of the primary creation who by their own will have entered into the world. But the One retains an ultimate authority, and (or so it seems as viewed in serial time) reserves the right to intrude the finger of God into the story: that is to produce realities which could not be deduced even from a complete knowledge of the previous past, but which being real become part of the effective past for all subsequent time (a possible definition of a 'miracle'). (Letters:235)

According to Tolkien, Elves and Men are the first of these intrusions, while the story was not yet realized but still only a story. Furthermore, this quotation shows that Tolkien was aware of the problems of time in regard to God ("seems as viewed in serial time").

In this context, I have to mention the Secret Fire since this signifies a divine element in the world: because "it is with Ilúvatar" (Sil:16), he has sent it "to burn at the heart of the World" (Sil:25) and said to the Ainur: "And since I have kindled you with the Flame Imperishable, ye shall show forth your powers in adorning this theme, each with his own thoughts and devices, if he will." (Sil:15) The Secret Fire seems to be identical with the 'Flame Imperishable', which means "the Creative activity of Eru (in some sense distinct from or within Him), by which things could be given a 'real' and independent (though derivative and created) existence." (MR:345, cf. Caldecott 2003:107f) This is a reference to Eru's 'authorship', by which an author is present in his work, while remaining independent and outside of his work. Since it means Eru's creative activity, it seems appropriate to regard the subcreative capacity of his creatures as combined with it. Kilby (1976:59) reports a personal conversation with Tolkien, who told him "that the 'Secret Fire sent to burn at the heart of the World' in the beginning was the Holy Spirit." This identification of the Secret Fire as creative activity of

Ilúvatar with the Holy Spirit is theologically possible since according to Christian creation doctrine God's spirit is live-giving and live-preserving. By the means of his Spirit (and Man's response to it), God can act through his creatures in his world without diminishing their freedom. According to Link (2005:424ff), an understanding of Providence within the context of the acting of the Spirit is theologically necessary.

But God's actions are not restricted to his creatures; other forms of divine intervention are also possible and indeed are a fact of Tolkien's cosmos. But Eru's interventions are deeply connected with his remoteness and the errand of the Ainur to prepare the dwelling and the coming of the Children of Ilúvatar and to guide them. He only acts in cases in which the Valar are not authorized.

The first intervention of Ilúvatar in the affairs of Eä concerns Aulë's making of the Dwarves (Sil:43f) and leads to their existence as the adopted Children of Eru. This example shows the limitation of the power of the Valar, because they cannot create independent beings of their own; their acceptance by Eru is indispensable. Furthermore, Ilúvatar integrates the Dwarves into his world, but will not suffer a fundamental change to his design, "that these should come before the Firstborn of my design, nor that thy impatience should be rewarded." (Sil:44)

An interesting example of the relationship between the Valar and Eru occurs with regards to Finwë and Míriel. While in some versions (MR:205ff, 225ff, 254ff), after a long debate of the Valar, Mandos declares the law of Ilúvatar and refers to "the right of lawgiving that Ilúvatar committed to Manwë" (MR:206, 259), the matter is different in the appendix 'The Converse of Manwë and Eru' to *Athrabeth Finrod ah Andreth* (MR:361-366). In the latter, Manwë explains the problem to Eru and asks him what he has designed. Manwë expresses their doubts to use their "power upon the flesh that Thou hast designed, to house the spirit of Thy Children, this seems a matter beyond our authority, even were it not beyond our skill." (MR:362) Eru gives the Valar the authority to re-make the former houses of the spirits of his children.[6] Concerning the sons of Eärendil and Elwing, it is explicitly stated: "The Valar indeed may not withdraw the gift of death, which comes to Men from Ilúvatar, but in the matter of the Half-elven Ilúvatar gave to them the judgement" (Sil:261).

The most remarkable event in *The Silmarillion* and the second intervention, in which Ilúvatar's responsibility is explicitly stated, is the *Akallabêth*, as the host of the Númenóreans broke the Ban of the Valar:

> Then Manwë upon the Mountain called upon Ilúvatar, and for that time the Valar laid down their government of Arda. But Ilúvatar showed forth his power, and he changed the fashion of the world; and a great chasm opened in the sea between Númenor and the Deathless Lands, and the waters flowed down into it, and the noise and smoke of the cataracts went up to heaven, and the world was shaken. [...]
>
> But the land of Aman and Eressëa of the Eldar were taken away and removed beyond the reach of Men for ever. And Andor, the Land of Gift, Númenor of the Kings, Elenna of the Star of Eärendil, was utterly destroyed. (Sil:278f)

The text does not explicitly mention the reasons why the Valar laid down their government, but it is probable that they did not wish to fight against the host of the Númenóreans for they doubted their authority to destroy the host and Númenor. Furthermore, it is possible that the Valar feared that a battle could be as disastrous as the War of Wrath. Be that as it may, the destruction of Númenor and the death of most Númenóre-

---

[6] The concept of an Elvish rebirth present in this converse was rejected by Tolkien in his later writings (cf. MR:363, and *Peoples of Middle-earth* [PM]:390).

ans is a result of an intervention of Ilúvatar, though he does not act without the consent of the Valar but because of their request.

Not mentioned in *The Lord of the Rings*, but in a draft to Robert Murray from 4th November 1954, is the third direct intervention of Eru, namely Gandalf's return. Gandalf states that he "was sent back – for a brief time, until my task is done" (LotR:491) and Tolkien explains that this was not "by the 'gods' whose business is only with this embodied world and its time; for he passed 'out of thought and time'." (Letters:203) 'The Authority' mentioned in this draft obviously is Ilúvatar.

Tolkien's (supernatural) belief in a personal God, who is the creator of the world and the master of history, is present in these explicit interventions of Eru in the affairs of Eä. This can be held only by believers in a personal God and is in contrast to a naturalistic view which excludes 'miracles' and denies God's presence as acting subject in history. But since it is present explicitly only in the mythological texts of *The Silmarillion* and only implicitly in *The Lord of the Rings*, it is not necessary to share this belief for enjoying the works.

Distinguished from these explicit interventions in the affairs of Eä is a further way of the acting of God in history, namely providence. A part of this takes place with the influence of the Valar and Maiar in Middle-earth, be it Ulmo's warnings or his design with Tuor or the Istari in the Third Age.

PATTERNS OF DETERMINATION AND PROVIDENCE IN MIDDLE-EARTH

The term 'providence' does not occur in Tolkien's (fictional) works (it can be seen in Letter # 246), but the concept is present in his mythology, although due to narrative linguistic usage it is mainly expressed by the terms 'doom', 'fate', etc.[7] In my discussion of the *Narn i Hîn Húrin*

---

[7] In this case, a reference to the 'Elvish' origin of the texts in *The Silmarillion* might be helpful since an understanding of the Elvish usage of words like 'doom', 'fate'

(Fornet-Ponse 2005:166-178), I stressed the freedom of Túrin and explained his fate mainly as a consequence of his character and his own free deeds. I indicated a possibility of combining this with providence, for the situations in which Túrin can decide freely emerge from events which are not caused by him. He is free to decide in these situations, but not free to determine the situations in which he has to decide. Tolkien's comment about the heroes in the world of *Beowulf* seems applicable to Túrin: "men caught in the chains of circumstance or of their own character, torn between duties equally sacred, dying with their backs to the wall" (Beowulf:17). While the *Narn* emphasizes Túrin's character, the aspect of a preordained 'fate' is more strongly present in the story of Beren and Lúthien than in the story of Túrin. Shippey (1992:226) mentions two meanings of 'fate' in 'Of Beren and Lúthien': on the one hand fate as an external force, and on the other hand, "rather the personal possession of someone or something", which suggests "that fate is not something external and organising, like Providence, but something individual, like 'life' – something however, unlike 'life', which *has been organised*. The very use of the word thus brings up a question of free will." The word 'doom' is more complicated, it can appear as an overmastering Power, with the sense of 'future disaster', but also in its original sense as decision or judgement. Both words "indicate the presence of controlling powers" (Shippey 1992:227). I propose an interpretation within the context of a theological understanding of providence which means both something individual like God's plan for every individual human and something organised like God's plan for his

---

as meaning an impersonal and external power which determines events would lead to conflicts with the Eldarin knowledge of the Ainur and their knowledge of Eru as creator communicated by the Ainur.
  Differences in tone between 'Of Túrin Turambar' and the other stories of the *Quenta Silmarillion* can be explained by the human authorship of this tale, for "the *Narn i Hîn Húrin* was the work of a Mannish poet, Dírhavel, who lived at the Havens of Sirion in the days of Eärendil" (*Unfinished Tales* [UT]:187).

world. Such an interpretation can avoid the denial of logic mentioned by Shippey (1992:227) concerning the indication of controlling powers as well as the freedom of persons to determine their own fate. A theological understanding thus combines the experience of an external organization with the experience of free will.

Since a detailed analysis of *The Silmarillion* and *The Lord of the Rings* is not possible, I restrict myself to 'Of Beren and Lúthien' and the main lines of *The Lord of the Rings*.

FREEDOM AND PROVIDENCE IN 'OF BEREN AND LÚTHIEN'

The word 'fate' occurs firstly in the story 'Of Beren and Lúthien' in the account of Beren pursuing the orcs who had slain his father: "Then Beren sprang from behind a rock, and slew the captain, and taking the hand and the ring he escaped, being defended by fate; for the Orcs were dismayed, and their arrows wild." (Sil:164) The defense by fate is explained by the incapability of the Orcs and should therefore be understood as a subsequent explanation, but it may – like in 'Of Túrin Turambar' – "mean nothing, be just what people say when they cannot find a better one." (Shippey 1992:233f) No one knows how Beren found a way to Doriath, but he passed through the Girdle of Melian, "even as she had foretold; for a great doom lay upon him." (Sil:165) Her foretelling was to Galadriel: "And one of Men, even of Bëor's house, shall indeed come, and the Girdle of Melian shall not restrain him, for doom greater than my power shall send him" (Sil:144). Similarly, the coming of Carcharoth is explained by fate but also combined with the power of the Silmaril (Sil:184). Since no other Valar or Maiar with a greater power than Melian's is mentioned as leading Beren to Doriath, this indicates that this doom is in the design of Ilúvatar.

During the first meeting of Beren and Lúthien in which Beren calls Lúthien 'Tinuviel' it says: "But as she looked on him, doom fell upon her, and she loved him" (Sil:165), although she flees. This conceptualises 'doom' as an external force, but it can also mean the providential pattern by which Ilúvatar designed a union of Elves and Men. Tolkien expresses this view in his draft letter to Peter Hastings (Letter # 153, Letters:194): "The entering into Men of the Elven-strain is indeed represented as part of a Divine Plan for the ennoblement of the Human Race, from the beginning destined to replace the Elves."[8] Thus, he wrote (Sil:165f):

> And wandering in mind he groped as one that is stricken with sudden blindness, and seeks with hands to grasp the vanished light. Thus he began the payment of anguish for the fate that was laid on him; and in his fate Lúthien was caught, and being immortal she shared in his mortality, and being free received his chain [...].[9]

What is meant by Lúthien's freedom and Beren's chain? It could mean mortality, but since this is mentioned separately and not understood as 'chain' but as freedom, based on the respective lines of the *Lay of Leithian*, I think it refers above all to their love and with this perhaps to Beren's part in the divine plan. This passage expresses the power of love, but also the freedom of both protagonists, for Lúthien returns to

---

[8] Cf. Gwindor's words to Finduilas concerning her love to Túrin: "It is not fitting that the Elder Children of Ilúvatar should be wed with the Younger; nor is it wise, for they are brief, and soon pass, to leave us in widowhood while the world lasts. Neither will fate suffer it, unless it be once or twice only, for some high cause of doom that we do not perceive." (Sil:210) Similarly Finrod tells Andreth: "Nay, *adaneth*, if any marriage can be between our kindred and thine, then it shall be for some high purpose of Doom. Brief it will be and hard at the end. Yea, the least cruel fate that could befall would be that death should soon end it." (MR:324)

[9] Cf. Lines 786-793 of *The Lay of Leithian* (Release from Bondage) (*Lays of Beleriand* [LB]:184): "And thus in anguish Beren paid / for that great doom upon him laid, / the deathless love of Lúthien, / too fair for love of mortal Men; / and in his doom was Lúthien snared, / the deathless in his dying shared; / and Fate them forged a binding chain / of living love and mortal pain." The main points of 'doom' or 'Fate' as individual and organised, but not effective without consent of the individuals are present yet in this 1931 abandoned lay.

Beren. As she leads him before the throne of Thingol, and Thingol questions him, it seemed to Beren "that words were put into his mouth" (Sil:166) and he says: "My fate, O King, led me hither" and expresses his desire for Lúthien. Therefore, Thingol wants to kill him, but Melian counsels him to "forgo his wrath". "'For not by you,' she said, 'shall Beren be slain; and far and free does his fate lead him to the end, yet it is wound with yours. Take heed!" (Sil:167) Here both aspects, the individual freedom and the external organization, are expressed. She does not force Thingol but counsels him – an expression of his freedom. Thingol's part in the divine plan to overcome Melkor/Morgoth consists in the request to bring him a Silmaril, which he thinks is deadly. "Thus he wrought the doom of Doriath, and was ensnared within the curse of Mandos" (Sil:167). This is in accordance with a passage much later when grief and silence have come upon Doriath, and Thingol turns to Melian. She says "that the doom that he had devised must work to its appointed end, and that he must wait now upon time" (Sil:183), which indicates clearly the working of a providential pattern through the actions of individuals who are not wholly aware of the consequences of their decisions. But these decisions are necessary for the appointed end. "Words overpower intentions. In any case intentions are not always known to the intenders. This is the sense of 'doom' which Tolkien strivess to create from oaths and curses and bargains, and from the interweaving of the fates of objects, people and kingdoms." (Shippey 1992:231)

The combination of the Oath of Fëanor is also perceived by Felagund, who states, that "it seems that this doom goes beyond his [= Thingol's] purpose, and that the Oath of Fëanor is again at work." (Sil:169) By his own vow to Barahir, Felagund too is ensnared. As he and Beren are captured by Sauron, only Lúthien comes with Huan[10] to their

---

[10] Huan's fate decreed in Valinor "that the should meet death, but not until he encountered the mightiest wolf that would ever walk the world" (Sil:173) can be under-

aid, after being held fast by Celegorm and Curufin. Combined with the later meeting of Beren, Lúthien and Celegorm and Curufin, by which Beren tooks Angrist, now all is provided which is needed to fulfill the task. This can be interpreted as chance but also as providence, since the text leaves no doubt about their freedom. This is clearly stated in the choice which Lúthien puts before Beren:

> You must choose, Beren, between these two: to relinquish the quest and your oath and seek a life wandering upon the face of the earth; or to hold to your word and challenge the power of darkness upon its throne. But on either road I shall go with you, and our doom shall be alike (Sil:177).

While this expresses above all Lúthien's love for Beren, it also hints at a providential pattern which demands the consent of free creatures, rather than fate as a power which overrules all wills. The same concept is present in the words of Huan when he speaks for the second time. According to him, Beren can deny his doom, but this denial is combined with danger:

> You can turn from your fate and lead her into exile, seeking peace in vain while your life lasts. But if you will not deny your doom, then either Lúthien, being forsaken, must assuredly die alone, or she must with you challenge the fate that lies before you – hopeless, yet not certain. (Sil:179)

In this scene, Beren recognizes the inseparable bond between his and Lúthien's doom and that they can only fulfil their task together. The

---

stood in terms of a task for Huan since he has to stay alive until he fights Carcharoth and thereby saving the Silmaril. Sauron's "thought that he himself would accomplish it" (Sil:175) turned out to be incorrect but was it necessary for him to be overthrown by Huan.

snapping of Angrist as Beren tries to cut out another Silmaril indicates another doom for them and can be understood in the context of a providential pattern that provides sufficient help for the accomplishment of one's task but not beyond. The rescue of Beren and Lúthien by Thorondor and his vassals as "the Quest of the Silmaril was like to have ended in ruin and despair" (Sil:182) bears the main points of a eucatastrophe, "the sudden joyous 'turn' [... which] denies (in the face of much evidence, if you will) universal final defeat and in so far is *evangelium*" (*On Fairy Stories* [FS]:68f).

Beren at last persuaded Lúthien to return to Doriath for he could not forget his oath and would not withhold her from Thingol. "So their doom willed it." (Sil:183) They return in the time of Carcharoth's onslaught and listening to their tale,

> it seemed to Thingol that this Man was unlike all other mortal Men, and among the great in Arda, and the love of Lúthien a thing new and strange; and he perceived that their doom might not be withstood by any power of the world. Therefore at the last he wielded his will. (Sil:184f)

Since Thingol's will is spoken of, his perception that the doom of Beren and Lúthien might not be withstood should rather be interpreted as expression of a providential pattern which demands the consent of free creatures than as expressing a power which overrules all wills. But because of Carcharoth, the Quest is not yet fulfilled, so they have to encounter him. According to Shippey (1992:227), three meanings are present in Beren's last words to Thingol ("Now is the Quest achieved [...] and my doom full-wrought" (Sil:186)): "That sentence on him has finally been executed[,] that disaster has come at last[, and] that his life has now reached a proper close, with all debts paid, promises and curses fulfilled". In my opinion, the last meaning is the most present one.

The events after the first death of Beren are of central importance. Initially, at Lúthien's request, he does not leave the world like every other human being but waits in the Halls of Mandos. Lúthien comes to Mandos and moves him to pity with her song. But because he "had no power to withhold the spirits of Men that were dead within the confines of the world, after their time of waiting; nor could he change the fates of the Children of Ilúvatar" (Sil:187), he goes to Manwë to whom the will of Ilúvatar is revealed. Lúthien is given the choice to dwell without Beren in Valimar or to become mortal and dwell in Middle-earth.

> This doom she chose, forsaking the Blessed Realm, and putting aside all claim to kinship with those that dwell there; that thus whatever grief might lie in wait, the fates of Beren and Lúthien might be joined, and their paths lead together beyond the confines of the world. (Sil:187)

Throughout this story, the free acceptance of the appointed plan of an authority is present. This illustrates the concept of providence and the combination of an appointed plan and the freedom to consent to it and thereby fulfil it.

FREEDOM AND PROVIDENCE IN THE LORD OF THE RINGS

The significance of themes such as providence, fate, chance or free will were recognized early in Tolkien criticism and evidenced by Tolkien scholars (cf. Dubs, Spacks, Pirson, Urang and many others), and thus it is not necessary to prove it with many examples.

> Providence acting in the world is obvious in many episodes, and a recitation of them all would prove tedious. The 'fortuitous' appearance of Strider at *The Prancing Pony*, and the 'lucky' rescue by elves who

> aren't usually seen in those parts but who just 'happen' by, are but two of the many episodes which illustrate the providential pattern. (Dubs 1981:38)

Spacks (1959:57) speaks truly of a "repeated emphasis on the importance of free will and on Fate which is not chance", of the "necessity for free decision" which "is to become a central issue of the trilogy", of the implied structured universe, a "plan in the universe", an "ordering force in the universe", "one ordering power in the universe" (Spacks 1959:59). She combines this with the Valar and the One mentioned in the appendices and states – still valid: "So it is that the Fate which governs all here is not arbitrary. Indeed, as has been hinted already in relation to Bilbo's act of mercy, it is to some extent determined by individual acts of will." (Spacks 1959:59) Without being explicit, this is a clear reference to a theological understanding of the interaction between providence and free will. But Tolkien (Letters:201) states

> [I] purposely kept all allusions to the highest matters down to mere hints, perceptible only by the most attentive, or kept them under unexplained symbolic forms. So God and the 'angelic' gods, the Lords or Powers of the West, only peep through in such places as Gandalf's conversation with Frodo [...].

This hidden presence may be a reason for the success of *The Lord of the Rings*, since it does not force a theological understanding upon the reader but leaves the conclusions to his or her freedom. Regarding the significance of Boethius for medievalists, it is small wonder that Dubs explains this by referring to Boethius' concept of providence, fate and chance. It is important to note

> that Boethius presents a universe created and governed by a benevolent providence, a universe of

order and harmony in which everything – including fate and chance – has purpose, even if that purpose is beyond the perception of human understanding.
(Dubs 1981:37)

The main aspects of a theological understanding of the interaction of providence with free will as dependent upon each other (as in Boethius' view) are clearly present in the debate between Gandalf and Frodo in *The Shadow of the Past*. Gandalf emphasizes the providential pattern which, on the one hand, chooses individuals and puts them in situations in which they have to act,[11] but on the other hand depends on the free decisions of these chosen individuals. The individual has to be aware of his role in the larger pattern but is not forced to act according to this role. In this way, individual freedom challenges providence since the individual can deny or accept the appointed task. The view that each individual has a special role to play, is emphasized by Elrond's reaction to Frodo's decision to take the Ring: "I think that this task is appointed for you, Frodo; and that if you do not find a way, no one will." (LotR:264) This raises the question of what would have happened if Frodo had chosen not to take the Ring. Bullock (1985:29) thinks because of the importance of free will "someone else would have", which is possible if we regard Eru's power to integrate free decisions in his own plan. But this scene can be read also as expression of the theological view of grace as enabling the creature to accept the grace offered by God and thus supporting the free will thesis. Tolkien himself comments upon Frodo's failure as a hero in his drafts to Eileen Elgar (Letters:326):

---

[11] "But you have been chosen, and you must therefore use such strength and heart and wits as you have." (LotR:60) "I can put it no plainer than by saying that Bilbo was *meant* to find the Ring, and *not* by its maker. In which case you also were *meant* to have it. And that may be an encouraging thought." (LotR:54f) The chosenness may be encouraging since the notion of an ordering power may provide hope as long as this power is regarded as good.

> But grace is not infinite, and for the most part seems in the Divine economy limited to what is sufficient for the accomplishment of the task appointed to one instrument in a pattern of circumstances and other instruments.

This can be seen as valid for the entire plot of *The Lord of the Rings*. Tolkien expresses his belief of a continuous acting of Providence. Drury (1980:9) refers to the paradoxical coordination of affairs by a providential design while it does not force actions upon characters and sees a parallel to "the traditional Christian view of God at work through history".

Dickerson (2003:182f) refers to Elrond's welcoming of the Council where he says, each person present was called thither but not by him and interprets Elrond's phrase "by chance as it may seem" (LotR:236) as "a clear implication that it is not by chance at all, but by some greater intentional purpose that only seemed like chance." Elrond indicates the existence of an ordering power.

The importance of choices recurs throughout the work and they appear *ex eventu* as the right ones. In this way Aragorn's choice to follow Merry and Pippin, his choice to take the Paths of the Dead, the Ents' choice to attack Isengard, Faramir's choice to let Frodo and Samwise go, Samwise's choice to take the Ring, Merry's insistence of riding with the Rohirrim and many others are, in retrospect, all necessary to overcome Sauron. Thus they are interesting examples for the interaction of divine will and individual will in fulfilling the plan of the providential power. The different alternatives within the interaction of fate and free will (to accept one's fate) is expressed in Frodo and Gollum:

> Perhaps the ultimate refinement of Tolkien's concern with interactive fate and free will is embodied in these two, for one willingly accepts his fate while

> the other is fated to follow his will. [...] Frodo freely accepts what is destined to happen. [...] Gollum is destined to be driven by his own desires.
> (Flieger 2002:151)

In my understanding, 'destined' does not mean that this is inevitable but that this is the plan and role appointed by Providence for each individual. Even though Gollum does not accept his role, his desires combined with the mercy of Frodo and Sam can be used by Providence to destroy the Ring without denying their freedom.

Another aspect of providence are the many prophecies and visions in *The Lord of the Rings* and their impact on the plot. But even this does not deny free will, rather it is "somehow used by the manager to bring about the very events that were fated and foretold by prophecy." (Dickerson 2003:181) Dickerson combines this with Ilúvatar's power to use free individual choices for his own ends. Regarding the *Ainulindalë*, these prophecies may partly be derived from a knowledge of the Music – directly or indirectly.

Having stressed the existence of free will throughout *The Lord of the Rings* I should at least mention the one example in which free will is not present, Frodo's declaration: "But I do not choose now to do what I came to do. I will not do this deed. The Ring is mine!" (LotR:924) Flieger (2002:153f) states that Frodo believes he is acting freely but "his will has been perverted and his choice preempted", whereas Shippey (2000:140) regards the choice of words as accurate and indicating that Frodo's will is subdued, "Frodo does not choose; the choice is made for him". Like Spacks (1959:64), he refers to the statement that in the heart of the realm of Sauron "all other powers were here subdued." (LotR:924) The domination of other wills is the declared purpose of Sauron and the Ring is the means by which he wants to achieve it. But this is not a proof for a lack of free will in Middle-earth. Instead it expresses the experience of a situation in which a free decision is limited or no longer possible. In my opinion, Tolkien himself offered a valid interpretation: "Frodo had done what he could and spent himself completely (as an instrument of Providence) and had produced a situation in which the object of his quest could be achieved." (Letters:326) But it is not necessary that he himself achieves the object of his quest, since grace is not infinite and Tolkien himself was aware of a Divine economy of grace. In another draft he wrote that by a 'grace' the last betrayal of Gollum "was at a precise juncture when the final evil deed was the most beneficial thing any one cd. have done for Frodo!" (Letters:234). Flieger (2002:154) comments, regarding the freedom of Frodo and Gollum beyond the Music: "Fate and free will have come together to produce the inevitable, unpredictable, and necessary end." Hibbs (2003:170) expresses pointedly how the destruction of the Ring depends on earlier events: "Gollum is, as Gandalf had predicted, an unwitting instrument of divine providence, but he manages to serve this role only because Frodo had earlier recalled Gandalf's words and taken to heart his plea for mercy and patience."

Concerning Frodo, Dubs (1981:38) explains clearly the interaction: "Fate helped Frodo because he helped himself." The destruction of the Rings can be understood as an act of Providence by the means of Gollum without stating a direct intervention of Eru. This is in accordance with Tolkien's statement in a letter to Amy Ronald: "The Other Power then took over: the Writer of the Story (by which I do not mean myself)." (Letters:253)

Comparing *The Silmarillion* and *The Lord of the Rings*, one cannot deny that there are great differences in the presentation of the problem of free will and providence. But I hope to have shown that the patterns are the same, that is, that Providence exists in Middle-earth and that this does not deny but rather challenge the freedom of the individual. Providence is the will of Ilúvatar and he has the power to use the free decisions of the protagonists to his own ends without limiting their freedom. This appears often as paradoxical but accords with our own experience of free will and a providential pattern, 'luck' or 'chance'. Maybe one of the reasons for the great success of *The Lord of the Rings* is its authenticity and complexity regarding the concepts of chance, fate, providence, freedom of will, etc. Furthermore, Dickerson's observation (2003:171) is worth considering: "For part of the wonder of the Hobbits' existence in Middle-earth is precisely their anachronistic nature: the fact that we see regular people placed in heroic situations, situations that require heroic actions." A similar view is expressed by Shippey (1992:240) who sees in *The Lord of the Rings* a balance "between ancient and modern modes of presentation, and between ancient and modern theories of virtue." I would add that the hidden character of the highest matters also adds to the applicability of *The Lord of the Rings*.

FREEDOM AND PROVIDENCE AS ANTI-MODERN ELEMENTS?

Returning to our starting question we can ascertain that Tolkien provides a more or less traditional theological concept of the interaction of providence and free will. In this way, Tolkien's works explain the interdependence of freedom and providence and this does not contradict necessarily a modern conviction of freedom. Since the free will is not limited by Providence, but challenged by it, this does not necessarily result in a conflict with modern (a-theistic) concepts of freedom. A conflict with these arises out of the origin of freedom (and thereby out of the question of the proper use of freedom) for Tolkien declares the One God to be the creator and origin of freedom. Combined with this is the great significance of a providential pattern both in *The Silmarillion* and *The Lord of the Rings*. This and the emphasis on God's acting in history both by means of interventions and providence are indeed anti-modern elements in the sense that they express old and continuous theological convictions and stand against the modern questioning of these concepts.

But since these theological concepts are only implicitly present in *The Lord of the Rings*, the reader may be aware of them but he can explain them with other concepts. Even the explicit mentioning of Ilúvatar in *The Silmarillion* can be explained as due to the use of mythological language. Both texts, *The Lord of the Rings* more than *The Silmarillion*, can be classified as 'open texts' with a wide range of applicability and a strong ethical impact (which can be shared also by modern readers). By not denying paradoxical experiences their authenticity contributes to their success and significance.

Furthermore, with its strong emphasis on free will Tolkien's work contradicts naturalistic positions. If naturalists enjoy reading *The Lord of the Rings*, they should be aware that they are enjoying a book which contains with its strong emphasis on free will and freedom views that are – according to their own view – wrong. But since they are naturalists, they have to be convinced not to have an alternative to enjoying this book. But I prefer enjoying Tolkien's book because of its quality rather than because of merely biochemical processes.

Thomas Fornet-Ponse studied Catholic theology, philosophy, and ancient history in Bonn and Jerusalem. He is working as a research assistant at the seminar of Fundamental Theology at Bonn University. His research interests focus on philosophical and theological analyses of Tolkien and other (fantasy) authors, ecumenical problems, Jewish-Christian dialogue and 'classical' questions of Fundamental Theology. He is a committee member of the German Tolkien Society and is the conceptual coordinator of the Tolkien Seminars as well as *Hither Shore*. He has published several articles on theological and philosophical questions in the works of Tolkien and Pratchett.

Bibliography

Bullock, Richard P., 1985, 'The Importance of Free Will in *The Lord of the Rings*', in *Mythlore* 41, 1985, pp. 29, 56.

Caldecott, Stratford, 2003, *Secret Fire: The spiritual vision of J.R.R. Tolkien*, London: Darton, Longman and Todd.

Curry, Patrick, 1997, *Defending Middle-earth: Tolkien: Myth & Modernity*, London: HarperCollins.

Deuser, Hermann, 2003, 'Vorsehung I. Systematisch-theologisch', in *Theologische Realenzyklopädie* 35, 2003, pp. 302-323.

Dickerson, Matthew, 2003, *Following Gandalf: Epic Battles and Moral Victory in The Lord of the Rings*, Grand Rapids, MI: Brazos Press.

Drury, Roger, 1980, 'Providence at Elrond's Council', in *Mythlore* 25, 1980, pp. 8-9.

Dubs, Kathleen E., 1981, 'Providence, Fate, and Chance: Boethian Philosophy in *The Lord of the Rings*', in *Twentieth Century Literature* 27.1, 1981, pp. 34-42.

Flieger, Verlyn, 1997, *A Question of Time: J.R.R. Tolkien's Road too Faërie*, Kent: Kent State University Press.

---, 2002, *Splintered Light: Logos and Language in Tolkien's World*, Kent: Kent State University Press.

Fornet-Ponse, Thomas, 2005, "'In the webs of fate': Freiheit und Determination in der Ainulindalë und der Narn', in *Inklings* 23, 2005, pp. 153-179.

Geyer, Christian (ed.), 2004, *Hirnforschung und Willensfreiheit. Zur Deutung der neuesten Experimente*, Frankfurt a.M.: Suhrkamp.

Hibbs, Thomas, 2003, 'Providence and the Dramatic Unity of *The Lord of the Rings*', in Gregory Bassham and Eric Bronson (eds.), 2003, *The Lord of the Rings and Philosophy*, Chicago: Open Court, pp. 167-178.

Kilby, Clyde, 1976, *Tolkien and The Silmarillion*, Wheaton: Harold Shaw Publishers.

Link, Christian, 2005, 'Die Krise des Vorsehungsglaubens: Providenz jenseits von Fatalismus', in *Evangelische Theologie* 65, 2005, pp. 413-428.

Nida-Rümelin, Julian, 2005, *Über menschliche Freiheit*, Stuttgart: Reclam.

Pirson, Ron, 2004, 'Göttliches Eingreifen in Tolkiens Universum', in *Concilium (D)* 40, 2004, pp. 454-462.

Purtill, Richard, 2003, *J.R.R. Tolkien: Myth, Morality, and Religion*, (first edition 1984), San Francisco: Ignatius Press.

Ratzinger, Joseph, 2000, *Salz der Erde*, Augsburg: Bechtermünz.

Shippey, Tom, 1992, *The Road to Middle-earth*, (first edition 1982), London: HarperCollins.

---, 2001, *J.R.R. Tolkien: Author of the Century*, London: HarperCollins.

Singer, Wolf, 2004, 'Verschaltungen legen uns fest: Wir sollten aufhören, von Freiheit zu sprechen', in Christian Geyer (ed.), 2004, *Hirnforschung und Willensfreiheit. Zur Deutung der neuesten Experimente*, Frankfurt a.M.: Suhrkamp, pp. 30-65.

Spacks, Patricia Meyer, 1959, 'Power and Meaning in *The Lord of the Rings*', (first published 1959), in Neil D. Isaacs and Rose Zimbardo (eds.), 2004, *Understanding The Lord of the Rings: The Best of Tolkien Criticism*, Boston: Houghton Mifflin, pp. 52-67.

Tolkien, J.R.R., 1994, *Morgoth's Ring*, (edited by Christopher Tolkien, *History of Middle-earth* 10), London: HarperCollins.

---, 1995, *The Lord of the Rings*, (first edition 1954/55), London: HarperCollins.

---, 1996, *The Peoples of Middle-earth*, (edited by Christopher Tolkien, *History of Middle-earth* 12), London: HarperCollins.

---, 1997, 'Beowulf: The Monsters and the Critics', in Christopher Tolkien (ed.), 1997, *The Monsters and the Critics and other Essays*, (first edition 1983), London: HarperCollins, pp. 5-48.

---, 1998, 'Ósanwe-Kenta', in *Vinyar Tengwar* 39, 1998, pp. 21-34.

---, 1999, *The Silmarillion*, (edited by Christopher Tolkien, first edition 1977), London: HarperCollins.

---, 2000, *Unfinished Tales of Númenor and Middle-earth*, (edited by Christopher Tolkien, first edition 1980), London: HarperCollins.

---, 2001, 'On Fairy-Stories', in *Tree and Leaf*, London: HarperCollins, pp. 1-81.

---, 2002, *The Lays of Beleriand*, in *The History of Middle-earth. Part One. Vols. I-V*, (edited by Christopher Tolkien, first edition 2000), London: HarperCollins.

---, 2002, *The Letters of J.R.R. Tolkien*, (edited by Humphrey Carpenter and Christopher Tolkien, first edition 1981), Boston: Houghton Mifflin.

Urang, Gunnar, 1969, 'Tolkien's Fantasy: The Phenomenology of Hope', in Mark Hillegas (ed.), 1969, *Shadows of Imagination*, Carbondale: Southern Illinois University Press, pp. 97-110.

Weinreich, Frank, 2004, ''It was always open to one to reject': Zur Möglichkeit philosophischer Interpretationen Tolkiens fiktionaler Werke am Beispiel der Willensfreiheit', in *Hither Shore* 1, 2004, pp. 71-83.

Democracy in Middle-earth: J.R.R. Tolkien's *The Lord of the Rings* from a Socio-Political Perspective

ALEXANDER VAN DE BERGH

Abstract

The various peoples of Middle-earth differ not only in their languages, but also in their ways of living together as a nation or at least a community. It is not so much the microanalysis of individual cooperation, as in the Fellowship, but the (by critics lesser valued) governments that are of interest in this article. The possibilities range from the totalitarian dictatorship in Mordor to the human monarchies to the idealized self-control of the Hobbits. We assume that these forms of government are not arbitrarily placed by Tolkien; instead, they relate to the respective peoples and to the fictional world of Middle-earth, hence adding substance to the novel as a whole. We can further assume that the events of the early and middle 20th century, among them the rise of the European dictatorships, had their share in contributing to the novel as it is now. Yet this does not mean that each and every aspect of the fictional governments could be allegorically translated into patterns of reality. It will become clear that there is indeed a close relationship between the peoples and their respective governments; that they share strengths and weaknesses. Comparing the implicitly and explicitly judging commentaries of the forms of government, we will see that the narration does not actively support democracy as a whole, but instead focuses on each individual's own responsibility.

INTRODUCTION

Tolkien's ingenious cosmos Middle-earth is filled with a rich variety of peoples. They differ not only in their physiology and their languages, but also in the ways they organize themselves in living together. Much has been written about the microlevel of cooperation concerning individuals, namely the Fellowship of the Ring itself. The following analysis, however, focuses on the macrolevel of the politics and forms of government of the peoples of Middle-earth. By classifying and comparing, I will show that Tolkien has integrated several different forms of government and ways for a society to live together in his novel. We shall see whether there are implicit or explicit commentaries to these forms presented. How are these forms structured? What impact does the, at that time, threatening topic of fascism have on these? And what can we extrapolate about the importance of democracy?

In addition, I will examine the movie version by Peter Jackson, with the same questions in mind. Which of the previously extrapolated statements can be applied to the movie as well? Which cannot? Is there a different focus? How is this presented? What are the consequences hereof? This way, the novel and the movie can be compared successfully as two distinct versions because not every fault of the movie is also a fault of the novel.

ALTERNATIVE FORMS OF SOCIETY IN *THE LORD OF THE RINGS*

The various alternative forms of society which are presented in *The Lord of the Rings* are indeed worth closer examination, for they are an important part of the extremely detailed and sophisticated background of the novel. In his appreciation of this background, Auden (1987:45f.) says:

> By the time the reader has finished the trilogy, including the appendices to this last volume, he knows as much about Mr. Tolkien's Middle-earth, its landscape, its fauna and flora, its peoples, its languages, their history, their cultural habits, as, outside his special field, he knows about the actual world.

However, our knowledge about the non-fictional reality, which we can experience with all our senses at first hand, will always – without exception – be greater than our knowledge about a fictional world, regardless of how detailed this world may be described. In addition, the knowledge about different forms of politics and society presented in the world of *The Lord of the Rings* is indeed very small, compared with the vast amount of knowledge concerning its history, names, and especially languages. Petzold (2004:54) agrees with this:

> With the use of a chronicle-like narration (in *The Silmarillion*) and the recounting of tales of old (in *The Lord of the Rings*), the peoples receive a historical dimension und thus a certain individuality. But (except for the Hobbits) we do not know much about their political organization, their social structure and their way of life.[1]

And Stoddard (1992:7) adds correctly: "Law and government were not, to be sure, Tolkien's primary interest." But these fields have to be examined nonetheless, as well as and especially when Tolkien is concerned. Petzold (2004:68) advocates this as follows: "When the problem of power is concerned, and when the historical-political situation is emphasized in such a manner, the questions about the use of power in a just political system must not be neglected altogether."[2] Therefore we will examine these questions with regard to the just political systems as well as to the unjust ones. Because of their prominence in the novel

---

[1] All translations, unless explicitly stated otherwise, are by the author. The German original is given in the footnotes. "[D]ie Völker erhalten durch den Chronikstil (im *Silmarillion*) oder das Erzählen alter Überlieferungen (im *Herrn der Ringe*) eine historische Dimension und damit eine gewisse Individualität, doch über ihre politische Organisation, ihre Sozialstruktur und ihre Lebensweise erfahren wir – die Hobbits ausgenommen – recht wenig" (Petzold 2004:54).

[2] "Wenn es um das Problem der Macht geht, und wenn die historisch-politische Dimension so weit in den Vordergrund rückt, dann darf die Frage nach der Machtausübung in einem gerechten Staatswesen nicht so restlos unter den Tisch fallen" (Petzold 2004:68).

and the comparatively detailed description of their life, the Shire-hobbits will be analyzed more closely.

Tolkien's novel was received in a rather broadly defined sociocultural group, primarily Western Europe und the United States.[3] In these countries democracy was then (and is today even more so) the dominant form of government. But apart from the many different variations of democracy, there are plenty of other forms of government, some of which are to be found in the novel. After some short explanations of seemingly well-known (and some not so well-known) terms of state theory, with a focus on the different possible forms of government, I will analyze, compare and to a certain extent evaluate the various societies in *The Lord of the Rings*. One of the questions to bear in mind will be: In which way can these societies be understood as possible alternatives to those we find in the primary world, in reality?[4]

STRUCTURES AND FUNCTIONS OF FORMS OF GOVERNMENT

In the context of political science, a form of government is defined as certain "politics, polity and policy"[5] (Nohlen 1998:610), being the foundation to exert power within a society in order to guide and control it. In the history of mankind there have been many ways of exerting political power, differing in numerous aspects.[6]

The manifestations of these possibilities are the forms of government. They differ in the number, the power and the authorization of

---

[3] The problems of defining these groups and culture(s) are dealt with in more detail in the corresponding chapter in van de Bergh 2005.

[4] It must be noted that merely perceiving these societies as alternatives does not necessarily mean that Tolkien intended them to be alternatives.

[5] "Institutionen-Aufbau, Struktur und Handlungsmuster polit. Herrschaft" (Nohlen 1998:610).

[6] Aristotle emphasizes the necessity for people to live in a state, hence under a form of government, including laws to define their coexistence (cf. *Politica*, Aristotle 1966, Book 1, Chapter 2).

their leader(s), the (non-)separation of powers, and the impact the government has on each individual citizen. To prevent chaos and confusion among the citizens, every state establishes certain rules. Gray (1980:3) calls this structure bureaucracy, by which he does not mean a paralyzing abundance of restricting rules, but rather their mere existence: "Bureaucracy is a formal attempt to organize the actions of a group of individuals. It parcels out power and specifies tasks so that the greater goals of the group can be accomplished. Bureaucracy is defined by a hierarchy [...], and by a set of rules." Since political systems, of which bureaucracy is a necessary part, are primarily concerned with the direct and indirect use of power, there is always a significant danger of those in power abusing their position. Tolkien's *The Lord of the Rings* has the question of power and its use at its very core, so it is only logical to examine how power is being used; not only by individuals, but also on the level of societies. The focus will be on how the abuse of power is restrained, how its exertion is nonetheless accomplished, and on the role of the individual citizen, be it Man, Elf, or Hobbit.

SHIRE

Critics do not agree on what exactly the form of government in the Shire is and how the Hobbits' society is structured. Koravos (2001:32) negates any organized system: "There is no government, but the Hobbits are peaceful and lawful by nature." Though the latter part of this is correct for most Hobbits, there is more government and bureaucracy in the Shire than he recognizes. This can be shown with the character of the Mayor, described by Stoddard (1992:6): "[The Mayor is] acting not as a legislator consciously designing a wholly new law, but as a magistrate extending existing law to cover a new case, in the traditional manner of English common law." The Mayor is the official leader of the Shire, yet his functions are limited to representative actions rather than executive ones (cf. *Fellowship*, Tolkien 1994a:13). He is elected, but not essential for the thriving society of the Hobbits. His relationship to the other authorities of the Shire, the Thain of the Tooks and the Master of Buckland, is examined more closely by Curry (1997:50): "Similarly, of the three positions of authority in the Shire, two are hereditary and only one elected. But these officers' powers, and duties, are minimal. [...] [M]ost decisions are taken at the lowest possible level, closest to those who are most affected by them." Similarly, Stoddard (1992:7) describes the form of government in the Shire as a "blend of aristocracy and republicanism".

This is correct for most parts. The Thain and the Master are characters of the aristocracy, which is a "form of government ruled by an elite who is superior in descendancy, property, experience, education and more, by their own definition as well as by definition of others"[7] (Nohlen 1998:48). But Curry's analysis also implies an element of anarchy. There are several possible connotations for this term,[8] but since the Hobbits are indeed of a very lawful disposition ("usually they kept the laws of free will"; *Fellowship*, Tolkien 1994a:12), they do not need much control or even dominance in their society; hence the positive connotation of anarchy fits better.

Another possible way to regard the Shire's form of government is to compare it to the ward system of the early American colonies, and there are indeed several similarities, for example the basic democratic structure, self-organization and a coexistence with but little violence, as pointed out by Weinreich (2005:93). However, we need to add that this system lasted only for some hundred years before becoming the more

---

[7] "Staatsform, in der eine nach eigenem Zuspruch und fremder Zuschreibung im Hinblick auf Abstammung, Besitz, Erfahrung, Bildung, u.ä. hervorragende Elite die Herrschaft ausübt" (Nohlen 1998:48).

[8] "Positive connotation: order without dominance [...]. Negative connotation: lack of laws, chaos, disorder." (Nohlen 1998:33; "Positiv besetzt i.S. von herrschaftsfreier Ordnung [...]. I. S. von Gesetzlosigkeit, Chaos, Unordnung wird A[narchie] negativ besetzt verwandt.")

permanent presidential democracy it is today, while the Shire has maintained this system for over 1400 years with no signs of change at all. This consistency, or rather stagnation, in Middle-earth is possible only because there have been no major changes (no industrialization, technological advance, and/or urbanization), and, of course, because of an astonishing lack of violence combined with an inherent lawful disposition of the Hobbits. They simply do not need any form of government more organized than the one they have. Weinreich (2005:93) hints at this saying that life in the Shire "is idyllic in an almost utopian way".[9]

This lawful disposition shows itself also in the numerous (although seemingly more ritualized) formalities obviously important to Hobbits: "[Bilbo's will] was [...] very clear and correct (according to the legal customs of hobbits, which demand among other things seven signatures of witnesses in red ink)" (*Fellowship*, Tolkien 1994a:51). These formalities are founded on law as well as on politeness and form, as shown by Sam in Ithilien, pondering "the courtesies, of which, as any hobbit would, he thoroughly approved. Indeed in the Shire such a matter would have required a great many words and bows." (*Two Towers*, Tolkien 1994b:321) But one cannot conclude from this that writing and reading in general are totally common for Hobbits. Stoddard (1992:4) speaks erroneously of a "widespread literacy of hobbits" and adds: "a large part of [the Shire's] populace could read and write" (Stoddard 1992:6). But Tolkien's text states explicitly otherwise: "All hobbits, of course, can cook, for they begin to learn the art before their letters (which many never reach)" (*Two Towers*, Tolkien 1994b:321).

However, at least a certain part of the Hobbits do master the letters and thus contribute to the Shire's economic system. De Camp (1976:225) may negate the existence of such a system: "[E]conomics has never come to Hobbit-land", but exports going on for years and

---

[9] "(Ein Leben, das] in nahezu utopischer Weise idyllisch ist" (Weinreich 2005:93).

several internal trade relations prove otherwise and are indeed an important factor in discussing matters of power.[10] However, it would be a little too bold to perceive this basic economic system as "evidence of a society well on the way to modernity" (Stoddard 1992:6). For it is for their general distrust of technology and the lack of any kind of class struggle that the Hobbits will probably never reach modernity as we know it – which, according to Tolkien's views on industrialism, may be a good thing for them.

In their everyday interaction with each other the Hobbits appear quite idealized by Tolkien. Minor affairs like the Baggins' quarrel with the Sackville-Baggins family or Ted Sandyman hanging around lazily are indeed the worst things that may occur in the peaceful land. Even the Shirriffs do not have much to do: "[T]hey were in practice rather haywards than policemen, more concerned with the strayings of beasts than of people. There were in all the Shire only twelve of them, three in each farthing, for Inside Work" (*Fellowship*, Tolkien 1994a:13).

Crimes of violence among Hobbits are more than unlikely, and fatal crimes are almost unknown. Such a positive society of pacifist individuals needs but few controlling elements in form of a government. Yet they risk being paralyzed by violence from 'outside' because they have never experienced violence from 'inside', thus they are unable to handle it: "Shirefolk have been so comfortable so long they don't know what to do" (*Return*, Tolkien 1994c:345).

Lacking this experience it is impossible for the Hobbits to show the necessary determination against aggression from outside the Shire. Ironically, in some Hobbits the invasion strengthens their potential of negative attributes: "[The Chief] wouldn't hear naught, if some of you weren't sneaks" (*Return*, Tolkien 1994c:337) This collaboration makes

---

[10] For more information about the will to power and its relationship with economical and financial matters, for example Lotho, see the corresponding chapter in van de Bergh 2005.

it much easier for the ruffians to take control. Their massive presence in the Shire is due to the doings of a Hobbit. It was Lotho Sackville-Baggins, who, driven by the greed for power, brought them into the Shire in the first place, which then results in the restructuring of the Shire's society. Plank (1975:109f.) explains this process: "The essential political innovation is the rise of an unprecedented police force, headed by the Chief Shirriff. The character of government is totally altered."

But those now in command do not have all tools necessary to sustain an effective control over the Shire's populace: "A problem arises [for the ruffians] that apparently was unknown in the Shire before: What should be done to a citizen who 'talks back' to the government? The solution is simple: He is imprisoned and often beaten" (Plank 1975:110). The question implied here can also be asked the other way round: What should be done to a government which talks back to the citizens? Even facing the danger, the Hobbits lack unity; it is not before Merry, Pippin, Sam and Frodo (who can hardly count as typical Shire-hobbits anymore) arrive that the masses are rallied.

The conditions of the invasion by the ruffians may remind a little of communism, especially concerning the policy of the "'gatherers' and 'sharers'"(*Return*, Tolkien 1994c:336), but Plank (1975:111) states clearly: "Communism is based on a theory of class struggle, while fascism preaches the unity of the people, which means in practice that everybody is treated equally badly, and this is certainly true in the Shire." This depiction of fascism can be seen as a form of critique against those who wish to establish such a regime or at least do not oppose those who would. Plank (1975:113) sums it up:

> Tolkien presents reasons why there was no effective resistance to fascism in the Shire [...]. One reason is cowardice: as one of the guardsmen utters some rather mild gripes, he is shut up by his comrades: 'You know talk o'that sort isn't allowed. The Chief will hear of

> it, and we'll all be in trouble.' Another reason is lack of solidarity: 'I've been itching for trouble all this year,' says my favorite witness, Farmer Cotton, but folks wouldn't help.' [...] The third reason is the most interesting and the most melancholy: 'I am sorry Mr. Merry, but we have Orders.' We heard something like this in the courtroom in Nuremberg. Tolkien [...] describes the overthrow of a tyrannical government as a quick and easy job. This seems surprising, but it can be explained [...] by the mildness of his description. [...] I must add that any earthly fascist regime has been much worse than what Tolkien shows.

This final point is one of the reasons why the Shire in particular and the novel in general should not be understood as a direct allegory (an approach which Tolkien has always refused). But the extrapolated parallels and the implicit criticism can motivate the alert reader to oppose such unwanted forms of government in time and with determination in order to preserve more positive conditions – or at least restore them, like they eventually do in the Shire.

After restoring the status of old in the Shire, there is no hint as to what happens to those who actively supported Lotho's and Saruman's plans, those who are described by Merry as "one or two rascals, and a few fools that want to be important" (*Return*, Tolkien 1994c:345).

Realization of their errors, regrets, reparations or legal actions are not mentioned at all. Therefore we may suspect that the recovered society of the Hobbits is able to reintegrate those individuals by means of the common good of their cause. A self-reflecting analysis of the possible reasons for them to do as they had done and also any form of punishment do not seem to be necessary. Here the idealization of the Hobbits as a society capable of healing itself miraculously becomes clear once again. Focused merely on the results, Finch (1994:112) states:

"[T]he Shire's strange form of government evidently worked." But regarding the aspect of idealization, this happy, content society of the Hobbits, in no need of any form of control cannot be seen as a realistic permanent alternative to forms of government in the primary world. The Hobbits are too peaceful, too modest and as individuals simply too good for humans to adapt their way of life.

LOTHLÓRIEN

Though the Elves do not have as peaceful a history as the Hobbits, Lothlórien is still a land of peace. The borders are guarded tightly: "We allow no strangers to spy out the secrets of the Naith. [...] I shall here blindfold the eyes of Gimli the Dwarf. The others may walk free for a while, until we come nearer to our dwellings" (*Fellowship*, Tolkien 1994a:455), yet inside the borders there are no controlling or restraining forces of government, except for Galadriel und Celeborn. Koravos (2001:32) states: "The Elven societies are also simple, but they do have some kind of authority, though not absolute." But we are not told where exactly this power has its limits, so it cannot be fully confirmed that it is indeed non-absolute. There is no separation of powers within the society, no organized police and no explicit law system. Thus the Elves appear even more idealized than the Hobbits; for the latter know at least their Shirriffs and some form of law, even though it is rather a ritualized convention among them. But nothing of this is to be found in Lothlórien, it simply does not seem to be necessary.

However, the Elves are a species of their own kind, and especially their longevity of several hundred and thousand years makes it difficult to establish a direct comparison to the human forms of government in *The Lord of the Rings*. Weinreich (2005:91) puts it this way: "It is not only the non-human or even super-human characteristics that Tolkien emphasizes with the Elves [...], but also their immortality (which cannot be compared to the human situation) which would lead to totally different social problems and solutions if we were to seriously imagine the political constitution of a society of immortals."[11] Therefore it is necessary to focus on the human forms of government in Middle-earth, which are different in many aspects.

ROHAN

The human realm of Rohan, ruled by a king, maintains a status of 'splendid isolation' at the beginning of the novel's events: "We do not serve the Power of the Black Land far away, but neither are we yet at open war with him; [...] we desire only to be free, and to live as we have lived, keeping our own, and serving no foreign lord, good or evil" (*Two Towers*, Tolkien 1994b:31). Yet this policy is quickly abandoned in favour of the old alliance with Gondor.

A monarchy like the one of Rohan turns out to be quite vulnerable. King Théoden can hardly resist the sinister counsels and whisperings of Wormtongue and finally falls into complete lethargy. His people do so as well, for they are not able to act against their king's will. Only Gandalf can free Théoden from this apathy, a state which would have been the king's responsibility to realize and reject in the first place. With his awakening his people come to life as well. Once he is restored to his former self, Théoden acts like a competent and respected, even beloved leader of his people. That is the big difference between him and Denethor, an opposition classified for example by Chance (2001:100):

> The leadership styles of tyrannical Denethor, Steward
> to the King of Gondor, and Théoden the King of Ro-

---

[11] "Dabei ist nicht nur auf den nicht- oder gar übermenschlichen Charakter hinzuweisen, den [...] Tolkien selbst den Elben zuweist [...]. Auch ist schon die Unsterblichkeit der Elben eine der menschlichen Lebenssituation unvergleichbare Eigenschaft, die, wenn man ernsthaft über die politische Verfassung einer Gesellschaft von Unsterblichen nachdenken wollte, zu völlig anderen sozialen Problemstellungen und dementsprechenden Lösungen führen müsste" (Weinreich 2005:91).

> han are complementary. [...] The tyrant commands his followers by edict, rule, and law; the true leader commands through respect and love, like a benign father to a son. Merry thus appropriately cries to Théoden, 'As a father you shall be to me' [...], while Pippin, like the ignored and unloved son Faramir, suffers from Denethor's selfish preference for his lost dead son.

It is only logical then that the people of Rohan show so much affection towards their king: "It is a joy to us to see you return into your own." (*Two Towers*, Tolkien 1994b:450) Denethor cannot and does not expect such a behavior of his people.

GONDOR

Since its foundation by Númenorians in the Second Age,[12] Gondor had been a monarchy led by a king. When the line of kings was broken, the stewards ruled instead, until the rightful king's heir shall return. Although Denethor, arrogant, hungry for power and acting against his duties, tries to prevent this, it happens at the end of the Ring War. Yet Denethor still is a leader with important functions for town and people. A well structured control[13] is indeed necessary for a society to function, as Gray (1980:4) proves with the example of Minas Tirith:

> Minas Tirith's gate is thrown down largely because the defenders are not bureaucratized. When a crisis separates them from their traditional leaders, the people of Minas Tirith don't know what to do or who to obey. When the Lord of the Nazgûl is destroyed the next official in the bureaucratic chain of com-

---

[12] "3320 [Second Age]: Foundations of the Realms in Exile: Arnor and Gondor" (*Return*, Tolkien 1994c:450).

[13] Which is Gray's understanding of 'bureaucratization'; see above.

mand, one Gothmog, takes control of the enemy forces and the battle goes on. But when Denethor lays down his traditional authority and his only surviving heir, Faramir, cannot succeed him, the city is left without adequate leadership.

Of course, this form of government must not lead to the dead end of irrational leadership, as in Denethor's case, or the limitation of the individual's freedom, as in the case of Mordor. Heeding these warnings, the new king Aragorn, whose decisions up to that point are no less than perfect, rules Gondor and Arnor, which means an extremely just and wise rulership can be expected (at least for those inside the lands he rules).

Yet the king of this Reunited Kingdom still is a ruler who fits the historical definition of the absolutistic monarchy, as Weinreich (2005:97) correctly states: "It can be said that Gondor and its predecessors were unconstricted absolutistic monarchies, juristically and practically."[14] More precisely, it is a form of government "in which the ruler claims to wield all power by himself alone, without being restrained by parliament or comparable institutions"[15] (Nohlen 1998:20). Stanton (2002:125) sees no problems with that: Aragorn "will be king in the highest sense of the word, not just head man, or arbitrary authority, but an epitome of his people, a distillation of his people's, Men's best qualities." Gray as well legitimizes the concentration of undivided power in one person, provided it is used for a good cause. He (1980:4f.) talks about "the fourth [sic!] Age, an age which must put together the fragmented pieces of Middle-earth, will be [...] a time of bureaucracy used for good purposes. Aragorn is charged with the bureaucratization of

---

[14] "Man kann festhalten, dass Gondor und seine Vorläufer juristisch wie praktisch uneingeschränkt absolutistische Monarchien waren" (Weinreich 2005:97).

[15] "[I]n welcher der Herrscher beansprucht, ungeteilte und nicht durch Mitwirkung ständisch-parlamentarischer Körperschaften beschränkte Staatsgewalt aus eigenem Willen [...] auszuüben" (Nohlen 1998:20).

Middle Earth." Petzold (2004:69), however, is much more critical in describing Aragorn:

> In Aragorn, the wishful thinking of this authoritarian 'theory' of state becomes clear. With him Tolkien has created the idealized figure of a most noble, just and legitimate leader for whom the adjective 'kitschy' is still a flattery.[16]

The dominant power of the state is wielded by one person alone. Luckily, for the peoples of Middle-earth, this person happens to be an idealized image of moral perfection. But for the primary world, this form of government is definitely not to be desired. In seeing this ambivalence, Petzold (2004:70f.) analyzes its roots:

> The concept of Aragorn is wishful thinking, just like the myths of Artus, Charlemagne and Frederik Barbarossa. It has been born from the dissatisfaction with political reality. It is especially attractive for ignoring all the weary intellectual pondering of political reality.[17]

For this political reality, which – according to Petzold – is largely ignored in *The Lord of the Rings,* presents several obstacles and difficulties for Aragorn's heirs and their contemporaries.

The form of government described holds a high degree of potential for abuse, since it focuses almost as much power on one person as

---

[16] "Der Wunschtraumcharakter dieser auf dem Autoritätsprinzip gründenden Staats-'theorie' wird besonders deutlich in der Gestalt Aragorns. Mit ihm hat Tolkien ein Idealbild des edlen, rechtmäßigen und gerechten Herrschers gezeichnet, das mit dem Adjektiv 'kitschig' noch wohlwollend umschrieben ist" (Petzold 2004:69).

[17] "Wie der Mythos Artus', Karls [des Großen] und Barbarossas ist auch der Aragorns ein Wunschtraum, der aus dem Ungenügen an der politischen Realität erwachsen ist. Seine Attraktivität liegt nicht zuletzt in dem Umstand, dass er die mühsame intellektuelle Auseinandersetzung mit der politischen Realität erspart" (Petzold 2004:70f.).

would have been gained by usage of the One Ring. Not to succumb to this amount of power is a challenging task, even for a firm and noble personality like Aragorn.

In addition, the fact that Aragorn is descended from the Númenorians does not give any reason to hope that his heirs, who will inherit his power after his death, will inherit his wisdom as well and use the power as wisely as he did. On the contrary: Taking a look at the history of Númenor one is inclined to fear history repeating itself. For back in the history of Tolkien's world, the Númenorians were so corrupted by the amount of power they wielded that they longed for life eternal and thus were punished by the devastation of their whole continent.[18]

For Tolkien the source of a given power is very important: The One Ring as an 'evil' source can only lead to its power being used for subjugation and destruction, regardless of the character of the person using it. But the hard-earned, legitimate power of the king as a 'good' source makes it possible for Aragorn to use the same amount of power to good ends. Obviously, the danger of the potential corruption of power, which is described and narrated very carefully and convincingly throughout the whole novel, loses a fair amount of forcefulness by this almost naïve depiction of Aragorn's idealized personality.[19]

---

[18] The Númenorian history, in particular their fall and their punishment, is summarized in the appendix of the third volume of *The Lord of the Rings* (*Return*, Tolkien 1994:383ff.).

[19] This conclusion is valid if restricted to the narrative covered by the text of The Lord of the Rings itself, which I have done here due to the limited space of an article such as this one. Regarding this matter on a wider scale, it must be added that in describing the history of Númenor and Gondor/Arnor (in the pre-Aragorn era), Tolkien does emphasize a warning concerning absolutistic monarchies, for these realms are worn down by corruption, pride and fatal stubbornness of their respective leaders. Weinreich (2005:98ff.) gives a thorough overview of these topics. In addition, this bears resemblance to Aristotle's criticism of the Platonian plea for strong leaders (cf. *Politica*, Aristotle 1966, Book 3, Chapters 14-17).

MORDOR

Forceful indeed is Tolkien's use of Mordor as a negative example of a form of government. At the time of the Ring War, the Dark Lord Sauron has been ruling in Mordor for about 70 years,[20] yet the land itself had been under his control for a much longer period. Neglecting the intervals of his unintended absence from this land, there is no hint of any other form of government there than open tyranny. Furthermore countries east and south of Mordor have to pay tribute to Sauron, his armies plunder and rob whatever they can, and his power is based on elements like fear, torture ("it is beyond all doubt that he [Gollum] went to Mordor and there all that he knew was forced from him"; *Fellowship*, Tolkien 1994a:334) and slavery in the "great slave-worked fields [...] by the dark sad waters of Lake Nurnen" (*Return*, Tolkien 1994c:236). This serves as the depiction of a thoroughly evil land, as Curry states. For him, Mordor is "an utterly authoritarian state, with a slave-based economy featuring industrialized agriculture and intensive industrialism" (Curry 1997:52).

The earth of the land has been tortured and broken under Sauron's rule, especially in Mordor itself, for there "all seemed ruinous and dead, a desert burned and choked" (*Return*, Tolkien 1994c:235). This destructive influence even extends beyond its borders:

> Even to the Mere of Dead Faces some haggard phantom of green spring would come; but here neither spring nor summer would ever come again. Here nothing lived, not even the leprous growths that feed on rottenness. The gasping pools were choked with ash and crawling muds, sickly white and grey, as if the mountains had vomited the filth of their entrails upon

---

[20] "2951 [Third Age]: Sauron declares himself openly and gathers power in Mordor" (*Return*, Tolkien 1994c:458). The events in the novel begin in 3018.

> the lands about. High mounds of crushed and powdered rock, great cones of earth fire-blasted and poison-stained, stood like an obscene graveyard in endless rows, slowly revealed in the reluctant light. They had come to the desolation that lay before Mordor; the lasting monument to the dark labour of its slaves that should endure when all their purposes were made void; a land defiled, diseased beyond all healing – unless the Great Sea should enter in and wash it with oblivion.
> (*Two Towers*, Tolkien 1994b:293)

Curry (1997:55) analyzes the dialogic dependency of the geographic landscape and the political system: "Mordor's landscape is one of industrial desolation, polluted beyond renewal; and [...] such desecration is inseparable from its autocratic, unaccountable and unrestrained exercise of political power." Then again, we must add that the last three adjectives named by Curry do also apply to King Aragorn in full extent, who, like Sauron, is also accountable to no one. But in contrast to Mordor, the people ruled by Aragorn are free as individuals. The narrator emphasizes that Sauron does not rule his people, but rather commands his slaves: "[Sauron] had few servants but many slaves of fear" (*Return*, Tolkien 1994c:205). Hence his need for a high degree of efficiency, as Gray (1980:3) explains:

> Sauron is very well organized – he has to be! Consider the nature of the individuals on whom he must rely: the orc is treacherous, cruel, greedy, foul-tempered, destructive and easily frightened. Trolls are worse. The men in Sauron's service are surly, cowardly and mean. Who could work with a crew like that? Only a very good administrator.

But even here there still is confusion about cause and effect: Does it take a brutal form of government to control the savage orcs, or are the orcs savage because they live under such a brutal rule? Though their reckless disposition is made quite clear indeed,[21] the ambivalence remains because there is no single orc in a free form of government presented to the reader, resulting in an inability to compare. It is, however, a vicious circle of 'evil' individuals and an 'evil' form of government which, on closer inspection, shows up in *The Lord of the Rings*. By these means it is stated that such a form of government forbids a peaceful coexistence of individuals.

But what exactly is the form of government depicted here? It seems to be a monarchy, as is the case in Gondor, a "form of state in which [...] one single, specifically legitimated person wields the highest power of state permanently on his or her own"[22] (Nohlen 1998:399). But Mordor is more than that; it is – and here is the difference to Gondor – a totalitarian state, relying on "an extensive ideology [of battle and war] enveloping all aspects of everyday life"[23] (Nohlen 1998:647f.), with a particular focus on a certain aspect of fascism, namely the "idolization of modern technology and technological advance"[24] (Nohlen 1998:176f.).

These are important differences between the countries of Gondor and Mordor, which, apart from these differences, are rather similar in their structures and the absoluteness of power wielded by the respective leaders. Because of these parallels Gondor runs the risk of becoming much more like Mordor, especially after the most noble king Aragorn dies. It is a warning which becomes clear only at a closer look but

---

[21] For further information concerning the depiction of the orcs and the topic of implicit racism see also the corresponding chapter in van de Bergh 2005.

[22] "Staatsform, in der [...] eine einzige, spezifisch legitimierte Person eigenständig und auf Dauer die höchste Staatsgewalt ausübt" (Nohlen 1998:399).

[23] "[E]ine umfassende, alle Lebensbereiche vereinnahmende Ideologie" (Nohlen 1998: 647f.).

[24] "Vergötzung des modernen technologischen Fortschritts" (Nohlen 1998:176f.).

nevertheless loses nothing of its impact – and which might be of even greater importance today.[25]

(UN?)DEMOCRATIC TENDENCIES

It has become clear that the contrast Gondor – Mordor is no binary opposition of complementary forms of government. The contrast is merely expressed in the different use of similar power, emphasized by the likeliness of the respective structures.[26] The absolute power in Gondor thus cannot claim moral superiority over the absolute power in Mordor; only the ruling individual could do so. Weinreich (2005:99) emphasizes this point: "The political quality of Númenor and of Gondor/Arnor [and of Mordor – remark by author] is directly related to the moral quality of their queens and kings."[27] Petzold (2004:68) strengthens this point on a different level by comparing the rulers Théoden and Denethor:

> Both negative examples, Théoden influenced by Wormtongue and Denethor's madness, emphasize the decisive importance of the ruling person: Woe to the land whose king does not have the right qualities to lead! The critical modern reader will sure enough rather discover the weaknesses of the

---

[25] Examples for similar patterns in the primary world and thus for a concrete 'applicability' of the extrapolated warning are the massive inhibition of civil rights by means of the 'Patriot Act' of the United States in 2001 and 2003 and the negation of civil or even human rights to 'enemy combatants' partly tolerated by the international community. For more information and statements on these topics see the American Civil Liberties Union: http://www.aclu.org

[26] Considering Aristotle, there is but little difference between Gondor and Mordor, since both monarchies are not constitutional (cf. *Politica*, Aristotle 1966, Book 3, Chapter 14).

[27] "Die politische Qualität sowohl von Númenor als auch von Gondor/Arnor [und von Mordor – Anm. d. Autors] hängt direkt von der moralischen Qualität seiner Königinnen und Könige ab" (Weinreich 2005:99).

> system. But surely Tolkien did not intend to show these weaknesses; no positive alternatives come to the fore. Even on the good side there is always the principle of authority[.][28]

Some of these weaknesses may indeed be extrapolated by a close reading of the text, especially concerning the dictatorial system of Mordor. But it is true that this is not the primary or most important aspect. The principle of authority does dominate the novel, but it is by no means absolute and without alternative. Petzold (2004:69) goes too far by stating:

> Insubordination occurs only on the evil side; with the Orcs for example it is totally common. But when it appears on the good side, e.g. when Denethor questions Gandalf's moral authority, then it is always a reliable indicator for an evil influence[.][29] (Petzold 2004:69)

Disobedience does occur on the good side as well; it is even depicted as necessary. Éowyn, Merry and Pippin, each in his or her own way, all disobey clearly stated orders, which is definitely not due to an evil influence, but instead leads to eventual victory for the good side by active and sensible use of their own ability to decide for themselves (cf. Chance

---

[28] "Die beiden negativen Beispiele, Théoden unter dem Einfluß Schlangenzunges und der Wahnsinn Denethors, unterstreichen die entscheidende Bedeutung des Herrschers: Wehe dem Land, dessen König nicht über die rechten Führungsqualitäten verfügt! Dem kritischen modernen Leser zeigen sie freilich eher die Schwächen des Systems. Doch auf die Aufdeckung dieser Schwächen kam es Tolkien ganz gewiß nicht an; positive Alternativen geraten gar nicht erst ins Blickfeld. Auch auf der Seite der Guten herrscht durchgängig das Autoritätsprinzip" (Petzold 2004:68).

[29] "Insubordination kommt daher nur auf der Gegenseite vor; bei den Orks z.B. ist dergleichen an der Tagesordnung. Tritt sie aber auf der Seite der Guten in Erscheinung, etwa wenn Denethor den moralischen Führungsanspruch Gandalfs anzweifelt (vgl. HR III, Kap. 7), dann ist das mit Sicherheit ein Zeichen für den Einfluß des Bösen" (Petzold 2004:69).

2001:101f.). And when the Hobbits return to the Shire, they ignore any rules and orders established and issued by the ruling regime (cf. *Return*, Tolkien 1994c:335ff.). Insubordination, therefore, is not necessarily a sign of evil, but instead a critical reaction to orders which are in conflict with one's own values. The focus here is clear: Tolkien emphasizes the responsibility of the individual – but this in itself is not yet a plea for democracy.

Both the good kingdom of Gondor/Arnor and the loose, self-regulating near-anarchy of the Hobbits lack a definite democratic legitimation to keep the balance between the people and the state. This is also not covered by the rhetoric question "'Shall he be king and enter into the City and dwell there?' [spoke Faramir.] And all the host and all the people cried *yea* with one voice." (*Return*, Tolkien 1994c:295) for several reasons. Surely, not the complete population of Gondor is present on this occasion (many had been evacuated before the war), and this question does not serve to found a solid basis of legitimization according to the definition of democracy. In this form of government "the power comes from the people and is exerted by the people"[30] (Nohlen 1998:112). This is clearly not the case when it comes to a king who rules absolutely and cannot be elected out of office.

Thus it becomes clear that democratic elements (apart from their minor occurrence in the Shire) are not implemented in the great realms of man, but only to be found in traces, for example in Rivendell, where the council of Elrond serves as "a model for democracy" (Chance 2001:48) – at least concerning the right of free speech and the fact that the people gathered there are representatives of their respective people.

---

[30] "[G]eht die Herrschaft aus dem Volk hervor und wird durch das Volk selbst [...] ausgeübt" (Nohlen 1998:112). This is directly opposed to a descending rulership where a leader rules because it is the will of God/the Gods. For further analysis of ascending and descending rulership with a focus on Middle-Earth, where the Valar have actively chosen Elros and his heirs (which includes Aragorn) to rule see Weinreich (2005:96f.).

In addition, there are the Ents, of whom Finch (1994:13) says wrongly: "[S]ome form of anarchy appears to be the order of the day." When they meet and discuss, we can see that they, according to Petzold (2004:68), live in fact "in a direct, but still ridiculously clumsy democracy".[31] In Tolkien's novel, democracy may indeed not be depicted as an efficient form of government that is to be desired.[32] But neither does he support fascist(ic) ideologies, regardless of all other aspects, as Curry (1997:49) states: "Tolkien was neither liberal nor socialist, nor even necessarily democrat; but neither is there even a whiff of 'blood and soil' fascism [in his work]."

A lack of balance between the people and the state described in several forms of government results from a lack of democratic legitimization and leads to the inability of the population to oppose the state even if necessary. An example can be found in the case of Minas Tirith ruled by Denethor, who is becoming engulfed in madness (*Return*, Tolkien 1994c:110f.). On the other side, it leads to the inability of the state to oppose the ruffians in a just and correct manner, as happens in the Shire:

> Old Will the Mayor went off for Bag End to protest, but he never got there. Ruffians laid hands on him and took and locked him up in a hole in Michel Delving, and there he is now. And after that [...] there wasn't no more Mayor, and Pimple called himself Chief Shirriff, or just Chief, and did as he liked; and if anyone got 'uppish' as they called it they followed Will. (*Return*, Tolkien 1994c:353)

---

[31] "[Ents leben] in einer direkten, aber auch lächerlich umständlichen Demokratie" (Petzold 2004:68).

[32] Though his depiction of the Shire is in several aspects similar to Aristotle's observation: "[T]he many are more uncorruptible than the few" (*Politica*, Aristotle 1966, Book 3, Chapter 15).

In both cases it has to be individuals who overcome the inability to oppose by ignoring and/or defying the rules in order to restore a just status. In case of emergency and catastrophe, neither of the depicted forms of government is able to maintain the necessary control by means of balance between people and state.

This fact is helpful and indeed almost necessary for the plot. A scouring of the Shire by means of formal protest and lengthy lawsuits would create significantly less suspense than a just uprising of the oppressed masses. The impressive, almost pathetic crowning of Aragorn to be a king for lifetime as a reward for all his toils and troubles might have been replaced by introduction of universal suffrage and the creation of a Parliament of Gondor, leading to a limited power for a limited time for Aragorn – but at the price of totally stripping this part of the epic of its (implied) heroic greatness.

Having analysed the structure and the resulting priorities of the novel, we can agree with Petzold (2004:71): "Tolkien's priority is not so much a critical discussion of political systems, but the question of how an individual should act in a world filled with conflicts."[33] Emphasizing individual responsibility, combined with peaceful cooperation, is an essential democratic value. But according to Tolkien, even this should not be forced upon the reader. Keeping this in mind, Shippey answers the question raised by Petzold concerning the behaviour of the individual and thus confirms the points stated earlier in this essay:

> The moral, obviously, is that one should never give up hope (like Denethor), nor on the other hand sit back and wait for things to change (like too many of the inhabitants of the Shire). But as Tolkien says, 'applicability [...] resides in the freedom of the

---

[33] "[W]ichtiger als die Auseinandersetzung mit politischen Systemen ist für Tolkien die Frage, wie sich der einzelne Bürger in einer Welt voller Konflikte verhalten soll" (Petzold 2004:71).

reader', and should only be suggested or provoked by the author. (Shippey 2001:174)

It might be a little restrictive to talk about one single moral which can doubtlessly be defined in the novel, for the potential impact of this novel is too great and the spectrum of difficult topics handled here is too broad, so that it is impossible to extract a simple 'message' in one sentence. But it is this very complexity of the book that provides the most interesting challenge for the reader – and for the viewer as well.

FORMS OF STATE AND GOVERNMENT IN PETER JACKSON'S MOVIE VERSION

Any viewer of Jackson's movie version of *The Lord of the Rings* is being confronted with the topics concerning forms of government already debated, though these aspects have been drastically reduced, favoring a shorter plot and a massively increased importance of battles.[34] For this reason we will examine the movie not as extensively as the novel, yet the aim is still to find out which aspects of alternative societies have been implemented in, left out of or have received a different meaning in the movie. It is to be expected that besides the shortenings (the necessity of which is debatable) Jackson was able to implement new elements and additional perspectives in his work.

Boromir's reaction in Rivendell when he learns about Aragorns heritage and right of the king is an example of a new yet fitting addition compared to the novel: "Gondor has no king. Gondor needs no king!" (*Fellowship*, Jackson 2001:23).[35] With these words, which are not to be found in this explicit form in the novel, yet that are nevertheless fitting, Jackson links the son to his father. For Denethor does oppose the return

---

[34] For further information on the topic of narrated violence see also the corresponding chapter in van de Bergh 2005.
[35] Whenever the movies are mentioned in the text, the number refers to the chapter on the DVD in question.

of the king to such a degree that he is acting against his duties as steward: "The rule of Gondor is mine, and no other's!" (*Return*, Jackson 2003:9). But in contrast to his father, Boromir does realize his errors on the brink of death and accepts Aragorn's claim, which happens in the movie even more pronounced (and pathetic) than in the novel: "I would have followed you. My brother, ... my captain, ... my king" (*Fellowship*, Jackson 2001:38). These words are very important for Aragorn; however, in the rest of the movie the power of words emphasized in the novel is extremely diminished in favor of battle.

The power of the spoken word (which is essential for Tolkien as a philologist) becomes especially clear in the novel when Gandalf offers Théoden honest criticism, true information and supporting hope, after which they leave the dark building to go outside, where sunlight and the fresh wind, the powers of nature, support the healing process (*Two Towers*, Tolkien 1994b:140ff.). But Jackson cancels this convalescence and replaces it with a quick and aggressive exorcism by Gandalf, full of unnecessary special effects (*Two Towers*, Jackson 2002:16). The difficult and complex situation of Théoden appears in a greatly simplified manner, and aggressive sorcery becomes more important than the subtle magic of words and nature.

Gandalf's lack of self-control in Jackson's movie version becomes even more obvious when confronting Denethor. In the novel, Denethor's mad orders[36] have little effect, because Gandalf takes improvised control by means of his natural authority, and is in body and spirit closer to the fighting men than Denethor in the Halls of the Dead. But when Jackson's Denethor gives the order to flee, Gandalf brutally knocks down the legal leader of Minas Tirith and takes control over the city by force (*Return*, Jackson 2003:28).

---

[36] "Why do the fools fly? [...] Go back and burn!" (*Return*, Tolkien 1994c:107). He does *not* order them to flee.

Later, Tolkien's Gandalf can save Faramir by gently carrying his body away. He is also able to use the power of words, persuasion and his natural authority to prevent the angry, mad Denethor from killing his own son (*Return*, Tolkien 1994c:144ff.). Even though he cannot prevent Denethor's suicide, the attempt to do so shows the significance of compassion in the wizard's personality. But Jackson's Gandalf does not even try to negotiate and does not show any form of compassion – once again he knocks Denethor down without further warning, and instead of carrying the mortally wounded Faramir, he does nothing to prevent him from falling down from the pyre, which is more than a meter in height (*Return*, Jackson 2003:36). In the movie, Gandalf shows a surprising and inappropriate lack of self-control, compassion and respect for the legal ruler of Minas Tirith; a respect which Tolkien's Gandalf, defying Denethor's growing madness, could sustain with dignity in the novel.

One of the most important aspects in the novel regarding the forms of government is the 'The Scouring of the Shire', which is totally missing in the movie. In the movies, every kind of danger and challenge ends with Frodo and Sam being rescued by the eagles instead. The Hobbits return to their peaceful Shire without problems, and the maturity and wisdom they gathered throughout their journey has absolutely no significance for the rest of their lives. Jackson totally neglects and negates the criticism of civilization of the novel as well as the depiction of the newly won potential of the Hobbit-protagonists. It is this chapter which can be regarded as an allusion to contemporary and current aspects of society. Within the novel, the chapter has several important functions. It shows how the Hobbits, having grown physically as well as in their personalities, can handle their own problems without any help from others, as Gandalf says: "You must settle its [the Shire's] affairs yourselves; that is what you have been trained for. [...] [Y]ou will need no help" (*Return*, Tolkien 1994c:332). Dickerson (2003:233) even regards this chapter as a summary of the whole novel:

> Indeed, the 'Scouring of the Shire' is not an appendix tacked onto the end of the story, but it is the real story; it is what the entire book is about. Gandalf is training the Hobbits so that they are prepared do [sic!] in the Shire what they have seen him and Aragorn do in Rohan and Gondor. That training succeeds. They don't need Gandalf anymore. The Hobbits are all grown up. Frodo shows to Saruman the same mercy that Gandalf does.

Of course, the novel covers far more aspects than can be summarized in a single chapter. But still this chapter is of major importance. For it is possible to understand Gandalf's statement as a request directed at the reader; a criticism of civilization in its most constructive form. In addition, the chapter shows the dangers which may threaten an uninformed, self-satisfied society – from within (as with Lotho) and from without (as with Saruman). Furthermore, it is a surprising turn of the plot that after having saved the world and enjoying a seemingly happy ending, problems may arise where they are least suspected, at home. This warning, that matters may change for the worse if not cared for, is one of the reasons why *The Lord of the Rings* continues to be a relevant work of literature for readers with open eyes and an open mind.

ALEXANDER VAN DE BERGH has studied English, American and German literature and psychology at the Justus-Liebig-Universiy of Giessen. His focus is on the fantastic branch of literature, including science fiction and fantasy. Currently he is working on his dissertation on the topic 'The Beauty of the Beast: Love Between Humans and Non-Humans in English and American Fantastic Literature'. His latest publication is: *Mittelerde und das 21. Jahrhundert. Zivilisationskritik und alternative Gesellschaftentwürfe in J.R.R. Tolkiens The Lord of the Rings*. Trier: WVT, 2005. He is chairperson of the section 'Phantastische Welten' at the 'Gießener Graduiertenzentrum Kuluiwissenschaften' and he is working as a translator for Nintendo of Europe.

Bibliography

Aristotle, 1966, *Politica*, (English translation by Benjamin Jowett), in W.D. Ross (ed.), *The Works of Aristotle Translated into English*, Vol. X, London: Oxford University Press.

Auden, W.H., 1978, 'At the End of the Quest, Victory', in Alida Becker (ed.), 1978, *The Tolkien Scrapbook*, New York: Running Press, pp. 44-48.

Chance, Jane, 2001, *The Lord of the Rings: The Mythology of Power*, Lexington: University Press of Kentucky.

Curry, Patrick, 1997, *Defending Middle-Earth. Tolkien: Myth and Modernity*, London: HarperCollins.

De Camp, L. Sprague, 1976, *Literary Swordsmen and Sorcerers: The Makers of Heroic Fantasy*, Sauk City: Arkham House.

Dickerson, Matthew T., 2004, *Following Gandalf. Epic Battles and Moral Victory in The Lord of the Rings*, Great Rapids, MI: Brazos Press.

Finch, Jason, 1994, 'Democratic Government in Middle-earth', *Amon Hen* 129, 1994, pp. 12-13.

Gray, Thomas, 1980, 'Bureaucratization in *The Lord of the Rings*', *Mythlore* 7.2, 1980, pp. 3-5.

Koravos, Nikolaos, 2001, 'Realistic Fantasy: The Example of J.R.R. Tolkien's *The Lord of the Rings*', *Mallorn* 38, 2001, pp. 31-35.

Nohlen, Dieter (ed.), 1998, *Lexikon der Politik*, Band 7: Politische Begriffe, München: C.H. Beck.

Petzold, Dieter, 2004, *Tolkien. Leben und Werk*, Eggingen: Edition Isele.

Plank, Robert, 1975, 'The Scouring of the Shire': Tolkien's View on Fascism', in Jared Lobdell (ed.), *A Tolkien Compass*, La Salle: Open Court, pp. 107-115.

Shippey, Tom, 2001, *J.R.R. Tolkien: Author of the Century*, London: HarperCollins.

Stanton, Michael N., 2002, *Hobbits, Elves and Wizards: Exploring the Wonders and Worlds of J.R.R. Tolkien's The Lord of the Rings*, New York: Palgrave Macmillan.

Stoddard, William H., 1992, 'Law and Institutions in the Shire', *Mythlore* 18.4 (70), 1992, pp. 4-8.

Tolkien, John Ronald Reuel, 1994a, *The Fellowship of the Ring. Being the First Part of the Lord of the Rings*, (first edition 1954), London: HarperCollins.

---, 1994b, *The Two Towers. Being the Second Part of the Lord of the Rings*, (first edition 1954), London: HarperCollins.

---, 1994c, *The Return of the King. Being the Third Part of the Lord of the Rings*, (first edition 1955), London: HarperCollins.

van de Bergh, Alexander, 2005, *Mittelerde und das 21. Jahrhundert: Zivilisationskritik und alternative Gesellschaftsformen in J.R.R. Tolkiens The Lord of the Rings*. Trier: Wissenschaftlicher Verlag Trier.

Weinreich, Frank, 2005, 'Verfassungen mit und ohne Schwert. Impressionen idealer Herrschaftsformen in Mittelerde als Ausdruck des politischen Verständnisses von J.R.R. Tolkien', in Thomas Fornet-Ponse et al. (eds.), 2005, *Hither Shore. Interdisciplinary Journal on Modern Fantasy Literature*, Düsseldorf: Scriptorium Oxoniae, pp. 89-104.

The Movies

Note: Although the titles of the DVDs used are in German language, they also contain the English version of the movie. That is the version used for this article. Whenever the movies are mentioned in the text, the number given corresponds to the chapter on the DVD in question.

Der Herr der Ringe: Die Gefährten, (DVD), 2001, Director: Peter Jackson. Actors: Elijah Wood, Ian McKellen etc. Screenplay: Fran Walsh, Philippa Boyens, Peter Jackson. USA: New Line Cinema.

Der Herr der Ringe: Die Zwei Türme, (DVD), 2002, Director: Peter Jackson. Actors: Elijah Wood, Ian McKellen etc. Screenplay: Fran Walsh, Philippa Boyens, Peter Jackson. USA: New Line Cinema.

Der Herr der Ringe: Die Rückkehr des Königs, (DVD), 2003, Director: Peter Jackson. Actors: Elijah Wood, Ian McKellen etc. Screenplay: Fran Walsh, Philippa Boyens, Peter Jackson. USA: New Line Cinema.

A

Agøy, Nils Ivar, 112, 118
Aldarion and Erendis, 62, 71, 72, 73
allegory, 88, 103, 121
amazon, 42, 61
anarchy, 22, 212
Anaxagoras, 150
Ancalimë, 74
Anglo-Saxon. see also Old English
anti-industrialism, 7
applicability, 88, 120, 121, 124, 204, 230
Aquinas, Thomas, 129, 153, 155, 162, 181
Aragorn
  and free will, 200
  as king, 221
Aredhel, 39
Aredhel and Eöl, 62
Aristotle, 129, 150
Arthur, 82
Arts and Crafts, 7
Arwen, 59, 60
  as parallel to Lúthien, 42
Arwen and Aragorn, 72
Ashbee, C.R., 7
Asimov, Isaac, 15

Auden, W.H., 106, 208
  The Age of Anxiety, ii
Augustine of Hippo, 150, 151, 155, 162

B

Baldwin, Stanley, 7
Barfield, Owen, 3, 120, 162
Barrie, J.M., 15
Belloc, Hilaire, 24
Beren and Lúthien, 64, 72
Berúthiel, 39
Bible
  on free will, 149
Blackwood, Algernon, 15
Blunden, Edmund, 17
Boethius, 151, 155, 160, 162, 198
  De Consolatio Philosophiae, 151
  on free will, 152
Book of Mazarbul, 11
Boromir
  as presented by Peter Jackson, 231
Boyens, Philippa, 59
Bradamante
  in Ariosto's *Orlando furioso*, 42
Bradley, Marion Zimmer, 70
Buckhurst, Helen McMillan, 64
Bullock, Richard P., 199

bureaucracy, 211
Burns, Marjorie, 43

C

Campbell, Joseph
  The Power of Myth, 118
Camus, Albert, ii
Carlyle, Thomas, 7
Carpenter, Edward, 7
Carpenter, Humphrey, 12, 14, 64
Catholic Church, 37
Catholicism, 90, 114, 155
  The Lord of the Rings as a
    fundamentally Catholic work, 86
Challis, Erica, 49, 61
Chance, Jane, 48, 127, 218
Chaos Theory, 138
Chaucer, Geoffrey, 15
chauvinism, 31, 56
Chesterton, G.K., 7, 10, 11, 24, 64, 153
  Autobiography, 11
  Orthodoxy, 12
  The Ballad of the White Horse, 12
Clorinda
  in Tasso's *La Gerusalemme liberata*, 42
Clutton-Brock, A.
  William Morris
    His Work and Influence, 13

Coleridge, Samuel Taylor, 15
communism, 215
consolation, 11
Cooper, Louise, 61
country walking, 16, 17
Crowe, Edith L., 57
Curry, Patrick, 125, 179, 212, 223, 224

D

d'Ardenne, Simonne, 35, 64
Dagnall, Susan, 64, 65
De Camp, L. Sprague, 213
de la Mare, Walter, 15
democracy, 228, 229
Democritus, 150
Denethor
  as presented by Peter Jackson, 232
Dennett, Daniel, 149
determinism, 135, 136, 138, 139, 142, 143, 147, 148
  in Middle-earth, 140, 180
Dickens, Charles, 15
Dickerson, Matthew, 179, 184, 186, 200, 201, 203
Disney, Walt
  Treasure Planet, 59
Donovan, Leslie, 43
Doughan, David, 2
Drout, Michael, 3, 8

Drury, Roger, 200
Dubs, Kathleen E., 197, 198, 202
Dunne, J.W., 3
Dunsany, Lord, 15

E

Ëarendil and Elwing, 62
economy
　of the Shire, 214
Eddison, E.R., 15
Eden, 98, 99
Empedocles, 150, 162
enchantment, 113, 114, 121, 122,
　124, 168
England, 1, 2, 20
　as a garden, 19
　rural, 16, 17, 19
English language, 82
Englishness, 83
Ents
　and free will, 200
Ents and Entwives, 62
Éowyn, 59
　as valkyrie, 43
Éowyn and Faramir, 70
Éowyn and Lúthien
　as representatives of modern vision
　　of women in Middle-earth, 40
Erasmus, Desiderius, 154, 155, 162
　De Libero Arbitrio, 154

Hyperaspistes diatribe adversus
　servum arbitrium M. Lutheri, 154
Erendis, 39, 61, 67, 71, 73, 74
eucatastrophe, 11

F

Faërie, 124
fantasy, 116, 117, 118, 122, 124
Faramir
　and free will, 200
fascism, 215
Fate, 198
feminism, 33, 57, 58, 59
Ferro, Jorge, 63
Finch, Jason, 216, 229
Flieger, Verlyn, 3, 120, 173, 179, 184
folklore, 1
Forster, E.M., 1, 2, 7, 17
free will, 136, 138, 140, 145, 146,
　147, 148, 149, 152, 156, 157, 158,
　178, 198
　and Aragorn, 200
　and death, 183, 185
　and divine intervention, 188, 190
　and divine providence in Beren and
　　Lúthien, 192
　and Elves, 166, 183, 184
　and Ents, 200
　and Faramir, 200
　and Frodo, 200

and Gollum, 200
and Melkor, 165, 181
and Men, 183
and pre-Socratics, 150
and providence, 164, 190
and Sam, 200
and the Music of the Ainur, 164
and the One Ring, 168
and the Silmarils, 166
as anti-modernist element, 203
Freeman, Edward, 8
Comparative Politics (1873), 8
French, 101
French culture, 100
Freud, Sigmund, 154
Frodo
and free will, 200, 201
Frye, Northrop, 14, 41

G

Galadriel, 40, 43, 48, 67
Galadriel and Celeborn, 67
Gandalf
as presented by Peter Jackson, 232, 233
Garbowski, Christopher, 22
Garth, John, 12, 14
genius, 119
Georgians, 7
Germanic languages, 82

Goldberry, 67
Gollum
and free will, 200
good and evil, 145
government
in Peter Jackson's movies, 231
of Gondor, 219
of Mordor, 223
of Rohan, 218
of the Elves in Lothlórien, 217
of the Shire, 212
Grahame, Kenneth, 7, 15
Pagan Papers, 17
The Wind in the Willows, 17
Gray, Patricia
theatrical adaptation of *The Hobbit*, 61
Gray, Thomas, 211, 219, 220
Griffiths, Elaine, 64, 65
Grundtvig, N.F.S., 112

H

Haggard, Henry Rider, 10
Eric Brighteyes, 11
She, 10
Hammond, Wayne and Christina Scull
The Lord of the Rings
A Reader's Companion, 170
Hardy, Thomas, 7
Harvey, Greg, 51

Heidegger, Martin, 91, 92

Helms, Randel, 127

heoric fantasy, 32

Heraclitus, 150

Hill, Joy, 64, 65

Hoggart, Richard

   The Uses of Literacy, 23

Hölderlin, Friedrich, 92

Homer

   Iliad, 65

Howard, Robert E., 32

Hudson, W.H., 17

Hume, David, 154

humility, 11

Húrin and Morwen, 67

Icelandic, 101

Icelandic sagas

   inspirations for Haggard and Tolkien, 11

indeterminism. see also nondeterminism

Inklings, 155, 157

insubordination, 228

Ioreth, 62

J

Jackson, Peter, 55, 59, 60, 70, 112, 127, 208, 231, 232

James, William, 154

Jefferies, Richard, 16

Jones, Diana Wynne, 62

Jordan, Robert

   The Wheel of Time, 32

Jung, Carl Gustav, 115, 116, 118, 122

K

Kafka, Franz, ii

Keats, John, 15

   La Belle Dame sans Merci, 48

Kilby, Clyde, 187

Kipling, Rudyard, 7, 9

   Puck of Pook's Hill, 9

Knoepfler, Nikolaus, 137

Koravos, Nikolaos, 211, 217

Kropotkin, Petr A., 24

L

Labour Party, 5

Lady Macbeth, 74

Lambert, J.W., 55

Lang, Andrew, 8, 126

language

   its creative power, 129, 130

Laplace, Pierre-Simon, 137, 154

Lawrence, D.H., 2, 7, 127

legends, 82

LeGuin, Ursula K., 56, 57, 59

Leucippus, 150

Levin, Henry
  Journey to the Center of the Earth, 59
Lewis, Alex and Elizabeth Currie, 43, 49
  The Uncharted Realms of Middle-earth, 35
Lewis, C.S., 10, 33, 57, 121, 155, 158
  Mere Christianity, 156
  on Boethius and divine foreknowledge, 160
  Studies in Words, 151
  The Discarded Image, 151
  '*The Four Loves*, 72
  The Problem of Pain, 156
Lewis, Sinclair
  Babbitt, 15
Link, Christian, 178, 188
Little Englandism, 20
Lobdell, Jared, 127
Lombard, Peter
  Libri Quattor Sententiarum, 152
  on free will, 152
Lonely Isle
  as England, 18
Lönnrot, Elias
  Kalevala, 12, 50
Luther, Martin, 154
  De Servo Arbitrio, 154
Lúthien, 67
  as contrast to Éowyn, 48

Lúthien and Éowyn, 61

M

MacDonald, George, 9, 10, 14
MacDonald, Ramsay, 7
Mackail, J.W.
  Life of William Morris, 13
Martinez, Michael, 68
Mathews, Richard, 12, 14
McKiernan, Dennis L., 135
McLeish, Kenneth, 65
McNew, Cynthia L., 61
medievalism, 7
Melian and Thingol, 67
Melkor
  and free will, 165, 181
Middle English, 101
Mills, Stella, 64
Milton, John, 161
misogyny, 31, 56
modernism, 4, 5
modernity, 115
monarchy, 22
  unconstitutional in Middle-earth, 25
Morris, William, 7, 10, 12, 14, 24
  Heimskringla, 13
  News from Nowhere, 13
  Sigurd the Volsung, 13
  The Earthly Paradise, 13
  The House of the Wolfings, 12, 13

The Life and Death of Jason, 12
The Roots of the Mountains, 13
The Sundering Flood, 13
The Volsunga Saga, 12
Under an Elm Tree or Thoughts in the Countryside, 16
Morwen and Túrin, 62
Muir, Edwin, 55
Müller, Max, 8
Murray, Simone, 127
Music of the Ainur, 27
mythology, 1, 64, 124
    and language, 130
    for England, 2, 61

N

Nesbit, Edith, 7, 17
Nietzsche, Friedrich, 154
Niggle, 27, 80, 85, 87, 103, 104, 105
nondeterminism, 137

O

Old English, 82
On Fairy Stories
    consolation, 11
    eucatastrophe, 11
    humility, 11
    recovery, 11
Orange Free State, 91
Orwell, George, 7, 19, 24
    Nineteen Eighty-Four, 26
    The English People, 23
    The Road to Wigan Pier, 23
Otty, Nick, 65, 66

P

Parish, 103
Parmenides, 150
Partridge, Brenda, 67, 68, 70
paternalism, 31
Pelagius
    On Free Will, 151
Petzold, Dieter, 209, 221, 226, 227, 229, 230
philology, 78
Pirson, Ron, 197
Plank, Robert, 215
Plato, 119
political correctness, 32, 38, 56, 74
political organization
    of peoples of Middle-earth, 209
practical realism, 139
predestination
    in Middle-earth, 159
predictability, 138
pre-Socratics
    and free will, 150
Priestley, J.B., 7, 19
providence, 178, 198, 200, 201, 202
Purtill, Richard, 179

Q

Quiller-Couch, Arthur, 21

R

Raffel, Burton, 126
recovery, 11
Renault, Mary, 15
Rimbaud, Arthur, 96
Rosebury, Brian, 3, 5, 62
Rosie Cotton, 59
Roth, Gerhard, 177
Ruskin, John, 7
Russell, Bertrand, 149
Ryman, Geoff, 66

S

Salu, Mary, 64
Sam
   and free will, 200
Sam and Frodo, 107
Sarehole, 7
Sassoon, Siegfried, 17
Sayer, George, 64
Sayers, Dorothy, 155, 158, 162
secondary worlds
   sub-created worlds, 136
Shakespeare, William, 39
   The Taming of the Shrew, 71

Shaw, George Bernard, 15
Shelob, 39, 67
Sherd of Amenartas
   model for Book of Mazarbul, 11
Shippey, Tom, 3, 5, 8, 12, 13, 41, 60, 101, 112, 145, 146, 179, 191, 192, 196, 201, 203, 230
Simplicius, 150
Singer, Wolf, 177
Skeparnides, Michael, 38
Spacks, Patricia Meyer, 197, 198, 201
Spinoza, 154
Stanton, Michael, 63, 65, 220
Stevenson, Robert Louis
   Treasure Island, 59
Stoddard, Michael, 211, 212, 213
Stoddard, William H., 209
Stoppard, Tom, 113, 114
Straight Road, 27
Straight, Michael, 173
Sturt, George, 17
sub-creation, 116
sub-creator, 119, 121, 130, 140
Suffield, Mabel, 63, 64
Suffields
   Tolkien's maternal ancestors, 91

T

Tennyson, Lord Alfred, 15
Thainship, 24

Index 245

The Shire
    as a model anarchist commune, 24
    as *Heimat*, 22, 105
theyocracy, 23, 24, 25
Thomas, Edward, 17
Thompson, Francis, 15
Tolkien, Edith, 34, 37
    as Lúthien, 37
Tolkien, Edith and John
    as Beren and Lúthien, 64
Tolkien, J.R.R.
    Athrabeth Finrod ah Andreth, 188
    Leaf by Niggle, 103
    On Fairy Stories, 11, 12, 94, 112, 116, 119, 123, 126
    The Book of Lost Tales, 14
    The Fall of Gondolin, 14
    The Man in the Moon Came Down Too Soon, 94
    Túor's Coming to Gondolin, 13
    Wanderings of Húrin, 13
Took, Belladonna, 64
Trevelyan, G.M., 7
Tyler, Liv, 60

U

Ungoliant, 39, 67
Unwin, Rayner, 78
Unwin, Stanley, 78
Urang, Gunnar, 197

V

valkyrie, 42, 43
Verne, Jules, 59
Vingilot, 27

W

Walsh, Fran, 59
Wawn, Andrew, 12, 14
Weinreich, Frank, 185, 212, 213, 217, 220, 226
Wells, H.G., 15
Williams, Charles, 162
Wilson, Edmund, 126
Wilson, T.P. Cameron
    Sportsmen in Paradise, 17
women's liberation movement, 36
Woolf, Virginia, 4
World War I, 6, 7, 8, 13, 17, 18, 19, 22, 88, 116
World War II, 5, 19
Wynne, Hilary, 3

Y

Yates, Jessica, 14

Z

Zimmerman, Morton Grady

first movie script of *Lord of the Rings*, 60

Walking Tree Publishers was founded in 1997 as a forum for publication of material (books, videos, CDs, etc.) related to Tolkien and Middle-earth studies. Manuscripts and project proposals can be submitted to the board of editors (please include an SAE):

Walking Tree Publishers
CH-3052 Zollikofen
Switzerland
e-mail: walkingtree@go.to
http://go.to/walkingtree

Cormarë Series

News from the Shire and Beyond. Studies on Tolkien.
  Edited by Peter Buchs and Thomas Honegger. Zurich and Berne 2004. Reprint. 1st edition 1997. (Cormarë Series 1)

Root and Branch. Approaches Towards Understanding Tolkien.
  Edited by Thomas Honegger. Zurich and Berne 2005. Reprint. 1st edition 1999. (Cormarë Series 2)

Richard Sturch. *Four Christian Fantasists. A Study of the Fantastic Writings of George MacDonald, Charles Williams, C. S. Lewis and J.R.R. Tolkien.*
  Zurich and Berne 2001. (Cormarë Series 3)

Tolkien in Translation.
  Edited by Thomas Honegger. Zurich and Berne 2003. (Cormarë Series 4)

Mark T. Hooker. *Tolkien Through Russian Eyes.* Zurich and Berne 2003. (Cormarë Series 5)

Translating Tolkien: Text and Film.
  Edited by Thomas Honegger. Zurich and Berne 2004. (Cormarë Series 6)

Christopher Garbowski. *Recovery and Transcendence for the Contemporary Mythmaker: The Spiritual Dimension in the Works of J.R.R. Tolkien.*
  Zurich and Berne 2004. Reprint. 1st edition by Marie Curie Sklodowska University Press, Lublin 2000. (Cormarë Series 7)

Reconsidering Tolkien.
  Edited by Thomas Honegger. Zurich and Berne 2005. (Cormarë Series 8)

Tales of Yore Series

Kay Woollard. *The Terror of Tatty Walk. A Frightener.* CD and booklet. Zurich and Berne 2000. (Tales of Yore 1)

Kay Woollard, *Wilmot's Very Strange Stone or What came of building "snobbits".* CD and booklet. Zurich and Berne 2001. (Tales of Yore 2)

www.ingramcontent.com/pod-product-compliance
Lightning Source LLC
Chambersburg PA
CBHW070731160426
43192CB00009B/1392